AGING AND HEALTH PROMOTION

Thelma Wells, R.N., Ph.D.

reprinted from
Topics in Clinical Nursing
and
Family and Community Health

AN ASPEN PUBLICATION®

Aspen Systems Corporation
Rockville, Maryland
London
1982

362.1
Ag 47

Library of Congress Cataloging in Publication Data
Main entry under title:

Aging and health promotion.

"Reprinted from Topics in clinical nursing and Family and
community health."

Includes bibliographical references and index.
1. Aged—Medical care—Addresses, essays, lectures.
2. Aged—Care and hygiene—Addresses, essays, lectures.
3. Aging—Addresses, essays, lectures. 4. Geriatric
nursing—Addresses, essays, lectures. I. Wells, Thelma J.
II. Topics in clinical nursing.
III. Family & community health.

[DNLM: 1. Geriatrics—Collected works 2. Health
promotion—United States—Collected works. WT 100 A264]
RA564.8.A39   362.1'0880565   81-12734
ISBN: 0-89443-398-9   AACR2

Library of Congress Catalog Card Number: 81-12734
ISBN: 0-89443-398-9

Printed in the United States of America

1 2 3 4 5

Table of Contents

Preface

From the family experiences of having grandparents or great grandparents to the public experiences of long bank lines on a social security check day we are conscious of growth in the older segment of our society. In this decade a twenty percent increase in the population over age sixty-five is expected.[1] While old age in itself has never been a unique happening, the large number of old people in recent years has created a novel impact on society. The single elder in a family or community might blend into the social fabric but multiple elders constitute a new thread. In many ways the current older population serves as pioneers in determining the strength and consistency of this new thread. The remainder of society will ordain the pattern of the weave. Thus, it is essential that knowledge and issues relevant to old age be widely disseminated during this period of social change.

A Harris survey found that sixty-two percent of the public and seventy percent of those over fifty thought that the worst thing about being over sixty-five years of age was poor health or poor physical condition.[2] Health is a significant issue for older people who, compared with other groups in the population, report more health problems and greater health costs. For example, twenty percent of those over sixty-five report activity limitations due to health as compared to two or three percent of those aged seventeen to sixty-five.[3] In fiscal year 1977 percapita personal health care expenditures for those over age sixty-five were 3.4 times greater than those under sixty-five with the elderly paying twenty-five percent of the costs out of pocket.[4,5] It is not too late to foster good health among the old nor reduce or eliminate health barriers in old age.

On an individual basis, most of the present younger generation will live to be at least seventy. Thus, we have a personal investment in learning about old age. Although research has yet to identify the cause of aging, considerable work has been done to identify its normal decrements, the altered presentation of disease in old age, and the interplay between normal age loss and an abnormal pathologic state. The current elderly are our best guide to patterns of adjustment and to methods of coping with the changes of age. But future elders will bring specific factors to aging phenomena.

If you were a World War II baby, perhaps you grew up near a neighborhood shoe store where foot x-ray devices appeared in the late forties. Will the fun of seeing your toe bones wiggle and the resulting radiation your feet received create a problem for you in later years? For those born in the fifties and sixties will the ingestion of increased preservatives, salt, and sugar in baby food, cereals, and snack food, effect individual health in the year 2015 or 2025? Perhaps our increased education will give us the knowledge to respond sensibly as the future unfolds. Exploration of different health care models and continued research offer great promise. In the meantime we would be well served to consider some fundamental questions about aging and health.

1. The Federal Council on the Aging, U.S. Department of Health and Human Services, *The Need for Long Term Care*, Information and Issues, Washington, D.C., 1981, p. 2.
2. Harris, Louis, and Associates for the National Council on the Aging, *The Myth and Reality of Aging in America*, Washington, D.C., 1975, p. 20.
3. U.S. Department of Health, Education, and Welfare, *Healthy People*, The Surgeon General's Report on Health Promotion and Disease Prevention 1979, Washington, D.C., p. 75.
4. U.S. Department of Health, Education, and Welfare, *Health United States 1979*, Washington, D.C., 1980, p. 182.
5. Federal Council on Aging, p. 50.

Thelma Wells
September 1981

Delivery of Care to Older People: Issues and Outlooks

Pearl S. German, ScD
Health Services Research and Development
  Center
The Johns Hopkins University
Baltimore, Maryland

THE RANKS of the elderly population have been increasing so steadily that issues of their care and the training and research associated with it are highly visible whenever concerns about health care delivery are raised. It is ironic under the circumstances that the elderly get the least attention in areas that might be most positive (i.e., health education aimed at prevention and rehabilitation), while they receive a great deal of attention in tertiary care, high technology care, and, ultimately, institutional care.

SOCIO-DEMOGRAPHICS AND HEALTH STATUS

The demographic trend in this country makes it highly unlikely that the focus on the needs of the older population will diminish. In 1900 those aged 50 and over were 13 percent of the population and those aged 65 and over were 4 percent. By 1978 those 50 and over were 26 percent of

1

Table 1. Percentage of population aged 50 and over in selected years

	1900 Percentage of total population	1978 Percentage of total population	2000 Percentage of total population
50 years and over	13.3	25.9	27.6
65 years and over	4.1	11.0	12.2

Source: Estimates and projections of the U.S. Bureau of the Census—Current Population Reports: Series P-25, Nos. 311, 519, 614, 800, and 704.

the population and those 65 and over were 11 percent. It is predicted that by 2000, those 50 and over will represent about 28 percent of the population and those 65 and over will represent about 12 percent.[1]

Table 1 summarizes this trend and shows the differences that have been taking place and that are predicted to take place through the year 2000.

Of greater significance for health care professionals than these overall increases are the growing numbers of adults at the upper end of the last third of life, the so-called "old-old." Table 2 shows the changing composition within the 50 and over group.

The demographic picture described here is one of several highly interrelated factors that serve to make the health of the elderly population a complex issue. The incidence and prevalence of disease and the symptomatology and disability associated with

Table 2. Percent distribution of population aged 50 and over by age in selected years (estimates and projections as of July 1, 1979)

Age	1900	1930	1970	1978	Projections (series II) 1980	Projections (series II) 2000
50 years and over	100.0	100.0	100.0	100.0	100.0	100.0
50 to 54 years	29.4	28.4	22.4	20.9	20.2	23.5
55 to 59 years	22.0	22.2	20.0	19.9	19.7	18.2
60 to 64 years	17.9	17.8	17.4	16.7	17.0	14.1
65 to 69 years	13.0	13.2	14.1	15.2	15.1	12.8
70 to 74 years	8.8	9.3	10.9	11.2	11.8	11.5
75 to 79 years			7.7	7.4	7.5	8.9
80 to 84 years	8.9	9.2	4.6	4.9	4.9	5.9
85 years and over			2.9	3.9	4.0	5.2

Source: Estimates and projections of the U.S. Bureau of the Census—Current Population Reports: Series P-25, Nos. 311, 519, 614, 800, 704.

Table 3. Life expectancy at selected ages by color and sex, 1949-1951 to 1976

	White			Nonwhite		
	1976	1969-1971	1949-1951	1976	1969-1971	1949-1951
Males						
Birth	69.7	67.9	66.3	64.1	60.9	58.9
55	20.5	19.5	19.1	19.2	18.1	17.4
65	13.7	13.0	12.8	13.8	12.8	12.8
75	8.5	8.0	7.8	9.7	8.9	8.8
Females						
Birth	77.3	75.4	72.0	72.6	69.0	62.7
55	26.1	24.8	22.6	24.3	22.3	19.6
65	18.1	16.9	15.0	17.6	15.9	14.5
75	11.2	10.2	8.9	12.3	11.0	10.2

Source: National Center for Health Statistics: Vital Statistics of the U.S., Life Tables, 1960, 1977.

advancing age, for example, combined with the overall increasing numbers of elderly ensure a large population at risk for heavy use of medical care.[2,3] There are differences by race and sex but a consistently longer life expectancy, with its increased chronic conditions, can be observed. Table 3 gives life expectancy by color and sex at three points: (1) 1949 to 1951, (2) 1969 to 1971, and (3) 1976. In 1966 additional expected years of life for those 65 years old ranged from 13.7 years for white males to 18.1 years for white females.

There is a problem in the way in which the elderly population is viewed; the problem is that, in general, the view of the elderly is distorted. Age 65, which has become the magic cutoff point, is in fact an accident of history set in the Social Security Act. Also, because of the dramatic nature of the needs of the frailest and sickest of the older population and the cost to society of meeting those needs, there is an inevitable focus on the institutionalized, a focus that is out of proportion with their representation in society. These factors obscure issues of health care and are related to some of the current problems in health care delivery.

PROMISING APPROACH

A more logical and promising approach to health care for the elderly considers the problems in the last third of life, and covers ambulatory as well as institutionalized populations. The rationale for this approach rests on evidence that new needs for health care and human services, because of increases in incidence and prevalence of chronic disease,[4-6] and changes in family structure, begin to emerge as major considerations 10 to 15 years before age 65.[7-9] These needs greatly influence the events after that point. In this case age 65 should serve as a transition point rather than a separation line that divides the population into two distinct groups. Interest should focus on ambulatory care as well as institutional care because this is the

4

major concern of the greatest number of individuals in the population.

Health care during the last third of life appears on one level to be concerned with simple questions of quantity and quality and the costs associated with these two dimensions. Overall use of a wide range of health care resources increases steadily, beginning roughly at age 55. The growing use is paralleled, obviously, by increasing cost. Cost and quality of care, therefore, have relevance and significance for practitioners, educators, and planners. In addition quality and cost encompass the interrelated and complex areas out of which practice issues emerge.

VARIOUS FACTORS

The interrelationships among biomedical factors,[10-12] psychological and social influences, and the environment[13,14] are complex. While individuals differ in timing and rate, all older people face the stress of physical, social, and environmental changes, many of which are for the worse. Unique to the phase of life beginning at age 55 are the series of stresses often referred to as the "insults" of aging: loss of employment, reduction in income, death of family members and friends. All take place at a time when coping ability has begun to diminish and physical and mental capacities may be deteriorating. Left unchecked these changes may lead to irreversible disability and cognitive impairment. The challenge, then, is to understand the interplay among these factors and to initiate interventions when and where they will have the greatest effect.

Environmental factors, such as housing,

income maintenance, employment, and social supports, are areas where interventions can be made.[15,16] The role of social support systems in maintaining function in the older population has been receiving an increasing amount of attention. These systems include family, friends, social organizations, and others that influence attitudes and behaviors; formal support mechanisms include the many human service organizations active in the community. The effects of this combination of forces on the use of health services and on health status are important enough to deserve emphasis.

Studies of health status in the older population stress the importance of the interactions among individual characteristics and resources in the immediate social milieu, the characteristics and resources of the community and larger society, and the biomedical factors of disease and deterioration. To date no means have been found to halt the aging process, the eventual decrease in functional capacity, or the increase in chronic problems. Furthermore, no hard answers exist as to which of these occurrences are preventable or amenable to moderation so as to make the last third of life as positive as it can be for the elderly while being the least costly to society.

This sketch of the various areas of concern when speaking of health care delivery to older individuals includes, tacitly, the importance of the various levels of personnel and different professionals, and the diverse and often fragmented services within a community. Provision of comprehensive services to the older population, particularly the oldest or most ill

Provision of comprehensive services to the older population, particularly the oldest or most ill and disabled members, requires the coordination and integration of many disciplines and professions.

and disabled members, requires the coordination and integration of many disciplines and professions.

It is sobering to consider the multitude of forces that interact with and affect health and health care. The overview of the complex number of facts associated with health supports the conviction that caring for the elderly requires an integrated, knowledgeable, innovative approach.

ISSUES OF QUALITY

Definitions of what constitutes quality health care have existed for many years. The definition that has best stood the test of time is the one formulated by Lee and Jones in the mid-1930s.[17] In this definition there was the first shift from concentration on technical aspects, and quality was considered to include, among other things, prevention, community services, physician-patient relationships, and accessibility for all. In more recent times consideration of quality revolves around a framework that Donabedian developed[18] that organizes care into elements of structure (characteristics of the system), process (the nature of the delivery and the interaction between consumer and system), and outcome (the

measurable effect on individuals and society) of health care.

5

Structure of care

In considering the framework presented here for the population in the last third of life, certain factors take on different meaning and significance. In considering the structure of medical care delivery to this group, it is apparent that, while primary care remains important, the increasing prevalence of chronic conditions makes recourse to secondary and tertiary care more frequent, and more options in the care of patients are necessary. The result is that the structural requirements for an effective health care system for the large proportion of people who reach their 70s and 80s are highly complex and depend on a broad array of skills and services, including knowledge about other human services and mechanisms to assure appropriate and timely use.

Integration of different levels of care becomes important so that, for example, easy access to specialty care with continuity of contact with primary care providers is an essential part of health care delivery. The type of provider and the amount of time spent with the patient are especially important in the late 50s and early 60s because it is often in these years that chronic conditions are first diagnosed, and information and education are most needed.

Process of care

Process as well as structure begins to have a different emphasis for this age group. For example in the early stages of

6   this period, when chronic conditions become increasingly detectable and associated changes in functional capacities become overt, a particularly important component of care is the nature and content of the provider-patient relationship. A focal point in this relationship would be the attention given to enlarging patient understanding of the respective roles of patient and provider in health maintenance and delay of secondary complications of conditions that will persist over a long period. As age advances this consideration persists with greater intensity until very old ages are reached.

Another aspect is that with increased prevalence of multiple chronic conditions, a larger array of providers and institutional settings for care become involved. Coordination, referred to under discussion of structure and often dependent on the provider-patient relationship, becomes a critical element in the process of care.

Mortality and morbidity have always been outcome measures of great importance. For the elderly, however, other outcomes, such as level of disability, satisfaction, and comfort, may have higher relative importance. Morbidity for this age group is a given and mortality not unexpected. The other outcomes, which measure quality of later life, become more salient. The goal is to maintain independent functioning and, when this is no longer completely possible, maximize functioning within the constraints imposed by the condition. Furthermore, how changes in functional ability are handled in the early stages may foreshadow later capacity to function and whether institutional care is required. A great deal of attention is directed toward functional

capacity, relief from symptoms, early detection of disease, rapid recovery from acute episodes of illness, and reduction in risk for respiratory disease (e.g., through influenza immunizations). All of these goals are significant objectives of health care at these ages. The potential or iatrogenic effect and misuse of drugs is particularly high because of the multiplicity of conditions that require protracted drug prescribing, and, in studies of quality of care, this issue is assuming increased prominence.

Outcome and cost

Clearly in considering an overview of the care delivered during the last third of life, not all or even a significant part of these complex considerations can be addressed. They serve instead to point up the important areas that practitioners, researchers, teachers, and planners may be addressing in part. Attention has been concentrated over many years in the relationship of structure and process, with less evidence concerning outcome.

In addition to questions of assessing outcome, the issue of rising costs has been increasing in intensity. The interest in cost-effectiveness analysis is in the need seen by policymakers and planners to use such analyses for decisions in allocating resources not only across conditions but in weighing alternative approaches to the care of population subgroups with long-term needs. Economists say the following:

the underlying premise of cost-effectiveness analysis in health problems is that, for any given level of resources available, society (or the decision-making jurisdiction involved) wishes to maximize the total aggregate health benefits conferred. Alternatively, for a given health-benefit goal, the objective is to minimize the cost of achieving it.[19]

Implicit in this statement is the notion that individuals are faced with choices between types of care. In practice this means that a cost-effectiveness analysis requires parallel sets of information for two or more alternatives. It is hoped and expected that the results will help identify the choice to be made and why. But it is recognized by all methodologists in this field that, in the end, other considerations may override the results of the "arithmetic" in the decision-making process.

For the elderly a particularly difficult question connected to the cost of health care concerns the time frame for measuring costs. Most often attention is focused on short-run costs incurred during highly circumscribed intervals defined by, for example, an episode of illness. "Long term" takes into account the health care costs for the sequelae of the condition. This becomes important when a change in mortality is followed by a change in disability or significant morbidity. That is, as life expectancy increases and mortality rates fall among the younger old population, illness and disability connected to that illness will increase. For the last third of life directing attention to long term represents a recognition that, for many individuals, no clear picture of costs for alternative care patterns will emerge unless the time frame covers a sequence of care.

This discussion of quality and cost-effectiveness has drawn on aspects of each that link the two when the interest is in the aggregated experience of patients or a population, rather than in the technical performance of a provider. In both, the end point sought is a positive impact on health status for an efficient, acceptable expenditure of resources. For both it is necessary to compare alternatives or to have a validated standard against which observations can be judged.[20] These aspects of care often are neglected in the pressure of service delivery. They are essential however to any long-term policy considerations, and providers are queried about them by administrators, regulators, and policymakers.

DISEASE PREVENTION AND TREATMENT

There are several central areas that are highlighted by current understanding of the elderly. The first of these concerns health promotion and disease prevention. The Surgeon General's Report, "Healthy People,"[21] focuses on disease prevention and will influence future interest in the topic.

A second area concerns treatment of specific conditions. This is an area of heavy investment in research and in demonstration programs. A great deal needs to be learned by the older population about the effect of multiple conditions, problems of functioning and coordination, and continuity of care over long periods of time. This includes a strong focus on technology, its use and misuse, and on different levels and intensity of care.

Related to both these areas is the area concerning population, the community in which the population lives, and the resources of the community. Essential to

8

all experiments in delivery of care, including reorganizations of services, and to the practitioners involved in all types of care, is an understanding of how the factors in these areas interact.

Prevention in its broadest sense, which includes maintenance and rehabilitation, overlaps with all aspects of care and is one of the cornerstones of nursing. The developments that are occurring in nursing, as well as the basic philosophy of the profession, interface with the particular, complex needs of the elderly to make health care of the older population an area where nurses can and should take major responsibility.

CHRONICITY

The elderly are prime candidates for health care directed at positive maintenance for a broad array of chronic conditions. Definitions of chronicity, as well as the health care needs they engender, reflect the type of care required. What constitutes a chronic condition? The 1956 Commission on Chronic Disease concluded with the following definition as quoted by Katz and colleagues: "... all impairments or deviations from normal which are permanent, leave residual disability, ... require special training, a long period of supervision, observation or care."[22] More recently the National Health Survey has defined chronic disease as any condition lasting more than three months.

These definitions imply the need for a life style adapted to chronicity, which includes a serious commitment by the patient to compliance with recommended regimens and cooperative interaction with the provider in all aspects of health care.

Mannay[23] argues that, for continuous monitoring and prevention, health education is crucial for an older age group because of isolation and immobility combined with tendencies to ignore early symptoms of new conditions or complications of old ones. More recently Berki and Koheshigawa have demonstrated both direct and indirect effects of chronic disease: the direct effect is the obvious need for care of the disease or condition, while the indirect (and some claim greater) effect is the relationship of the presence of a chronic condition to increased episodes of illness.[24] All of these findings represent important reasons for monitoring chronic conditions and for educating professionals about their role in the care of these conditions.

These conclusions support the argument that active involvement of elderly patients in their own health care is vital. To extend life and improve its quality it seems imperative that delivery of care be focused on the problem of chronicity and that strategies be devised for involving the population in their own care. There is reason to believe that involvement of patients in their own care and an active health education approach in conjunction with medical care by medical practitioners is not a phenomenon likely to sweep the practice of medicine. A number of factors lessen active involvement of providers with those

There is a widely accepted belief that learning processes deteriorate with age, that memories fail, and that old age brings loss in control over mind and body.

consumers who may need such involvement the most. Providers find chronic disease less satisfying to treat than other conditions and the elderly less satisfying patients in general.[25]

There is also a widely accepted belief that learning processes deteriorate with age, that memories fail, and that old age brings loss in control over mind and body. These form the bases for stereotypes about the elderly that are held by many individuals who have never had direct experience in working with this group.[26,27] Changes occur during aging in many areas of functioning. However, evidence produced in the controversy over the educability of the elderly raises doubt as to the inflexibility of sensory loss and the specific etiology of these changes and failings of the senses. It has been demonstrated in several studies that the elderly can overcome difficulties in learning if specific care is given to the pace, the relevance of material, and the appropriateness of the feedback.[28]

There is also evidence that nurses may be spearheading innovations in their care of the elderly. A study undertaken in 1973 examined health care delivery to the elderly in four different settings. The overall findings have been reported elsewhere, but certain findings support the importance of nurses in delivering care, offer insights into content of care given, and inevitably raise additional questions.

A STUDY OF HEALTH CARE DELIVERY TO THE ELDERLY

A study launched in Baltimore in 1972 investigated health care delivery to those aged 65 and over in four ambulatory care settings. Data were gathered through a household survey of those in this age group and through a survey of the providers of care within each of the settings. As well as serving different patient populations, each of the settings offers a different approach to the delivery of health care.

One setting, Highlandtown, is a community that is predominantly white, with low to middle incomes. The group of elderly studied were receiving care from a fee-for-service group practice and had the approximate expected proportions of elderly people (10 percent of the 3,500 registrants). This setting is probably the most typical of the settings in which the elderly receive care in the United States in terms of staffing population and method of delivery.

The East Baltimore Medical Plan, located in the eastern section of Baltimore, is in an inner-city area. The plan is a newly organized, health maintenance organization (HMO) of physicians, health associates, and health advocates that serves a low-income black population. The aged population is relatively small (5.6 percent of the 3,500 registrants).

The Columbia Medical Plan is also a prepaid HMO group practice but differs in almost every way: it serves a large middle- to upper-income white population in a newly designed city in the Baltimore-Washington corridor. It has a mix of personnel—physicians, health associates, and assistants. Its proportion of elderly is the lowest of all the settings (1.5 percent of the 13,800 registrants). Columbia is made up primarily of young to early middle-aged families.

The Broadway-Orleans Health Center is the most distinctly different of the four settings. It is a clinic serving a low-income

10 black population in a high-rise public housing unit whose 230 residents are either aged 65 and over or are aged 55 and over with a chronic condition. Care is delivered primarily by nurse practitioners who use physician backup, either consultatively or on request of the patients who represent 60.9 percent of the total enrollees aged 65 and over. Referrals are made to the outpatient department of The Johns Hopkins Hospital; this clinic is technically a satellite of the outpatient department.

Within these four settings broad areas of information were collected and analyzed, including the attitudes and behaviors of the population as well as of the providers. One of the aims of the study was to collect information on and analysis of the process by which individuals sought care and how they perceived the care they were receiving.

The process of care for chronic diseases was an important focus because of the age of the study population. Although the objectives of the study did not include a direct evaluation of preventive care and patient education, the information gathered inevitably focused attention on a process of care that could be described as preventive and educational. A series of questions was asked concerning directions from a provider that were for other than direct care for an episode of illness or a specific medical regimen. These questions, which concerned general instructions for daily diet, exercise, rest, care for some part of the body, and miscellaneous "other" instructions, were viewed as related to maintenance of health, to positive health habits, and to care as a source for general instructions on life style.

Table 4 shows the proportion of individuals who reported receiving each of the five types of instructions. The settings differed significantly in the proportions of individuals who reported receiving the four specific types of directions. For each of these categories the Broadway-Orleans setting has higher proportions of individuals who reported receiving instructions: approximately 57 percent on diet compared to ranges of 22 percent to 49 percent in other settings; 41 percent on exercise versus 12 percent to 29 percent; 39 percent on resting versus 11 percent to 32 percent; and 19 percent on care for part of the body

Table 4. Percentage of individuals reporting health care instructions received—by setting and type of instructions

Instructions received	Setting			
	Highlandtown	East Baltimore	Columbia	Broadway-Orleans
What to eat*	47.8% (54)	41.6% (32)	22.0% (28)	56.7% (59)
Exercise*	23.0% (26)	28.6% (22)	11.8% (15)	41.3% (43)
Resting*	31.9% (36)	26.0% (20)	11.0% (14)	39.4% (41)
Care for part of body**	12.4% (14)	15.6% (12)	6.3% (8)	19.2% (20)
Other instructions	14.2% (16)	10.4% (8)	6.3% (8)	14.4% (15)

*Significantly different across settings at the .001 level.
**Significantly different across settings at the .05 level.

Table 5. Percentage of individuals reporting directions given who report compliance for these directions—by setting and directions

Able to follow instructions	Setting			
	Highlandtown	East Baltimore	Columbia	Broadway-Orleans
What to eat	81.5% (44)	84.4% (27)	88.5% (23)	83.1% (49)
Exercise	84.6% (22)	68.2% (15)	80.0% (12)	86.0% (37)
Resting	91.7% (33)	90.0% (18)	85.7% (12)	97.6% (40)
Take care of body	85.7% (12)	75.0% (9)	75.0% (6)	90.0% (18)
Other	56.3% (9)	62.5% (5)	87.5% (7)	84.6% (11)

versus 6 percent to 16 percent. (This is the smallest difference, but in this case the numbers are small.) Such findings might have been anticipated in view of the type of care and its delivery at the Broadway-Orleans Health Clinic. Nurse-practitioners deliver the primary care there, and their training, skills, and philosophy are congruent with a focus on preventive care, on education, and on dealing with the totality of problems faced by patients. These reported instructions indicate an approach to general maintenance of health and attempts to influence life style.

What is the influence of this approach on actual health care? There are further findings from this study indicating that whether or not directions are given may be important, because the elderly appear to take seriously the advice they receive.

Table 5 shows the percentage of individuals who reported complying with directions they received. While a caveat is necessary for self-reported compliance, these data are highly suggestive for providers. The differences noted in proportions among settings reporting directions do not exist for reported compliance. Almost all those reporting that they received directions also reported complying. The lowest

proportion so reporting (discounting the miscellaneous group of "other") is 68 percent in East Baltimore with regard to exercise. In most other groups, 80 percent to 90 percent reported compliance.

These data lend credence to speculation that the elderly have a high potential for active participation as consumers of health care, not only because of the nature of their needs, but from indications of a readiness to act on directions given. Programs aimed at the elderly with an emphasis on self-care are an area of great interest currently.[29,30] Hopefully, verification of compliance and effectiveness of health education strategies will be forthcoming.

These data also provide evidence that changes in the delivery of care, which are aimed at special needs of the elderly and which hold promise for positive outcomes, are underway among nursing professionals.

SUMMARY

Demographic trends ensure that there will be increasing numbers and proportions of elderly individuals in this country.

12 Furthermore, these increases are in the direction of higher proportions of the "old-old" or those over 75. The age-related incidence and prevalence of chronic disease mean that the proportion of people with conditions and symptoms requiring continuing treatment and monitoring will be growing. Delivery of health care to this growing sector of the population will require approaches that take into account demographic, social, cultural, and psychological influences and that make use of providers attuned to the special needs of this group.

REFERENCES

1. U.S. Bureau of the Census. Current Population Reports, Series P-25 (Washington, D.C.: Government Printing Office). Nos. 311,519,614,704,800.
2. Havinghurst, R.J. and Sacher, G.A. "Prospects of Lengthening Life and Vigor." *Extending Human Life Span* (Chicago: Report prepared for National Science Foundation by Committee on Human Development of the University of Chicago 1977).
3. U.S. Department of Health, Education, and Welfare. *Health: United States* (Washington, D.C.: Public Health Service 1978) DHEW Pub. No. PHS 78-1232.
4. U.S. Department of Health, Education, and Welfare. "Data From Health Interview Survey." (Washington, D.C.: National Center for Health Statistics).
5. Nagi, S. "An Epidemiology of Disability among Adults in the United States." *Milbank Memorial Fund Quarterly* (Fall 1976) p. 439-467.
6. Atchley, R.C. *The Social Forces in Later Life* (Belmont, California: Wadsworth Pub. Co. 1972).
7. Hershey, D. *Life Span and Factors Affecting It* (Springfield, Illinois: Charles C Thomas 1974).
8. Palmore, E. "Total Choice of Institutionalization among the Aged." *Gerontologist* 16(1976) p. 297-302.
9. Palmore, E. ed. *Normal Aging 11: Reports from the Duke Longitudinal Studies, 1970-1973* (Durham, North Carolina: The Duke University Press 1975).
10. Birren, J., Finch, C.E., and Hayflick, L., eds. *Handbook of the Biology of Aging* (New York: Van Nostrand Reinhold Co. 1975).
11. Exton-Smith, A.N. and Evans, J.G. *Care of the Elderly* (London: Academic Free Press 1977).
12. U.S. Department of Health, Education and Welfare. *Our Future Selves* (Washington, D.C.: National Institute on Aging, 1977). DHEW Pub. 77 p. 1096.
13. Shanis, E. and Sussman, M.B., eds. *Family, Bureaucracy and the Elderly* (Durham, North Carolina: Duke University Press 1977).
14. Chatfield, W.F. "Economic and Sociological Factors Influencing Life Satisfaction of the Aged." *Journal of Gerontology* 32:(September 1977) p. 593-599.
15. Cutler, S.J. "Aging and Voluntary Association Participation." *The Journal of Gerontology* 32:(July 1977) p. 470-479.
16. Sheppard, H.L. "Work and Retirement" in Binstock, P.H. and Shanas, E., eds. *Handbook of Aging and the Social Science* (New York: Van Nostrand Reinhold Co. 1977).
17. Lee, R.I. and Jones, L.W. *The Fundamentals of Good Medical Care* (Chicago: University of Chicago Press 1933).
18. Donabedian, A. *A Guide to Medical Care Administration. Vol 11: Medical Care Appraisal; Quality and Utilization* (New York: The American Public Health Association 1969).
19. Weinstein, M.C. and Stason, W.B. "Foundations of Cost-Effectiveness Analysis for Health and Medical Practices." *The New England Journal of Medicine* 296:(March 31, 1977) p. 716-721.
20. Shapiro, S. "Cost and Quality of Medical Care in the Last Third of Life." (Baltimore: The Health Services R & D Center of The Johns Hopkins University, October 1979). Mimeographed.
21. U.S. Dept. of Health, Education, and Welfare. *Healthy People: The Surgeon General's Report on Health Promotion and Disease Prevention* (Washington, D.C.: Government Printing Office 1979). DHEW Pub. (PHS) No. 79-55071.
22. Katz, S., Halstead, L., and Wierenga, M. "A Medical Perspective of Team Care." in Sherwood, Sylvia, ed. *Long-Term Care* (New York: Spectrum Publications, Inc. 1975).
23. Mannay, J.D.J. *Aging in American Society.* Chapter 11. (Ann Arbor, Michigan: Institute of Gerontology 1975).
24. Berki, S.E. and Koheshigawa, B. "Socioeconomic and Need Determination of Ambulatory Care Use." *Medical Care* 14:5 (1976) p. 405-421.
25. German, P. et al. "Symposium: Health Care of the Aged." *Gerontologist* 14:(1975) p. 311-332.
26. Botwinick, J. *Aging and Behavior* (New York: Springer Publishing Co. 1973).
27. U.S. Department of Health, Education, and Welfare.

Secretary's Committee to Study Expanded Roles for Nurses Extending the Scope of Nursing Practice. (Washington, D.C.: Government Printing Office 1971).

28. White House Conference on Aging. *Background and Issue: Physical and Mental Health* (Washington, D.C.: Government Printing Office 1971).

29. Lewis, C.E., Resnik, B.A., Schmidt, G., and Waxman, D. "Activities, Events and Outcomes in Ambulatory Patient Care." *New England Journal of Medicine* 280:(1973) p. 645.

30. Simmons, J., ed. "Making Health Education Work." *American Journal of Public Health* (supplement 1975).

Physical Assessment of the Elderly

Patricia A. Bailey, RN, MSEd, MSN
Senior Associate Professor
Department of Nursing
Bucks County Community College
Gerontological Nurse Consultant
Newtown, Pennsylvania

NURSES TODAY, regardless of the setting they work in, need to understand the normal aging process and its implications for physical assessment. In the hospital setting RNs are responsible for interviewing new admissions. They must accurately obtain a history and physical review of body systems to adjust care. A larger number of patient admissions today than in past years are of geriatric age.

Because institutionalization has profound effects physiologically, psychosocially, and financially, careful assessment of the need for health care services is imperative as the aged have decreased reserve energy to cope with confinement. Nursing home residents also have the right to be evaluated holistically so that they may lead full lives.

Nurse practitioners, in their extended role as primary health care nurses, must possess a higher level of assessment skill to be able to manage holistic care for their clients in any situation. They may be an

16 excellent source for gerontological consultation in all fields of nursing.

An understanding of age-related effects on body functions is an integral part of nursing care for the elderly. There is a growing realization, supported by more and more new literature, that many conditions attributed to the aging process are due to specific and identifiable disease. No one becomes ill simply because he or she is old but because of a definite, identifiable disease. Current misconceptions about senility and aging must be dispelled.

Multiple pathology is the main clinical manifestation in the elderly. The process of aging complicates diseases of later life; therefore, manifestations of the disease are different. The most important difference is the frequent lack of symptoms, as multiple pathology makes diagnosis difficult. Adequate assessment, however, must precede treatment.

INTERVIEWING TECHNIQUES

The object of taking a clinical history is the same at any age, but the differences lie in the technique by which the history is taken in older adults and also in the interpretation of the symptoms. For example nurses should take more time and have more patience during interviews, taking into account the elderly adult's prolonged need for response time and the possibility of various hearing deficits. Memory impairment and digression from the subject also may greatly impede the normal process of question and answer. It may be necessary to rely on information provided by people other than the patient.

Questions need to be simple and straightforward and progress from an impersonal to a personal nature. The room should be quiet and devoid of distractions. For example, if the patient has a hearing problem, the interviewer should face the client directly, adjusting position to meet the patient's specific needs. The expenditure of time in initial assessment saves time in ensuing encounters with the older person. It is difficult for the client to collapse 80 years of living into an hour and a half interview.[1] The interviewer should initially spend more time with the client and should employ proficient interviewing skills.

THE AGING PROCESS

Before any assessment process for the elderly can take place the assessor must have a working knowledge of the normal aging process. Changes associated with the aging process occur in three areas:
- Physical, which includes posture, weight, contour, features, and hair.
- Body composition, which includes fat, lean body mass, water, cell solids, and bone.
- Organ function, which includes cell population, oxygen consumption, tissue blood flow, and functional efficiency.[2]

Physiology

The physiological parameters of aging are illustrated by a kyphotic posture and the resulting appearance of long arms and shorter neck and trunk due to dehydration of the vertebral discs and bone calcification. The weight of an older adult decreases with age due to decrease in lean muscle mass and accumulation of fat in the body. This can be an important consideration when ordering and administering drugs on a weight basis. Toxicity due to accumulation of the drug may result.

Decrease in cell population promotes a decrease in oxygen consumption, which leads to low metabolic rate and decreased blood flow. This directly affects the changes in the body's organ functioning. Decreased blood supply to organs and loss of elasticity of collagen fibers causes age changes in organ systems.

Vital functions

The older adult's heart shows less ability to respond to stress. There is a more rigid myocardium, resulting in a 25 percent increase in the thickness of the left ventricle. The speed of the mitral valve closure decreases by 5 percent.[5] Fatty deposits are increased in the intimal layers of the arteries, also enhancing vessel rigidity and circulating insufficiency. These changes in the aorta are responsible for the increased workload of the heart, so that peripheral resistance is increased. By age 70 systolic blood pressure may normally be 150 mm Hg and diastolic 90 mm Hg, leading to persistent arterial hypertension. There is a decrease in cardiac output, leading to a decreased heart rate and stroke volume and a resultant diminished blood supply to the liver and kidneys.

The nurse should educate the patient in the importance of exercise to improve physiological functioning and in the importance of a low sodium and cholesterol diet to maintain blood flow and reduce the strain on the heart, and explain how slower position changes may help orthostatic hypotension. Antihypertensive drugs should be used with caution, and side effects should be judiciously explained.

The kidneys have a decrease in the number of functioning nephrons and a lower glomerular filtration rate. If there is 50 percent decrease in renal blood flow certain drugs probably will take longer to be eliminated and will accumulate in the body when multiple dosages are administered.

The kyphosis and contraction of the accessory muscles of inspiration lead to an increase in the diameter of the thoracic cage. There is also a decrease in the contraction of expiratory muscles, making it difficult to expire air. Oxygen transport is impaired and utilization through the vessels is decreased. The elderly compensate by elevating the amount of oxygen in their lungs by increasing their depth of respiration. Serious illness or increased activity makes prolonged work difficult to sustain; the cough reflex is decreased and lung disease is a major threat. The liver decreases in size, but function remains adequate.

Hormone and nervous systems

There is a decrease in hormonal secretions and a shift in ratio of catabolic to anabolic activity due to decrease in gonadal steroids. Glucose tolerance decreases with age. Thyroid functioning decreases, but hypothyroid is not a common finding.

Diminished brain weight and the number of neurons lead to a progressive

18 slowing of response to verbal instruction. Short-term memory is impeded, and learning is hindered. Long-term memory storage however is not affected by chronic hypoxia. A decrease in the number and sensitivity of sensory receptors in the central nervous system contributes to dulling of the sensations of temperature regulation, pain perception, and tactile discrimination. This is of vital consideration in the care and assessment of the elderly, as fatigue may be the only symptom of chest pain.

Misuse and overuse of drugs, especially tranquilizers, narcotics, and sedatives, result in unnecessary falls and confusion. Any stressor, such as illness or a new environment, interferes with the compensatory mechanisms established by the elderly to deal with neuron loss. They compensate by doing tasks slowly and avoiding stressors. The elderly do this well, so nurses must recognize the response for what it is and not for what it might wrongly be evaluated to be. In testing the elderly, the ability to judge what is normal improves clinical diagnosis and prevents overtreatment.

CULTURE AND ENVIRONMENT

Nurses should take into account the age group they are dealing with and place special emphasis on cultural beliefs and

Nurses should take into account the age group they are dealing with and place special emphasis on cultural beliefs and environmental exposures.

environmental exposures. For example, nurses must find out not only what clients eat but where and how often; who does their cooking; whether they eat alone; and how they go and shop for food. Nurses must also evaluate if poor dietary habits are based on a lifetime pattern of eating.[3]

Clients' adjustment to retirement and their previous occupations should be evaluated to judge better their use of spare time and choice of recreational activity. Nurses should ask clients how they feel about their health status. Are they victims of polypharmacy?

Hearing and visual difficulties might make the person appear confused, so this should be evaluated carefully to avoid assessment errors.

Sometimes positive symptoms go unnoticed if clients consider them part of the aging process and feel they must cope with them. Activities of daily living should be assessed in terms of independence, interdependence, and dependence.[4]

Older people are often handicapped by their own bodies, which respond to challenges with less energy. A rapid number of losses can leave individuals with layers of unresolved grief.[5] Documentation of mental health is essential both objectively and subjectively. It must be noted if the elderly express loneliness, depression, or feelings that life is not worth living.

SPECIAL NOTATIONS

Physical examination specialty skills necessary for helping the elderly require even greater knowledge of the aging process. The absence of fever, for example, does not exclude the possibility of an infection, and hypothermia (over 90%) is of mild concern. An onset of fatigue or restlessness usually signifies an infection. Auscultation of the chest is limited due to decreased expansion. Special attention must be paid to venous pulsations in the neck, because these are a guide to rhythm disorders. Any mention of cardiac pain, no matter how slight, should be taken seriously. The apex of the heart may be displaced, making determination of an apical pulse more difficult. Heart murmurs are more difficult to assess in an elderly person whose control of respiration is imperfect, and gallop rhythms are an important clue to the presence of heart failure. Blood pressure must be taken in a sitting, lying, and standing position to determine correctly the baseline significance.

The site of abdominal tenderness is much more reliable in locating the pain than any description given by the patient. Urinary stasis is common in the elderly due to decreased bladder tone and urethral strictures, so urine cultures are more frequently ordered.

Limitation of movement requires that nurses take more time with range of motion and reflexes examinations and pedal pulses. Reflexes are often reduced, and pedal pulses are decreased due to the high incidence of peripheral vascular disease.

Another challenge for nurses in assessing the elderly is eliminating prejudices and stereotyping that connote that all elderly people are homogeneous and that aging only means degeneration.

REFERENCES

1. Caird, F.C. and Judge, T.C. *Assessment of the Elderly Patient* (Kent, England: Pitman Medical Publishing 1974).
2. Malasanos, L.J. and Tichy, A.M. "Physiological Parameters of Aging." *Journal of Gerontological Nursing* 1:5 (January-February 1979) p. 42-45.
3. Quinn, J.L. and Ryan, N.E. "Assessment of the Older Adult: A Holistic Approach." *Journal of Gerontological Nursing* 1:5 (March-April 1979) p. 14-18.
4. Riley, G.A. "How Aging Influences Drug Therapy." *U.S. Pharmacist* (November-December 1977) p. 29-35.
5. U.S. Department of Health, Education, and Welfare. *To Understand the Aging Process, What Do We Know about Aging Now?* No. (NH) 78-134 (Washington, D.C.: Government Printing Office) p. 10-14.

Hearing Loss and Aural Rehabilitation of the Elderly

Barbara R. Heller, RN, EdD
Assistant Dean
College of Nursing
Villanova University
Villanova, Pennsylvania

Edward B. Gaynor, MD, FACS
Otolaryngologist
Private Practice
Norwalk, Connecticut

HEARING rivals vision as a means of deriving highly complex and detailed information from the environment, and in humans is the most important channel for interpersonal communication.[1] For the elderly, because of deterioration of other sensory systems, hearing plays an even more vital role in orientation and adaptation to environment and surroundings.

HEARING LOSS AND SENSORY DEPRIVATION

Hearing is progressively lost with age. It is estimated that 55 percent of those over age 65 have some degree of hearing loss, and by age 80, 66 percent have serious hearing problems.[2]

Because hearing loss is often a gradual process, the older person is often unaware of the subtle effects of hearing change until there is significant impact on life style and social interaction. The response to this loss may take a number of forms, including such behaviors as confusion, anger, depression, and paranoia. Continued reduction and deprivation of sensory input and variability can ultimately result in withdrawal, alienation, and isolation.

Hearing change in the elderly must be considered in relation to concurrent changes in physiological, psychological, and social functioning. Unfortunately many individuals, including nurses and other health professionals, fail to recognize significant and correctable hearing problems in the elderly and instead may interpret these as age-related mental deterioration or "senility."

REACTIONS TO HEARING LOSS

Research data indicate that many elderly with impaired hearing tend to underestimate their degree of hearing loss.[3] Older people often do not admit the existence of a hearing problem. They attempt to deny their deficiencies by such statements as: "It is not my hearing; it is that everybody mumbles," "If people would speak up, I wouldn't have any problem." These reactions are reinforced by family members who blame them for "hearing what they want to hear." Although a degree of hearing selectivity is entirely possible, it is not always voluntary on the part of the older person.

A lack of awareness of an elderly client's hearing impairment may cause nurses to react negatively to inappropriate responses in verbal interactions by labeling the client "confused" or "uncooperative" and by limiting contacts with the client. Such avoidance may contribute to further client withdrawal and isolation and may provoke

similar negative reactions by the client's family or friends.[4] Increased understanding of hearing problems of the elderly and heightened sensitivity to the impact of hearing loss could do much to improve the quality of interaction between elderly clients and significant others.

ANATOMY AND PHYSIOLOGY OF HEARING

Relevant to an understanding of hearing changes that occur with age is a review of the anatomy and physiology of hearing.

Sound

The ability to hear is a direct response to sound stimuli that are produced and thus perceived by the individual from the immediate environment. Sound is an energy form that consists of a series of waves traveling outward from a source, similar to the ripples of water produced when a rock is thrown into a pond. These waves have two major characteristics: intensity and frequency. The intensity (loudness) of sound is measured logarithmically in decibels (dB), usually as hearing level; frequency (pitch) is measured in hertz (Hz).

Sounds that are normally perceived are complex signals comprising a mixture of many pure tones of different intensity and frequency. It is the combination of many and varied sounds that provides for the differences in the character of "noises" that are heard. Human speech usually is heard in the frequency range below 2,000 to 3,000 Hz. Losses of hearing in these lower frequencies are more critical than a loss in the higher frequency range.

The human ear of a newborn has the ability to perceive sounds as high as 25,000 to 30,000 Hz. Deterioration actually occurs from that time with marked acceleration in the elderly. Sound energy reaching the level of 100 to 120 dB (the louder the sound, the higher the decibel level) can become a painful stimulus, and if sufficiently loud or prolonged, permanent hearing deficits can result.

Transmission of sound

The human ear is divided into three portions: the external ear, which acts as a funneling device for sound waves; the middle ear, which is both a transmitting and amplifying apparatus; and the inner ear, which receives, transmits, and probably codes acoustic stimuli for transmission to higher centers for perception.

The external ear consists of the auricle and cartilaginous and bony ear canals. Within the external ear canal are the ceruminous and other apocrine glands. The tympanic membrane (eardrum) separates the external canal from the middle ear.

Within the middle ear are three small bones that comprise the ossicular chain: the malleus (hammer); the incus (anvil); and the stapes (stirrup). The stapes is in a bony opening known as the oval window, which serves as an entrance from the middle ear to the inner ear. The ossicular chain and tympanic membrane act to amplify acoustic stimuli approximately 35 times.

The cochlea is the auditory portion of the inner ear. It consists of a snail-shell-shaped area of bone medial to the middle ear in which the organ of Corti and many other delicate neural structures are located.

For sound stimuli to be recognized the cochlea must be stimulated. Acoustic stimuli reach the cochlea either by direct vibration of the skull bones (bone conduction) or pass via the external ear canal and strike the tympanic membrane, resulting in vibration of the ossicular chain. The vibrating of the stapes in the oval window provides a direct pathway for sound transmission to the inner ear. The resultant wave in the inner ear causes hair cell motion in the organ of Corti. This motion is believed to produce a form of electro-acoustic energy or nervous stimulation and a subsequent neural response that passes to the higher centers of the brain for perception of sound on a conscious and subconscious level.

HEARING PROBLEMS OF THE AGED

Hearing problems of the aged are of two major types: (1) conductive hearing loss and (2) sensorineural (perceptive) hearing loss. Regardless of type and etiology, the effects of hearing loss can result in similar problems for the individual concerned, but the treatment may vary dramatically from simple removal of impacted cerumen to neurosurgical excision of a tumor of the auditory nerve.

Conductive hearing loss

The majority of hearing problems in the older age group are of the sensorineural type, but conductive problems are not uncommon. A conductive hearing loss can occur when there is blockage of sound transmission from the external ear through the tympanic membrane and ossicular

24 chain in the middle ear to the cochlea. Any impairment of this mechanism can produce a significant hearing loss that may be amenable to surgical or medical therapy.

It is not unusual to encounter elderly clients whose only hearing problem is cerumen occluding the external ear canal. Treatment usually consists either of lavage and irrigation or mechanical removal of the impacted cerumen and, at times, the use of cerumenolytic agents, such as Debrox. Ears are not irrigated if there is a history of a perforated eardrum or ear drainage, and the water used must be at body temperature to avoid provoking caloric stimulation of the balance portion of the inner ear.

Other, more common conductive hearing problems are serous otitis media and otosclerosis. Serous otitis media produces negative pressure or fluid accumulation in the middle ear, causing a feeling of blockage or fullness as well as an associated conductive hearing loss. This can result simply from an upper respiratory infection, but if the blockage is unilateral, it may signify an obstructive tumor occluding the eustachian tube orifice in the nasopharynx. Medical treatment usually consists of inflation of the middle ear, antihistamines, and decongestants. If refractory to medical treatment, a myringotomy (incision into the tympanic membrane), with or without insertion of a ventilating tympanotomy tube, may be desirable.

Otosclerosis is usually an autosomal dominant condition of varying penetrance, more frequent in females, which results in the fixation of the stapes because of new and abnormal bony growth in this area. As a conseqence vibration of the ossicular chain is impaired, and there is a subsequent conductive hearing loss. Treatment consists either of amplification with a hearing aid or surgery. Stapedectomy, the preferred surgical treatment in otosclerosis today, can be performed under a local anesthetic, usually with supplemental sedation and monitoring by an anesthesiologist. The postoperative disability is minimal, and recovery is quite rapid, even in the elderly.

A conductive hearing loss may also be a result of damage to the tympanic membrane (perforation) or to the ossicular chain, usually as a result of trauma, chronic otitis media, or cholesteatoma (ingrowth of epithelium into the middle ear). These problems can be surgically corrected with minimal postoperative disability.

Sensorineural hearing loss

Sensorineural hearing loss is by far the most prevalent hearing problem of the elderly. With age there occurs the loss of cochlear hair cells, initially involving the higher frequency range, commonly known as presbycusis. This loss can be of varying degree and becomes especially severe when the lower frequencies in the speech range (2,000 Hz and below) are involved.

The older individual may retain the ability to hear pure tones, but when these pure tones are grouped to form words, the ability to understand and perceive these sounds as intelligible speech may be lost. This is known as impairment of discrimination ability. The individual will have increased difficulty hearing high-frequency stimuli; sibilant sounds (*f*, *s*, *th*, *ch*, and *sh*) are usually the most severely affected. The ability to hear low-frequency vowel sounds is retained. As a result the client will be able to recognize only a portion of the spoken word, and the sounds that are perceived may be heard but are unintelligible. In addition for reasons as yet unknown, central perceptual problems occur in the older age group that are frequently associated with peripheral or cochlear hearing losses.

Present treatment of sensorineural hearing loss is by aural rehabilitation, which includes amplification utilizing hearing aids. Surgical correction is not yet feasible, although significant investigative efforts are being made in this area. The surgical insertion of cochlea implants has been attempted in a few selected cases. Although this method appears to hold considerable promise, it is far from ready for use by the general population.

ASSESSING THE HEARING PROBLEM

Early detection is an important first step in the treatment of impaired hearing, and nurses can take initiative in casefinding

---

Early detection is an important first step in the treatment of impaired hearing, and nurses can take initiative in casefinding and referral.

---

and referral. All elderly clients should be routinely screened for hearing or communication problems.

Behaviors and history

The assessment effort is multidisciplinary and aims to determine the level at which an elderly person is able to hear and communicate. Nursing observations are an essential part of the hearing assessment and can provide much valuable data about the hearing efficiency and communication ability of the elderly client. The following behaviors may indicate a loss of hearing: inattentiveness; inappropriateness of response to the spoken word; difficulty in following directions; speech that is unusually loud; habitually turning one ear toward the speaker; and unusual voice quality. Other signs are frequent requests to have statements or questions repeated; irrelevant comments during verbal interaction; and tendency to withdraw from activities that require verbal communication.

The client's history is also significant. Head trauma, exposure to loud noises (especially over a prolonged period), frequent ear or upper respiratory infections, exposure to ototoxic medications, tinnitus, ear drainage, and a family history of hearing loss should be noted. Aspirin is a common offender in producing hearing loss in older persons because many elderly people take large daily doses of aspirin for arthritic problems. The effects of aspirin on hearing, however, generally are reversible once this medication has been discontinued.

Objective evaluations

In addition to inspecting the ear canal for obstruction and examining the tympanic membrane for signs of inflammation, the nurse can employ a variety of

26 objective techniques in making a hearing assessment, including the use of a ticking watch or whispering. Both techniques screen for the existence of high-tone hearing loss. Several other screening tests that differentiate between conductive and perceptive hearing loss involve the use of the tuning fork.

The older client with a suspected hearing problem should be referred to an otologist or otolaryngologist for diagnosis, then to an audiologist for audiological evaluation. Audiological evaluation consists of pure-tone testing with acoustic stimuli ranging from 250 Hz to 8,000 Hz and speech testing to obtain speech reception thresholds, including the client's ability to discriminate speech. Additional testing is performed if sufficient pathology is present.

NURSING INTERVENTION

The objectives of an aural rehabilitation program are to maximize hearing and to increase or maintain the client's ability to communicate and interact with others. This is accomplished by "establishing goals with the client related to the acceptance of adjustments to hearing changes and compensation for the deficiencies present."[5] The nurse's role is supportive and educative throughout the process and includes: counseling the elderly client and family; assisting with amplification; and facilitating communication and effective social interaction with others.

Rehabilitation begins as soon as the problem is identified. The success of the aural rehabilitation program depends on the client's interest and willingness to participate as well as the cooperation and encouragement of the family. The client and the family may view the hearing loss as a normal part of aging that must be accepted, and may be reluctant to invest money and effort in a rehabilitation program. Concern over expense is a realistic consideration because Medicare does not provide for hearing aids or aural rehabilitation.

Because motivation plays an important part in successful rehabilitation, it is essential that the nurse help the client and the family to become actively involved in establishing the goals of the rehabilitation program and in accepting responsibility for its outcomes. The nurse should also provide opportunity for the client and family to identify and discuss their attitudes and feelings about the value of the program.

FACILITATING AMPLIFICATION

Optimum amplification is important to the progress of the aural rehabilitation program.[6] If a hearing aid is prescribed the nurse can assist the elderly client in making a decision regarding the use or type of hearing aid that is compatible with the individual's life style.

The client's reactions to using the hearing aid should be determined. The client may view the hearing aid as a social stigma and reject the use of it. Cosmetic considerations may take on greater importance than therapeutic value. Other factors related to use of the hearing aid include comfort needs as well as the client's manipulative abilities.

The nurse should explain to the client

the benefits and limitations that can be expected from amplification. The hearing aid is designed to assist in hearing acoustic stimuli; it does not correct the auditory disorder. In addition the client should be advised that a hearing aid amplifies all acoustic stimuli within the frequency response of the microphone. Consequently it makes extraneous background noises louder as well as amplifying meaningful sounds. This can be disconcerting to the user and is one of the major obstacles to amplification.

Types of hearing aids

There are three main types of hearing aids: the behind-the-ear; the in-the-ear; and the body aid. Although the body aid is the most powerful, it requires external wiring and is large and cumbersome and therefore objectionable. Space age technology has revolutionized the design of hearing devices, and the widespread use of microcircuitry has enabled hearing aid manufacturers to reduce the size of wearable hearing instruments. This means that most clients can be fitted with either behind-the-ear or in-the-ear aids.

The in-the-ear aid, which is considered cosmetically less obvious, is frequently the first selection of many clients even though it may not be as beneficial as the behind-the-ear aid, which provides more flexibility, less distortion, and greater durability and amplification. The behind-the-ear aid is the most commonly worn type of aid and can be attached to eyeglasses.

In addition, the use of Contralateral Routing of Signals (CROS) and more elaborate hearing aid fittings has greatly enhanced the dimension of hearing aids.

For example, an elderly client with nonamplifiable hearing loss in one ear and normal hearing in the other ear can have a signal routed from the impaired ear via an eyeglass frame wire or radio frequency signal to the hearing ear. This allows binaural hearing and consequently increased ability to localize sounds.

An earmold, usually constructed of a clear, flesh-colored, synthetic material, is necessary for all types of hearing aids. To properly serve the wearer, the earmold must closely approximate the anatomic structure of the external ear canal. A skilled technician must fit the earmold and educate the client about its use and maintenance.

The nurse should explain that, for protection of the elderly client, a recent FDA regulation requires medical clearance before purchase of a hearing aid, although this can be eliminated if a waiver is signed by the client. A one-month trial period must also be provided by the dealer before purchase of the aid.

Adjustment to the hearing aid

The elderly client may need assistance in adapting to life with a hearing aid. The orientation period is critical to the outcome of the aural rehabilitation program. Although some difficulty in adjustment can be anticipated initially, the client should be encouraged to utilize the instrument as much as possible.

The nurse should determine the extent to which the elderly client understands and remembers instructions regarding use and maintenance of the hearing aid. Aspects of routine care of the device should be reviewed and reinforced. When not in use

28 the aid should be stored in a dry place. The battery should be disconnected and can be refrigerated to preserve its life. It is advisable for the earmold to be cleaned weekly. If the client is unable to care for the appliance, the nurse can assist with this or teach a family member how to do so.

The nurse should check to see if the elderly client is encountering operating difficulty with the aid. Too often the nurse may ignore the client's problems with a hearing aid because of lack of understanding of the mechanism. Complaints of malfunction are usually the result of an inoperable battery, a clogged earmold, or a switch turned to off or telephone instead of microphone setting. A squeaking or high-pitched whistling noise may indicate a problem with the earmold fit or tubing, and it is recommended that the client contact the dealer from whom the aid was purchased for the necessary modifications.

FACILITATING COMMUNICATION AND SOCIAL INTERACTION

Effective communication is essential to the mental health and social well-being of the elderly client. There are specific principles that can be employed by the nurse that may facilitate communication with the hard-of-hearing older person. By using appropriate techniques, barriers to communication with the elderly can be overcome.[7]

Because older people may take longer to perceive and interpret what is said, it is important to allow more time and patience for each communication. Communication is assisted by closeness and by directly

Because older people may take longer to perceive and interpret what is said, it is important to allow more time and patience for each communication.

facing the client when speaking. Older people need all kinds of sensory stimulation and it may be necessary for the speaker to touch the client for attention before attempting to communicate. The nurse should keep in mind however the individual's response to touch and personal space requirements.

The nurse should speak not only loudly but slowly. Shouting should be avoided as it promotes distortion of sound and is embarrassing to the client. Exaggerated lip movements may be confusing and should also be avoided.

It is helpful to use short phrases rather than lengthy sentences. If the message is misinterpreted, the information should be repeated using different words. Pictures, demonstrations, or written key words or proper names may assist in the communication process. The nurse should also be aware of the tools of nonverbal communication. Facial expressions, gestures, and body language can convey moods and feelings that enhance comprehension of the spoken word.

The nurse can also help the client's family and friends to learn the techniques of communication that enhance reception of messages. Furthermore the elderly client can be taught to become appropriately assertive in managing communication of others for most effective reception.

Because social withdrawal often accompanies loss of hearing, there is significant nursing responsibility to assist the hearing-impaired elderly client to reenter the hearing world by encouraging social interaction with others. The nursing interventions necessary to accomplish this goal may indeed provide a greater challenge than any other aspect of the program of aural rehabilitation.

IMPLICATIONS OF AGE-RELATED CHANGES

The nurse needs to view the older person holistically, taking into account the behavioral, social, and cultural changes as well as the physiological alterations that occur with age. As the functional performance of various systems declines with advancing age, along with the accumulation of pathological events affecting these systems, the ability of the elderly person to adapt becomes impaired.

Hearing loss is thought to be one of the most devastating of the physiological detriments associated with the aging process because it may lead to withdrawal from interaction with society and meaningful people and loss of contact with the environment.

Assisting the elderly client to maximize hearing and communication potential presents a unique challenge. Although "normal" auditory function can not be restored, further disability can be limited or prevented through technology and sensitive nursing intervention.

REFERENCES

1. Best, C.H. and Taylor, N.B. *Physiological Basis of Medical Practice* 9th ed. (Baltimore: Williams and Wilkins Co. 1973).
2. Saxon, S.V. and Etten, M.J. *Physical Change and Aging* (New York: The Tiresias Press 1978) p. 64.
3. Yurik, A.G. et al. *The Aged Person and the Nursing Process* (New York: Appleton-Century-Crofts 1980) p. 354.
4. Ibid. p. 360.
5. Ibid. p. 361.
6. Hipskind, N.M. "Aural Rehabilitation for Adults." *The Otolaryngologic Clinics of North America* 1:2 (October 1978) p. 823-834.
7. Clark, C.C. and Mills, G.C. "Communicating with Hearing Impaired Elderly Adults." *Journal of Gerontological Nursing* 5:3 (May-June 1979) p. 40-44.

Maximizing Psychological Adaptation in an Aging Population

Jeanette Lancaster, RN, PhD
Associate Professor
School of Nursing
University of Alabama
Birmingham, Alabama

THE CENTRAL IRONY of aging is that everyone wants to live as long as possible, but no one wants to grow old. In many cultures the aged are revered and respected for their wisdom and experience. In contrast, in the United States, growing old is usually associated with decreased physical and psychological capabilities. The great American Dream is to live a long and productive life while still looking good, acting and feeling young, and being healthy.[1] Social, economic, and technological advances frequently present challenges and hurdles to the attainment of the "stay young dream."

In general the American population is growing older. Fewer children have been born since the 1940s and improved health practices have increased longevity. The size of the population over 60 years old has increased nearly seven times since 1900, while the number of those over 75 years old has grown tenfold.[2] The average life expectancy rose from 47 years in 1900 to approximately 73 years in 1976. At present

32

people over 65 account for 11 percent of the population and represent the fastest growing population group in the United States.[3] By the year 2030 it is estimated that 17 percent of the U. S. population will be over 65 years of age.

Probably no other age group is more affected by economic, social, and technological changes than the elderly. In most instances people over 65 have fixed incomes that do not escalate at the same rate as inflation. All too often economic constraints necessitate doing without most luxuries and often not even being able to afford the necessities for maintaining an optimal level of functioning.

Furthermore at a time when the body is beginning to slow down in its rate of responsiveness and general overall efficiency in functioning, rapid changes in urbanized society make strenuous and far-reaching demands on the older person for adaptation and accommodation. Since the 1950s, social and technological changes have occurred at an unprecedented pace. Older people have greater difficulty than younger ones in coping with rapid change due to the necessity for novel and often unexpected responses at a time when the capacity to adapt is already beginning to diminish. Continuous demands for responses to new situations, as well as the cumulative effects of multiple stressors over an extended period of time, may compound the much needed psychological adjustment of older people. Stressful stimuli are often characterized as ones that are novel, intense, rapidly changing, or unexpected.[4] The day-to-day existence of older people is too often replete with examples of such stressors.

Although age 65 does not mark the onset of a uniform physical and psychological decline, it does represent society's benchmark for what is called "aging" and the legal age to be called a "senior citizen." Despite this societal expectation that people automatically become an "older person" at age 65, it is important to remember that each person ages at a unique rate due to a complex, interacting relationship of biological, psychological, social, and environmental factors. Although debate exists as to whether the psychological changes observed during the latter part of the life span are due to physiological or emotional alterations, the most useful view seems to be one which acknowledges the interplay of a variety of factors. Furthermore it is of critical importance to distinguish between the actual concomitants of aging—which vary from one person to another—and society's myths and expectations about the behavior of this segment of the population.

The behaviors typically ascribed to people over 65 tend to occur largely as a result of two entirely different sets of circumstances. First society expects this group to behave in ways that generally reflect less competence, and second there are physiological changes that alter the person's ability to respond as spontaneously and, at times, as appropriately as they previously did to environmental cues. Although there are various approaches for describing ways to maximize the coping capacity of the aging population, an ecological framework is particularly useful. An ecological approach utilizes a systems theory framework, which is founded on the belief that all people are open systems constantly affecting and being affected by both internal and external environmental forces. It is possible to conceptualize people as hierarchies of natural, open systems that are connected by exchanges of information, energy, and matter.[5]

ECOLOGICAL VIEW

From an ecological perspective aging is an experience that is determined by the quality of the interactions between older people and their combined internal and external environments. Birren[6] purports that people age in three ways: biologically, psychologically, and socially. A person's biological age can be viewed as either the number of years remaining or the extent to which people have already "used up" their biological potential for existence. Psychological age is considered as the level of adaptive capacities, which includes the ability to adapt to the environment in terms of accuracy, speed of perception and reaction, memory, learning, and reasoning. Social age is defined by the differentiated social roles that people play.

To adapt along these three dimensions several basic human needs must be met:

- Physiological supplies of oxygen, food, fluids, temperature, rest, sleep, and elimination must be adequate to meet the person's demands.
- Safety must be provided.
- The person must feel worthwhile and valued.
- The person must experience purpose in life.

Thus from an ecological view health is defined as a harmonious interaction among all components of the system. Because all living systems attempt to maintain balance and stability, the interaction among physiological, psychological, and social factors must continually move toward balance. Disease results from disturbances that threaten the system's balance. Hence the role of nursing is to recognize sources of disruption to the system of the aging person and intervene to reduce these threats whenever possible.

By using an hourglass an analogy can be drawn to the myriad of forces affecting adaptation among the elderly. (See Figure 1.) The basic function of the hourglass is to measure time. In this context the sands can be considered the numerous ecosystems (subsystems) that make up the internal and external environments of the elderly person. Internal forces, as well as those in the community, affect the individual and vice versa. Behavior does not occur in a vacuum; elderly people affect their environments just as they are affected by the number and variety of environmental occurrences. The shifting sands represent the relationship between the elderly person and their environmental resources.

PHYSIOLOGICAL ASPECTS OF AGING

Many health problems of the elderly reflect the success that has been achieved in extending longevity. Because people live longer their bodies tend to wear out, resulting in 45 percent of the older population having some degree of activity limitation due to a chronic health problem.[7] Severe physical decline is not an inevitable

34

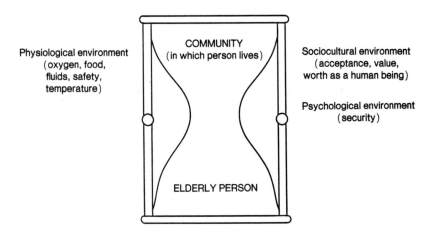

Figure 1. Hourglass analogy: relationship between the elderly person and the environment. The shifting sands of the hourglass represent the changing interrelationships between an individual and the community. Physiological, sociocultural, and psychological variables in the community influence the level and psychological adaptation of the elderly person.

part of the aging process. Furthermore there is considerable individual variability in the physiological changes that result from aging. Some general physiological changes include: (1) increased porosity and brittleness of bones; (2) decreased elasticity of muscles, which accounts for the increased numbers of falls among this age group; (3) decreased sensory acuity, which results in diminished ability to discriminate light, noise, odor, and pain; and (4) frequent loss of tastebuds, and tooth discomfort. This last change affects the elderly person's response to food, which may substantially decrease their nutritional adequacy.

Several commonly experienced physical conditions lead to decreased oxygenation of cells and subsequent confusion. For example several reversible causes of confusion due to hypoxia include heart failure, malnutrition, anemia, infection, head trauma, stroke, thyroid or vitamin deficiencies, and side effects from medication. When-

ever an older person appears confused and unable to respond appropriately to the environment, the first step taken should be to determine if a physiological imbalance is present. Nursing intervention can often bring balance to the physiological component of the hourglass by careful assessment for subtle cues of faulty adaptation.

SOCIOCULTURAL FACTORS AFFECTING AGING

Feelings of being valued and having purpose in life are particularly difficult for the elderly to sustain due to forced retirement and economic penalties for earning more than a minimal amount when receiving retirement benefits. Income is a significant factor in the maintenance of health and home, and the vast majority of elderly people can and do remain in their own homes. "In 1975, 77 percent had their own households, 5 percent lived with a spouse and 26 percent lived alone, 18 percent lived in a home with someone other than a spouse and only 5 percent were institutionalized."[8] In addition, the often held belief that older people have little contact with their families is a myth. Although the current trend is toward older people maintaining an independent household, there continues to be considerable family interaction. While only approximately 20 percent of elderly people live with relatives other than a spouse, 80 percent have living children. Of these elderly people with living children, 75 percent live either in the same household or at least within a 30-minute drive. Families provide considerable financial, emotional, and social support for members.[9] In addition, with the provision of adequate social, environmental, and health services, a greater percentage of elderly people could maintain their independence and experience a more productive quality of life.

While the number of elderly living in poverty has decreased by 60 pecent since 1959, approximately 14 percent still have incomes below the poverty level.[10] Moreover elderly black people are three times as likely to have below poverty level incomes than are their white counterparts. Women are also particularly susceptible to low levels of income because severe financial disadvantages accrue to elderly widows. Tibbitts emphasizes the economic plight of many elderly people when he says: "The problems of living arrangements for those living alone, paying for suitable housing, obtaining needed services, and meeting food costs are exacerbated by the low incomes characteristic of widowed persons, particularly women."[11]

At a time when income levels are shrinking, the elderly account for a significant proportion of personal health care costs. Although people over 65 represent 11 percent of the population, they account for approximately 30 percent of the health care expenditures.[12] In addition society's response to health costs for the elderly has been both fragmented and inadequate in amount. "In 1975, the per capita expenditure by the elderly for health care was $1,218 of which Medicare paid only $463."[13] Fear of the potential high cost of an illness often prompts elderly people to conserve their already restricted income and do without adequate food and heat in order to pay for health care should the need arise.

The elderly and stereotypes

At a time when they are struggling to maintain adaptation in terms of physiological and economic declines, the elderly often must contend with the societal prejudice referred to as "ageism." This term has been coined to refer to the way in which society views the elderly. Ageism is manifested in both individuals and institutional actions in discrimination in employment, housing, education, and general services to a specific segment of the population. Because of their age the elderly are deemed inadequate to participate in many activities that other people take for granted.

The prevalence of myths and stereotypes is particularly destructive to the elderly. Old age has a bad reputation and often is the recipient of cruel humor. It is not uncommon to hear references such as "he is a dirty old man," "that old coot," or "you can't teach an old dog new tricks." Another firmly held myth contends that older people cannot "learn, change, or grow emotionally.[14] These remarks influence perceptions about how older people "ought" to behave. In accord with the concept of a self-fulfilling prophesy, many older people internalize such stereotypes and behave accordingly. For many the word "elderly" conjures an image of a stooped, wrinkled person with thin, gray hair, a wobbly gait, and a penchant for talking about the good old days. If constantly expected to look and act in certain ways, the elderly soon learn what is expected of them and behave accordingly.

Health care providers often have beliefs about elderly people which interfere with effective service delivery. Hagebak and Hagebak[15] cite six hurdles which prevent the establishment of an effective therapist-client relationship. These stereotypes are not limited to mental health professionals, but they are seen in many provider attitudes. Specifically, providers often believe themselves in the "Can't teach an old dog new trick" syndrome which influence their goals and expectations for the elderly. A second hurdle is entitled "My, God, I'm mortal too" and refers to the provider's awareness of the reality of aging and one's own mortality. The third hurdle occurs when providers see little value in working with the elderly and essentially adopt "Why bother?" attitudes or else they believe that "Senility is natural" and expect the elderly to be forgetful, etc. Providers also can become involved in a role reversal which is seen as an "I'm the child" attitude whereby they respond to the elderly patient as though to a parent. In direct contrast, other providers participate in the "Patient is a child" myth whereby elderly people are treated as children.

The first step in dealing with such stereotypes as mentioned above is awareness. Once awareness takes place, introspection to search out personal beliefs and attitudes needs to occur followed by an acknowledgment that an older person is someone who has just grown older. The "unique personhood" remains with the same basic needs, drives, and desires as were evidenced during prior years.[15]

In recent years research findings have disputed many of these myths about aging by providing evidence that intellectual differences and abilities are generally due to genetic endowment and social, cultural, and educational influences rather than being an inevitable response to the aging process. Hence those who interact with the elderly have a responsibility to respect their abilities and to support their efforts as vital, contributing people.

PSYCHOLOGICAL FACTORS IN AGING

Marked psychological decline is not necessarily inherent in the aging process. Some changes do occur in most people, but many more can be prevented or lessened by paying attention to the environment as well as by strengthening the coping ability of the person. Effective interaction with the environment depends largely on the ability to receive information accurately. Impairments in perception, as well as sensory blurring due to decreased acuity to light, noise, pain, taste, or odor, influence how people react to their human and nonhuman environments. Also increased stress and agitation affect perception and sensory accuracy, and in extreme forms can lead to "physical disease which manifests or interacts with aging to increase degenertion."[16] Stressful situations tend to be those that are novel, intense, and rapid in occurrence as well as those that precipitate boredom, frustration, and fatigue. For any situation to elicit a stress response it must be perceived as threatening or in some way unpleasant or potentially damaging. Two people may perceive the same occurrence in entirely different ways, depending on their individual past experiences, perceptual acuity, intelligence, education, personality, and state of health.

How people handle stress also depends largely on their past experiences, innate ability to cope and problem solve, and the quality of their support systems. Older people are especially susceptible to rapid and sudden changes that require an immediate response as well as to the often stressful changes in life style brought about by retirement, physical disability, losses of friends and family due to death or relocation, and decreasing resources. Frequently observed behavioral responses to stress include fatigue, repetition, hearing impairment, faulty coordination, and increased errors.

The elderly and drug abuse

Older people, like those in all other stages of the life cycle, often use drugs in their attempts to cope with stress. Although older Americans are less likely to drink than younger ones, there are still a substantial number of elderly who are problem drinkers. The tendency to misuse alcohol by mixing it with medication is heightened in this group because of the

Older people, like those in all other stages of the life cycle, often use drugs in their attempts to cope with stress.

number of people with chronic ailments who must take medication regularly. The highest incidence of alcoholism occurs among widows, largely due to the stress of loneliness and dealing with problems that their spouses typically handled.

The incidence of alcoholism is higher in the West and Sun Belt regions, where large numbers of older people retire. It is also important to be aware that a substantial proportion of elderly alcoholics begin to abuse alcohol late in life at a time when they often have a simultaneous high rate of medical problems.[17] In contrast the geriatric opiate abuser does not typically reflect an adult onset of drug abuse, but rather is more often a person who has been involved in this activity for many years. There is a much greater chance for rehabilitation if the alcohol or opiate abuse resulted from stress than if it has been a lifelong pattern.

A third category of drug-abusers is the inadvertent abusers who accidentally take too much medication, do not take the designated medication, or mix alcohol and medication. The elderly, because of their decreased physical resilience, are twice as likely to react adversely to even normal doses of medication. They also experience side effects from a wider variety of medications than their younger counterparts.[18] Another variation of inadvertent abuse occurs when a group of elderly people, often living in close proximity, not only share drugs but hoard medications to the

38

extent that they become outdated and lose their effectiveness. Because persons age 55 and older are the largest group of consumers of legal drugs, they need to be counseled not to mix alcohol or over-the-counter medications with those that are prescribed.

Several over-the-counter medications produce side effects that may appear to be symptomatic of psychological dysequilibrium. Because the most frequently abused drugs of older people are sleeping pills, laxatives, and aspirin compounds, it is important to be alert for key symptoms. For example when bromide (as in Sominex and Bromo Seltzer) accumulates in the body, symptoms such as confusion and disorientation can mimic organic brain syndrome. Also antihistamines found in most cold remedies and anticholinergics, such as scopolamine, which is found in many over-the-counter medications, can also cause a state of confusion. Excessive consumption of aspirin compounds tends to produce both physical and psychological symptoms.

In general the more physiologically disabled people are, the more susceptible they are to stress. Intervention in the form of accurate assessment and immediate implementation of a plan to help manage stress is imperative. Astute observations and careful listening are often crucial to accurate assessment of stress-related symptoms.

Changes in behavior and personality

Personality is intimately related to psychological adaptation. Although some personality characteristics may change with aging, in general, personality traits are continuous throughout the life span. At any given time people are more like they were at an earlier developmental stage than they are similar to peers. Personality is a product of heredity and environment, and comprises the individual's unique way of perceiving, thinking, believing, acting, and feeling.

Behavioral responses tend to become more exaggerated in older people, but they still are reminiscent of earlier behaviors. Because of their decreased reaction time, learning capacity, and perception, many older people tend to become more inner-directed or introverted. This is evidenced by an increased preoccupation with themselves—their thoughts, bodily functions, and wants.

Consistent with a tendency toward introversion is a predisposition toward conservatism. In this sense convervatism refers to a general desire to avoid change in order to maintain the status quo. This trend is manifested in "behavioral rigidity, unyieldingness, greater consistency in social and political attitudes."[19] Older people are less tolerant of ambiguities and try to impose structure when possible. They also tend to be more hesitant in making judgments and taking chances. Although they are conservative in decision making and most behaviors, the elderly deviate from this tendency in certain social behaviors that are viewed as being outspoken or in wearing clothes that do not fit the occasion. Seemingly older people feel less need to be "socially proper" and indulge themselves in behaviors previously resisted.

Perception

Perception refers to an individual's ability to receive, register, process, and respond to a stimulus. Perception occurs at the points of contact between people and their internal and external environments and is largely determined by past experiences, quality of sensory receptors, biases, beliefs, values, and attitudes. "Sensory, cognitive, motor, conceptual and affective processes are all linked with one another in any given perceptual act."[20] Because perception reflects the psychological point of contact between an individual and the environment, it is a central element in effective adaptation. Debner emphasizes the importance of perception in understanding aging when he says: "changes in perception are of the greatest significance because they influence actual behavior more directly than changes in sensation."[21] Older people tend to have difficulty in differentiating stimuli from their background. They also need sufficient time to perceive complex or incomplete representations. Hurrying an older person tends to diminish perceptual acuity due to a tendency toward caution in arriving at judgments about what is seen as well as a need for more time to interpret accurately the stimuli.

It is important to watch and listen for verbal and nonverbal cues that reflect the older person's perception in order to clarify any possible inaccuracies. Reactions of fear, doubt, skepticism, or hurt feelings may signal perceptual confusion. When the older person's perception appears different it is often helpful to reconstruct the event and look at all aspects to determine what really occurred.

Faulty perception of environmental specifics may lead to seemingly inappropriate behavior. The older person's response might imply faulty thinking and

reasoning when the error was actually one of perception. Lighting can dramatically affect perception by clearly illuminating the environment; thus care should be taken to choose the most effective form of lighting. Fluorescent lighting, which has a low operating cost, often is avoided because of its tendency to cause glare and eyestrain.

Sensory acuity

Although alterations in sensory acuity have both physiological and psychological bases, they clearly influence psychological adaptability by reducing or altering the information received. Key psychological aspects of functioning, such as communication, thinking, problem solving, and to some extent self-image, are influenced by the degree of sensory acuity. Because loss of sensory acuity causes alienation from the environment, it is vitally important to determine if deficits exist and provide interventions, such as glasses, hearing aids, and altered environmental cues, where possible.

Hearing

Hearing deficits are common in older people, with changes often so subtle that the onset of impairment goes unnoticed. Carstenson found that approximately 70 percent of older people in the senior citizen and nutrition centers sampled had hearing deficits, as did approximately 90 percent of the nursing home population sampled. It was also found that, while hearing aids significantly helped only one-third of those with deficits, up to 80 percent could be aided to regain hearing capability by learning to read lips and by instructing people to speak to them more slowly to allow accurate processing.[22]

Hearing testing is usually done for tone; this measure is not useful in an aging group because most can pass a tone test. Many people who are considered hard of hearing suffer from a selective high-frequency loss rather than a general decrease in auditory acuity.[23] Thus voices, telephones, and doorbells with a low tone are more accurately heard. There is also decreased ability to discriminate the consonants *s*, *f*, *t*, and *g*. Older people also have difficulty with long sentences, fast speech, as well as discrimination of words from background noise. Because of difficulties it is important to speak slowly, concisely, audibly, and in a moderate volume (because loudness is heard as shouting).

It is also important to recognize that hearing loss due to degeneration of the central and peripheral auditory mechanisms as well as increased rigidity to the basilar membrane often leads to personality change.

The older person's suspicious or often seemingly paranoid behavior may be due to defective hearing; unable to accurately detect what is said, older people may think others are talking about them. A simple gesture, such as putting the hands over the mouth while talking, can markedly muffle words and decrease their clarity. Suspicion may lead to withdrawal due to a feeling of not belonging and a reluctance to confront others with such feelings.

Vision

Many of the visual changes that occur with aging can be remedied with corrective lenses or environmental alteration. Many factors seem to be responsible for visual changes. These factors include decreased light reaching the retina caused by reduced pupil size and reactivity, which results in progressive inability to adapt to darkness; decreased elasticity of eye muscles; impaired color vision; and a gradual shrinking of the visual field.[24] Older people also tend to have presbyopia, or difficulty in focusing on near objects, due to decreased elasticity of the lens.

A variety of simple environmental changes can increase visual acuity for older people. Impaired color vision tends to include difficulty in distinguishing blues, greens, and purples; this problem can be altered by avoiding these colors in areas occupied by older people and choosing reds, yellows, and browns for decor. Sharp color contrasts, such as pairing yellow and brown, may provide the greatest medium for color discrimination. Other mechanisms for increasing the distinctiveness of the environment include the use of handrails that can also serve as "landmarks," as well as wall decorations and signs that help distinguish one room from another.

Problem solving

Older people tend to be slower in problem solving than their younger counterparts because they frequently recall past experiences to provide clues for dealing

---

The older person's suspicious or often seemingly paranoid behavior may be due to defective hearing.

with current situations. They also tend to show poorer performance on such tasks as "describing similarities, completing analogies, constructing sentences from odd words, logical reasoning, tasks of analysis and synthesis, and tasks of inventiveness."[25] These difficulties in problem solving are attributed to errors in organizing complex materials, poor short-term memory, and lack of ability to make fine discriminations among stimuli.

Nursing assessment should reflect careful attention to each person's ability to solve problems. If the task seems overwhelming it can often be divided into several small parts that are more manageable for the elderly person and provide increased opportunities for success. Hurrying the elderly person inevitably impairs problem solving. Also offering alternative solutions from which the person can select is often more useful than expecting a unique solution each time.

Learning

It is difficult to assess accurately whether learning ability is directly affected by age because of the many variables that constitute learning. Debner states that learning ability decreases with age in the areas of new verbal learning and incidental learning. He poses the question, "Is rigidity in holding onto old ways inhibiting new learning, or is there also a deficiency in learning ability?"[26] In general, health, reaction time, and hesitancy to try new things impair learning ability rather than learning being directly related to age. The older person frequently has to do a great deal of unlearning before new learning can take place. Habits, beliefs, and biases are well-established and often resistant to change. This increases the time required to learn new information.

Older people learn better when they have ample time and believe that their efforts, if not correct, will neither be scorned nor be the source of ridicule. They tend to be cautious in new learning, and if hurried they commit omission errors.

Memory

Evidence from research on memory functions in elderly people indicates minimal impairment in the ability to recall the distant past but less accuracy in recall of recently learned information. For purposes of discussion, memory can be categorized into three groups:

1. Short term—immediate memory or the ability to recall items a few seconds after they have been presented;
2. Long term—ability to recall items that were presented from minutes to years before and that the person has not kept in short-term memory by constant use and recall; and
3. Remote—items learned many years ago.[27]

The capacity to store short-term memory is limited, so only items that have considerable meaning to the person are remembered. Elderly people also have difficulty in transferring information from short-term to long-term memory, so deficits occur at this juncture. Remote memory generally is least affected by age. In general, material learned when a person is between 15 and 25 years of age is retained best throughout life. Remote memory is involved in reminiscence.

42 Although studies have failed to support the contention that all older people live in the past, the value of reminiscing should not be underestimated. It is an adaptive process that can provide the nurse with considerable information about previous behaviors, beliefs, and experiences. Not only does reminiscing provide valuable information about the older person, it contributes to a feeling of self-worth and competence when discussing previous successes.[28]

In their book, *Culture and Aging,* Clark and Anderson[29] outline five adaptive tasks that present critical challenges to older people. They contend that successful adjustment at this stage depends on an accurate assessment of personal strengths and weaknesses so as to modify responses to deal appropriately with both internal and external stimuli. These tasks include:

1. Acknowledging that some physical and mental limitations are inherent in the aging process, which necessitates an alteration in activity level in order to cope successfully and conserve finite energy resources;

2. Changing both level and type of physical activities as well as social roles;

3. Finding new ways to fulfill physical, economic, and emotional needs;

4. Developing new criteria for self-evaluation by learning to relax, being more tolerant of others, and experiencing happiness at seeing others succeed; and

5. Establishing new values and goals by recognizing that some tasks will take longer than they previously took.

Nursing interventions provide a unique opportunity to help older people cope with these five tasks and make the later years rewarding rather than dreaded. Although how long people live is important, the quality of life during those years should be of prime concern. Nursing's basic mission is to provide holistic care, including attention to both internal and external stressors as well as strengths.

SUMMARY

The aging person's behavior is a function of the ability to adapt the resources available to the ever-changing environmental demands. Although these people are generally less energetic and physically competent than younger people, they do have the capacity to learn, remember, and reflect. The capability and potential contributions of the elderly should not be discounted or discouraged by harmful myths or stereotypes.

In all age groups, but especially with older people, the environment affects behavior. Declining sensory acuity necessitates environmental modification in the form of color usage, adequate lighting, and slow, clear speech. If older people are treated like children they will behave as such; nursing actions should encourage independence in order to promote self-respect and personal dignity. The value of an ecological view of aging is that it calls attention to the multitude of interacting factors that can maximize or mitigate against psychological adaptation. Deficits in psychological, physiological, or sociocultural resources influence the adaptation of an individual. Responsible nurses should identify deficiencies and seek ways to provide appropriate support and interventions so that the elderly person maintains a maximal level of homeostasis.

REFERENCES

1. Bruhn, J.G. "Is Growing Old Unhealthy?" *Health Values: Achieving High Level Wellness* 3:4 (July 1979) p. 202-205.
2. Tavani, C. "Meeting the Needs of the Oldest of the Old." *Aging* 291:1 (January-February 1979) p. 2-7.
3. Richmond, J.B. "Health Promotion and Disease Prevention in Old Age." *Aging* 295:3 (May-June 1979) p. 11-15.
4. Eisdorfer, C. and Wilkie, F. "Stress, Disease, Aging, and Behavior" in Birren, J.E. and Schaie, J.W., eds. *Handbook of the Psychology of Aging* (New York: Van Nostrand Reinhold Co. 1977) p. 251-275.
5. Miller, J.G. "Living Systems: Basic Concepts." *Behavioral Science* 10 (July 1965) p. 193-237.
6. Birren, J.E. "Psychological Aspects of Aging: Intellectual Functioning" in Kart, C.S. and Manard, B.B., eds. *Aging in America: Readings in Social Gerontology* (Sherman Oaks, Calif.: Alfred Publishing Co. 1976).
7. Richmond, J.B. "Health Promotion and Disease Prevention in Old Age." p. 11-15.
8. Ibid.
9. Shanas, E. "Social Myth as Hypothesis: The Case of the Family Relations of Older People" *Gerontologist* 19:1 (January 1979) p. 3-9.
10. Ibid., p. 13.
11. Tibbitts, C. "Older Americans in the Family Context." *Aging* 270:2 (April-May 1977) p. 6-11.
12. Richmond, J.B. "Health Promotion and Disease Prevention in Old Age." p. 11.
13. Bruhn, J.G. "Is Growing Old Unhealthy?" p. 204.
14. Manney, J.D. *Aging in American Society: An Examination of Concepts and Issues* (Ann Arbor: The Institute of Gerontology 1975) p. 8-50.
15. Hagebak, J.E. and Hagebak, B.R. "Serving the Mental Health Needs of the Elderly: The Case for Removing Barriers and Improving Service Integration" *Community Mental Health Journal* 16:4 (Summer 1980) p. 263-275.
16. Eisdorfer, C. and Wilkie, F. "Stress, Disease, Aging, and Behavior." p. 251.
17. Schukit, M.A. "Geriatric Alcoholism and Drug Abuse." *Gerontologist* 17:2 (February 1977) p. 168-174.
18. Ibid. p. 169.
19. Debner, A.S. "The Psychology of Normal Aging" in Spencer, M.G. and Dorr, C.J., eds. *Understanding Aging: A Multidisciplinary Approach* (New York: Appleton-Century-Crofts 1975) p. 67-90.
20. Weinberg, J. "On Adding Insight to Injury." *Gerontologist* 16:1 (January 1976), p. 4-10.
21. Debner, A.S. "The Psychology of Normal Aging." p. 72.
22. Carstenson, B. "Speech and Hearing Problems Among Older People." *Aging* 285:6 (July-August 1978) p. 24-27.
23. Manney, J.D. "Aging in American Society." p. 75.
24. Siegler, I.C. "Life Span Developmental Psychology and Clinical Geropsychology" in Gentry, W.D., ed. *Geropsychology: A Model of Training and Clinical Services* (Cambridge, Mass.: Ballinger Publ. Co. 1977) p. 87-109.
25. Debner, A.S. "The Psychology of Normal Aging." p. 78.
26. Ibid. p. 79.
27. Ford, J.M. and Roth, W.T. "Do Cognitive Abilities Decline with Age?" *Geriatrics* 32:9 (September 1977) p. 59-62.
28. Ebersole, P. "Reminiscing." *American Journal of Nursing* 76:8 (August 1976) p. 1304-1305.
29. Clark, M. and Anderson, B. *Culture and Aging* (Springfield, Ill: Charles C Thomas 1967) p. 67-68.

Promoting Healthful Aging through Strengthening Family Ties

Gretchen K. Brewer, RN, MS
Clinical Nurse Educator
National Institutes of Health
Bethesda, Maryland

A S INFORMATION from investigative studies becomes increasingly available, perceptions about the elderly are based more on reality than stereotypes. For instance recent data cite that the "over 55" population is larger (more than 38 million), wealthier, better educated, and in better health than ever before.[1] Because of this growth in the population of elderly people, families and professionals will become more involved with the issues of the so-called "aging process." What then, if anything, can families and professionals do to encourage as many individuals as possible to age in a self-responsible, optimally functional, and asymptomatic way?

SOME BELIEFS ABOUT BEHAVIOR

Differentiation of self

This question necessitates a look at certain assumptions about human behavior. These assumptions include the belief

46 that the quality of emotional bonds in a family varies greatly and depends largely on the level of "differentiation of self" of the various family members.[2] This refers to the "degree of fusion, or differentiation, between emotional and intellectual functioning."[3] As such this concept describes a characteristic common to all and addresses a broad range of human functioning.

When a person's intellect and emotions are deeply fused, his or her life tends to be directed by emotions and those things that "feel right" rather than by principles or beliefs. When using this kind of emotionally based behavior, people seem to have difficulty adapting and remaining flexible, becoming emotionally reliant on others. Such people tend to have many of life's "problems" and experience difficulty when trying to resolve dilemmas. In contrast, those persons with a higher level of differentiation tend to be more principle oriented, relying primarily on intellectual functioning. Decisions are based on facts and beliefs; the result is a life pattern of greater adaptability, success, and orderliness.[4]

Two important aspects of this idea of "differentiation of self" are a person's levels of "solid self" and "pseudo self."[5] The solid self consists of clearly delineated convictions, beliefs, and principles, which have evolved through life experiences. They evolve through making well thought-out decisions and taking responsibility for the consequences of those decisions. The beliefs form a framework that, through its consistency, becomes the basis for decision making, even during times of increased anxiety and stress. It is believed that everyone has some quantity of solid self.[6]

The pseudo self evolves through emotional pressure and, as a result, is altered in this same manner. The pseudo self consists of a variety of inconsistent beliefs that a person subscribes to because they are deemed "right." As such these beliefs constitute more of a "pretend self" and facilitate people having pretenses to being something they are not. During periods of intense closeness, one person's pseudo self will fuse with the pseudo self of another. The result is that one "loses" self while the other "gains" self.[7]

Family relationships

Assuming that a broad range of levels of differentiation exists, it follows that people at different levels of differentiation (and different levels of solid self) will use different emotional processes in establishing relationships with others. Relationships in families where members have higher levels of differentiation tend to be more open and flexible. Each person can define and pursue an independent, self-responsible life course. Each can experience close and intimate relationships with others yet become autonomous when the need arises.

Family relationships where the level of differentiation is lower tend to be more rigid and intense. People in this situation expend great energy seeking love and maintaining their "comfortable," dependent relationships. This pursuit becomes even more intense when anxiety increases. As a consequence little, if any, energy is left for defining life goals. Important decisions are made with the sense of wanting to perpetuate love and approval.[8]

Therefore, depending on the type of

relationships in a family, there may result a greater or lesser degree of "connectedness" among family members and across generations. The question that arises is whether the family emotional processes and the resulting connectedness, or lack thereof, serve as a prognosticator of the potential for development of symptomatic behavior in the elderly.

TRANSGENERATIONAL FAMILY RELATIONSHIPS

United States public policy statements on health care tend to focus on particular groups (i.e., the young, the elderly). It is as if the policymakers see little relationship between the functioning of these various groups or as if each of these groups is so totally and exclusively different from the others that there are no commonalities, no ties between them. Because the aging process in and of itself is not necessarily pathological, perhaps some of the problems (i.e., poverty, poor health) identified as belonging to the elderly are similar to the problems of other people, regardless of where people are in their life span. It might even be possible that "problem oldsters" were once "problem youngsters." Attempting to single out the elderly as having such special needs may actually be interfering with, rather than supporting, them. It has been suggested that, "a correlation might exist between a comparative lack of emotional 'connectedness' of elderly persons with younger generations of family members and the onset and development of symptomatic behavior in the same older persons."[9]

One study reveals that in families where the elderly have a personal, one-to-one relationship with various family members across the generations, they tend to be more effective in handling their lives, including such additional stressors as retirement, illness, and death.[10] In other families where there were symptomatic older people, the family members tended to be isolated from each other and rather superficial and constrained in their contacts. There did not appear to be much sense of connectedness between the family members.

In an attempt to identify some mechanisms that were operating in families where aging occurred as a less symptomatic process, it was found that relationships were personal, flexible (i.e., people could alternate between using dependent and independent behaviors depending on the circumstances), and transcended generations.[11] To the extent that this was able to occur, the elderly were functioning effectively at a rather high level, and were experiencing fewer personal, family, and societal crises. When stress did occur they were able to cope more effectively, leading to early resolution.

PROFESSIONALS AND THE "HELPING RELATIONSHIP"

Negative effects

Another investigator studied elderly hospitalized clients who were experiencing disorientation with respect to "significant life events."[12] Although the particular circumstances of each individual's situation were different, the investigator identified what was believed to be a common element. Specifically each of the elderly studied had relinquished his or her responsibility for deciding matters related to significant life issues (i.e., determining whether or not to be hospitalized, determining future care needs, determining whether or not to continue medical care).

Family members and health care professionals had tried to be "helpful" by making the decision for the clients, but the results were not to their clients' liking. Not being satisfied with the outcome of the decisions, the hospitalized individuals became less functional and began to develop a sort of disorientation. The effect of not having made their own important life decisions was that these people began to experience increased anxiety. This phenomenon probably played a part in precipitating limited functioning (i.e., increased anxiety led to more emotional-rather than principle-based decisions).

Other noteworthy characteristics were shared by the clients and their families. First the elderly person was seen as being incapable of "handling" certain kinds of information, such as knowing more about their current state of health and planning for future care. Consequently family members and health care professionals avoided relating directly to the client any information about these issues. However, the clients did not ask to be given any such information, so they, too, seemed to be taking a part in this cycle of being cut off from their surroundings.

Additionally both the family and the health care providers were operating in a "doing for" manner. They did not seem to remember that the clients had a history of successful accomplishments, and that they had once been more self-responsible. In all probability they could operate in a similar manner again. Instead the focus of the health care personnel was the disorientation and its degree of intensity.[13]

"Helping" versus support

Most health care providers are service-oriented people; consequently the professions tend to attract those persons intent on "being helpful." What, though, is being helpful? It is important to distinguish between true support and "help." Distinguishing between the two determines what a "helping" professional can do to provide an individual with the opportunity to live, grow, and remain functional.

Initially it is important that the professional determine exactly what it is clients are capable of doing for themselves. The real dilemma seems to be in deciding precisely what clients' capabilities consist of. When the "helper" (i.e., health care professional) falsely assumes or becomes convinced that individuals are as helpless as they would have others believe, then they can be "helpful."[14] Willingness on the part of professionals to be the helper can deprive clients of opportunities to know and do for themselves, and can, therefore, contribute to and perhaps potentiate underfunctioning and the development of symptomatic behavior. In most instances individuals may be capable of coping with their own problems if they are given the

Willingness on the part of professionals to be the "helper" can deprive clients of opportunities to know and do for themselves.

necessary objective information about a situation.

The health care professional who can remain objective about the issue at hand and relate to the client in a personal, one-to-one manner, can play a significant, supportive role. This happens as the professional supplements information known to the client. The client can then make a meaningful decision congruent with his or her needs. This seems to be more effective than trying to force clients to comply with decisions that others have made. Providing clients with such opportunities may encourage them to take a more principle-based approach to controlling their lives and environment in the present and future.

CAN PROFESSIONAL AND FAMILY RELATIONSHIPS MAKE A DIFFERENCE?

It seems, then, that attributing to the aging process the pseudo-significance of being responsible for, or the cause of, an individual's problems may well be giving the process more importance than reality would warrant. Encouraging people to "connect" across generations may be a more effective direction for professional concern. Some limited data tend to point to the desirability of encouraging people to have frequent, personal contacts with their family members. In so doing people have an opportunity to diffuse some of the anxiety and intense emotionalism that is frequently a part of symptomatic behavior. They can also begin to raise their level of

differentiation, which appears to be a critical component of improved functioning.

Should a time come for individuals to need help from professionals, then the professionals may actually do more by doing less. If clients seem to be managing their own life events, then professional assistance is probably not necessary. Conversely when clients decide the services of a professional are needed, it might be useful for the professionals to keep the following in mind[15]:

- Whose life is it?

- Whose decision is it?

- Who has to live with the consequences of this decision?

Using these questions as a guideline, professionals may find they can better maintain a sense of balance between what clients can know and do for themselves, and what professionals can know and do for clients, whether they are individuals or families.

There is need for continued investigation into the part that family relationships play in whether aging will occur as a symptomatic process. Do family relationships really make any difference, and, if so, why, in some families, do people age and remain quite functional while in other families there is much more symptomatic behavior? Likewise it might be useful to define more clearly what it is that operates in a supportive professional relationship— one that encourages clients to remain responsible, optimally functional, and in control of their lives to the greatest extent possible. It may well be that families and professionals do play a meaningful part.

50   REFERENCES

1. *U.S. News and World Report*. "Life Begins at 55." 89:9 (September 1, 1980) p. 50.
2. Bowen M. "Theory in the Practice of Psychotherapy" in Bowen, M., ed. *Family Therapy in Clinical Practice* (New York: Jason Aronson 1978) p. 362-370.
3. Ibid., p. 362.
4. Ibid.
5. Ibid., p. 364.
6. Ibid., p. 364-365.
7. Ibid., p. 365.
8. Ibid., p. 367.
9. Hall, M. "Aging and Family Processes" in Lorio, J., and McClenathan, L., eds. *Georgetown Family Symposia, Volume II* (Washington, D.C.: Georgetown Family Center 1977) p. 133.
10. Ibid., p. 133-151.
11. Ibid.
12. Nowakowski, L. "Disorientation—Signal or Diagnosis" in Sagar, R., ed. *Georgetown Family Symposia, Volume III* (Washington, D.C.: Georgetown Family Center 1978) p. 297-305.
13. Ibid.
14. Resnick, R. "Chicken Soup is Poison." 1970 (mimeographed).
15. Nowakowski. "Disorientation—Signal or Diagnosis." p. 303.

Health Promotion and the Assessment of Health Habits in the Elderly

Nancy C. Moyer, RN, MSN
Doctoral Candidate
Lecturer
School of Nursing
University of Pennsylvania
Philadelphia, Pennsylvania

THE terms *high-level wellness, health maintenance,* and *health promotion* have come into popular use among health professionals. In a survey of nurses, for instance, 61 percent claimed "health promotion and maintenance" as one of their functions.[1] Associated with this emphasis on health is the assumption that people's health habits affect or largely determine their health status.

Thus most health care workers would concur with Haggerty's statement that "one's life style, including patterns of eating, exercise, drinking, coping with stress, and use of tobacco and drugs, together with environmental hazards, are the major known modifiable causes of illness in America today."[2] The importance of a person's habits is underscored by research that demonstrates a positive correlation between health practices and health status.[3] In light of this evidence, it is clear that nurses have a responsibility not simply to help people cope with or recuperate from illness but also to assist them in developing wellness-generating patterns of behavior.

ATTITUDINAL BARRIERS

Certainly few nurses would seriously object to the previous statement . . . that is, *until* they began to contemplate the meaning of health promotion for the elderly. The seemingly inevitable deterioration of health status then becomes an issue. Suddenly there is the temptation to minimize the importance of altering deleterious habits. The frequently quoted statistic that 80 percent of older Americans have at least one chronic disease[4] can lead nurses to a fatalistic—and possibly ageist—attitude. This attitude is reflected in such statements as: it is simply too late in life to hope for any significant upgrading in the quality of health, or: why bother with attempting to modify patterns that have become ingrained over a lifetime?

In *Healthy People; The Surgeon General's Report on Health Promotion and Disease Prevention*, it is pointed out that "health promotion and disease prevention measures nevertheless should be applied to the elderly. After all, many will be 'elderly' for 10 or 20 years (half of those reaching 65 will live to be at least 80 years old . . .)."[5] In a longitudinal study of health habits in the elderly, Palmore reported that exercise, weight control, and avoidance of cigarettes contributed to better health in this age group.[6] A further reason for pursuing health promotion is that the life expectancy of Americans has not increased significantly over the last 20 years,[7] in spite of massive health care expenditures. We might project that, by reducing hazardous behaviors, unnecessary illness would be decreased and people would enjoy longer and more productive lives.

Regardless of interest in testing such a hypothesis, it would still be useful to determine the health habits of senior citizens. By using an assessment instrument that permitted the quantification of results, it would be possible to identify individuals and groups who are at higher risk of developing a preventable illness. It is this writer's opinion that the tool could also provide the rationale for health education efforts aimed at promoting health in demonstrable ways, rather than simply providing information. Hence the importance of assessing health habits is underlined.

PROBLEMS OF DEFINITION

Nurses and physicians generally assess health practices as part of a comprehensive client history. The information is thus rarely collected and analyzed in a systematic way. Even when an organized attempt is made, a number of problems arise. For example Steele and McBroom point out that "the range and typology of health behavior indicators is limited only by the imagination of the researcher and the purposes of the research."[8]

This statement is verified by an examination of the ways in which various authors have defined health practices, habits, or behaviors. Steele and McBroom themselves identify the use of professional services, including medical and dental checkups and health insurance coverage as "preventive health behaviors."[9] Belloc and Breslow depict health practices as "certain aspects of daily living that may be considered as personal habits related to health."[10] Pesznecker and McNeil describe health habits as "practices which are generally accepted by health professionals as being beneficial or detrimental to the maintenance of health."[11] Because the delineation of significant health practices, habits, and behaviors is by nature arbitrary, some lifestyle patterns that are crucial in promoting health may not yet have been operationalized.

It could be assumed that an individual's level of knowledge about and attitudes toward health-related matters could be an accurate indicator of that person's health status or habits. Unfortunately research studies largely negate this idea. Pratt, for instance, has noted that "general health knowledge was not found to be related to the level of health among the poor."[12] Minkler summarizes that "there is a wealth of . . . data indicating the often surprisingly low correlation between what people say they believe and what they in fact do with respect to health practices."[13] Thus, an older adult might have an extensive *knowledge* of nutrition and might *believe* that health is determined by nutritional patterns. However, if that adult is limited in mobility, finances, or the will to live, then the expression of attitudes and knowledge alone will be deceptive. Although nurses cannot discount clients' beliefs and levels of knowledge, the assessment of health habits is likely to yield more pertinent information with respect to the present concern with altering deleterious behavior patterns.

CRITIQUE OF RELEVANT ASSESSMENT TOOLS

A number of assessment tools published in the nursing literature focus on the needs, habitual activities, or health-related attitudes of senior citizens. None deals specifically with practices that could be considered health promotive for this age group. There is one tool that addresses the subject of health-related behaviors, but it is intended for use with adults of all ages. In the public health literature there are several instruments developed primarily for research purposes.

Reliability and validity

A framework for evaluating assessment tools is suggested in *Instruments for Measuring Nursing Practice and Other Health Care Variables.*[14] Reliability is defined as "the accuracy of the data in sense of their repeatability or stability."[15] Validity is described as "the extent to which the instrument actually measures what it seeks or purports to measure."[16]

Content validity refers to whether the instrument's content is "relevant to the test author's stated purpose."[17] Logical or sampling validity may be defined as "the inclusion of terms which adequately reflect the trait of concern; the aim is "to discriminate between those who possess the trait and those who do not."[18]

Determination of the criterion-oriented (predictive) validity of an instrument entails the correlation of the test's results with some other measure that is supposed to be predicted by the instrument.[19]

54 Belloc and Breslow test

Public health authorities Belloc and Breslow have constructed an instrument that could be useful to nurses. (See Table 1.)[20] It is a questionnaire with test items pertaining to habits of sleep, eating, exercise, alcohol consumption, and smoking. Based on a survey of 6,928 adults, Belloc and Breslow concluded that the test is "highly reliable."[21]

The purpose of this research is to "present data bearing on the association between 'good' health habits and physical

Table 1. Survey of health practices

1. Usual hours of sleep: 　　6 hours or less 　　7 hours or less 　　8 hours 　　9 hours or more
2. How often do you eat between meals? 　　Rarely or never 　　Once in a while 　　Almost every day
3. How often do you eat breakfast? 　　Almost every day 　　Sometimes 　　Rarely or never
4. Weight for height: 　　10% or more under desirable weight 　　5.0 to 9.99% underweight 　　Within 4.99% of desirable weight 　　5.0 to 9.99% overweight 　　10.0 to 19.99% overweight 　　20.0 to 29.99% overweight 　　30% or more overweight
5. How often do you do any of these things? 　　Often　Sometimes　Never 　　Active sports 　　Swimming or taking long walks 　　Working in the garden 　　Doing physical exercises 　　Taking weekend automobile trips 　　Hunting or fishing
6. Consumption of alcoholic beverages: 　　Never 　　Amount at one time: 　　　1 to 2 drinks 　　　3 to 4 drinks 　　　5 or more

Frequency:
　less than 1 per week
　1 to 2 per week
　more than 2 per week

7. Smoking habits:
　Smoking cigarettes:
　　Never
　　Formerly
　　Now
　Amount smoked daily—
　present smokers:
　　1 pack or less
　　More than 1 pack
　Amount smoked daily—past smokers:
　　1 pack or less
　　More than 1 pack
　Whether inhale—present smokers:
　　No
　　Yes, some
　　Yes, deeply
　Whether inhaled—past smokers:
　　No, or some
　　Yes, deeply
　Number of years smoked—
　present smokers:
　　Less than 10 years
　　10 to 19 years
　　20 years or more
　Number of years smoked—
　past smokers:
　　Less than 10 years
　　10 to 19 years
　　20 years or more
　Ever smoke cigars or pipe?
　　Never
　　Formerly
　　Currently

Source: Belloc, N.B. and Breslow, L. "Relationship of Physical Health Status and Health Practices." *Preventive Medicine* 1:3 (1972) p. 409–421. Reprinted with permission.

health status."[22] Most of the questions conform to this purpose. An exception is the inclusion of an inquiry about "weight for height" along with items exclusively concerned with behaviors. The authors justify these as indicators of nutritional status.

The topic of nutritional habits raises questions about the instrument's logical or sampling validity. In this tool there are only three items related to eating habits. They indicate nothing about the content of a person's diet, which is particularly important for the elderly, but rather are directed at meal patterns and body weight. In the case of alcohol consumption, the

---

An individual with undiagnosed, asymptomatic lung cancer could receive a better health status rating than one who complained of mild arthritis.

---

alcoholic content of typically consumed beverages is not taken into account. Only the number of drinks is assessed.

The criterion-oriented validity for Belloc and Breslow's tool appears to be excellent. Health practices as measured by this tool have been correlated with physical health status and with mortality statistics.[23] However physical health status has been self-assessed in this study; it may therefore be subject to a high degree of error. In addition subjects are ranked according to degree of physical disability, number of chronic conditions and symptoms, and energy level. Thus an individual with undiagnosed, asymptomatic lung cancer could receive a better health status rating

than one who complained of mild arthritis.

This assessment tool's weaknesses appear also to be its strengths. For example the instrument covers only a small number of habits in superficial detail; however, the assessment may be performed rapidly, and all of the gathered data are quantifiable. This quantification facilitates the identification of "at risk" individuals.

Oelbaum test

Oelbaum proposes an ambitious and seemingly relevant nursing assessment tool. (See Table 2.)[24] The author claims that "interest in promoting good health prompted me to write a list of criteria for determining levels of wellness in adults."[25] One of Oelbaum's premises is that the behaviors that she specifies are necessary to maintain health; those that are "performed poorly will influence the type of disease, disorder, or damage that will follow."[26] Listed are 26 criteria for assessing wellness, and Oelbaum suggests that a four-point scale be used to measure an individual's "self-reliance."[27] The latter statement calls the instrument's content validity into question. Is the purpose of the tool to measure a person's self-reliance, level of wellness, or health practices? Oelbaum is not clear about this.

Oelbaum has also attempted to consider such diverse facets as utilization of oxygen, humanistic expression of love, and minimization of role conflict. Although these aspects of life would appear to have a bearing on health, their inclusion leads to problems with the tool's logical or sampling validity. In other words the test's 26 items represent 26

Table 2. Hallmarks of adult wellness

A. Performs activities of daily living;	P. Demonstrates personality growth and creative expression appropriate to developmental level and prized by society;
B. Has a stable body image perceived as being socially acceptable;	
C. Provides for own comfort and relaxation (psychological and physical);	Q. Demonstrates high quality cerebral functioning (to remember, think abstractly, transfer knowledge, concentrate, and solve problems);
D. Efficiently disposes of metabolic wastes;	
E. Obtains and maintains an environment conducive to well-being;	
F. Has an appropriate intake and healthy distribution or excretion of fluids and electrolytes;	R. Mobilizes resources to meet needs (internal, significant others, community), begins by expressing needs freely to an appropriate person;
G. Guards against overwhelming changes; regulatory and defense systems intact and helpful;	
H. Maintains good hygiene;	S. Receives and recognizes sensory input (the five senses, balance, proprioception, and body scheme);
I. Builds and maintains meaningful interpersonal relationships, is comfortable with interdependence;	
J. Juxtaposes the tasks of various life roles with minimal conflict while keeping in touch with own needs;	T. Is a team member of own prevention/rehabilitation team, has sufficient understanding, initiative, self-control, and financial resources to maintain health;
K. Accumulates knowledge and skills that bring success in chosen life roles and self-esteem;	U. Recognizes and cherishes the uniqueness of his or her own identity and the uniqueness of each other person;
L. Holds expectations and makes decisions reflecting understanding of own limitations and situational realities;	V. Demonstrates functional verbal and nonverbal communication;
M. Maintains optimal motor function (strength, range of motion, locomotion, gross and fine coordination);	W. Attains healthful balance of productive work and rest;
	X. Humanistically expresses love and respect for all life and the quality of that life;
N. Obtains, digests, and metabolizes appropriate amounts of foods that promote good nutrition;	Y. May have symptoms, but they are yielding to prescribed therapy, uses therapies to help carry out wellness work; and
O. Efficiently utilizes oxygen;	Z. Demonstrates a zest for living.

Source: Oelbaum, C.H. "Hallmarks of Adult Wellness." *American Journal of Nursing* 74:9 (1974). Copyright © 1974, the American Journal of Nursing. Reprinted with permission.

categories. To discern whether an individual "demonstrates a zeal for living,"[28] for example, "zeal" would have to be defined unambiguously.

In some cases then, a number of items would be needed to distinguish those people who possess the specified trait from those who do not. Unfortunately this ambiguity is apparent in every item. The lack of definitions for terms would obviously lead to confusion, in that each person who is to be assessed might have very different preconceptions about the meanings of the terms. The assessment tool's reliability must therefore be seriously questioned.

The criterion-oriented validity of the tool is not indicated. There is no evidence that Oelbaum used the instrument in practice, and hence no effort could be made to correlate results with some other measure of health status. In light of the problems with the tool's reliability and content and logical validity, many modifications and additions would be necessary before using the tool.

Oelbaum's assessment tool represents a promising but unsuccessful attempt at identifying health-promotive practices. Whereas Belloc and Breslow have neglected the difficult task of objectifying a broad spectrum of wellness-promoting habits, Oelbaum has neglected more easily measurable behaviors.

Preferred instrument

Although both instruments have merits and disadvantages for assessing health habits in the elderly, Belloc and Breslow's seems to be more immediately useful. To be especially relevant to older adults, quantifiable items could be added pertaining to dietary content, home safety practices, and social interaction versus isolation. Certain authors imply that social isolation per se in the elderly is not directly related to mental or physical health status.[29] However data gathered through the assessment of this factor in large numbers of senior citizens might yield more objective indications about the validity of considering social isolation as a "risk factor."

MERITS

An assessment of health habits alone will obviously not yield all the information needed to provide care or to plan health promotion programs for older adults. It can be extremely useful, however, in primary care settings and in community settings, such as senior citizens' housing or recreation centers. It provides a means for rapidly evaluating large numbers of people and for identifying prevalent, potentially modifiable problems.

Schatzkin has urged that "to increase life expectancy in this period, we should marshal our resources not toward aging per se, our protoplasmic limitations, but *primarily* toward the *reversible* social determinants of the leading causes of death that keep us from reaching nine and perhaps ten decades of vigorous, healthy life."[30]

Health habits are certainly of prime significance as social determinants of preventable death. Nurses are in a position to contribute to the goal that Schatzkin has outlined: to promote the health of older adults through the assessment of health habits and through the planning of interventions with these factors in mind.

REFERENCES

1. Moses, E. and Roth, A. "Nurse Power; What Do Statistics Reveal about the Nation's Nurses?" *American Journal of Nursing* 79:10 (October 1979) p. 1745-1756.
2. Haggerty, R.J. "Changing Lifestyles to Improve Health." *Preventive Medicine* 6:2 (1977) p. 276-289.
3. Belloc, N.B. and Breslow, L. "Relationship of Physical Health Status and Health Practices." *Preventive Medicine* 1:3 (1972) p. 409-421.
4. Combs, K.L. "Preventive Care in the Elderly." *American Journal of Nursing* 78:8 (1978) p. 1339-1341.
5. U. S. Department of Health, Education, and Welfare. *Healthy People; The Surgeon General's Report on Health Promotion and Disease Prevention* DHEW Pub. No. 79-55071A (Washington, D.C.: Government Printing Office 1979) p. 367.
6. Palmore, E. "Health Practices and Illness among the Aged." *Gerontologist* 10:4 (1970) p. 313-316.
7. Siegel, J.S. "Demography of Aging" in Ostfeld, A.M. and Donnelly, C.B., eds. *Epidemiology of Aging* U. S. Department of Health, Education, and Welfare Pub. No. (NIH) 75-711 (Washington, D.C.: Government Printing Office 1975) p. 2.
8. Steele, J.L. and McBroom, W.H. "Conceptual and Empirical Dimensions of Health Behavior." *Journal of Health and Social Behavior* 13:4 (1972) p. 382-392.

58

9. Ibid. p. 385.
10. Belloc, N.B. and Breslow, L. "Relationship of Physical Health Status and Health Practices." p. 411.
11. Pesznecker, B.L. and McNeil, J. "Relationship among Health Habits, Social Assets, Psychologic Well-Being, Life Change, and Alterations in Health Status." *Nursing Research* 24:6 (1975) p. 442–447.
12. Pratt, L. "The Relationship of Socioeconomic Status to Health." *American Journal of Public Health* 61:2 (1971) p. 281–290.
13. Minkler, M. "Health Attitudes and Beliefs of the Urban Elderly." *Public Health Reports* 93:5 (1978) p. 426–432.
14. U. S. Department of Health, Education, and Welfare. *Instruments for Measuring Nursing Practice and Other Health Care Variables* (Volume 2) DHEW Pub. No. (HRA) 78-54 (Washington, D.C.: Government Printing Office 1979).
15. Ibid. p. 792.
16. Ibid. p. 792.
17. Ibid. p. 792.
18. Ibid. p. 792.
19. Ibid. p. 792.
20. Belloc, N.B. and Breslow, L. "Relationship of Physical Health Status and Health Practices." p. 409–421.
21. Ibid. p. 411.
22. Ibid. p. 410.
23. Belloc, N. "Relationship of Health Practices and Mortality." *Preventive Medicine* 2:1 (1973) p. 67–81.
24. Oelbaum, C.H. "Hallmarks of Adult Wellness." *American Journal of Nursing* 74:9 (1974) p. 1623–1625.
25. Ibid. p. 1623.
26. Ibid. p. 1625.
27. Ibid. p. 1624.
28. Ibid. p. 1623.
29. Butler, R.N. and Lewis, M.I. *Aging and Mental Health; Positive Psychosocial Approaches* (St. Louis: C.V. Mosby Co. 1977) p. 129–130.
30. Schatzkin, A. "How Long Can We Live? A More Optimistic View of Potential Gains in Life Expectancy." *American Journal of Public Health* 70:11 (November 1980) p. 1199–1200.

Sexuality in the Later Years

Harriet Yoselle, MSN, R.N.C.S.
Psychotherapist
Certified Sex Therapist
Private Practice and Partner
Chesapeake Mental Health
  Resources, Chartered
Washington, D.C.

ALTHOUGH AMERICANS have begun to talk about sex education for their children, the March 1980 *SIECUS Report* suggests that sex education should perhaps be directed to adults in society.[1] American society tends to be youth-oriented, thereby ignoring adults. Those working in the field of sex education have paid limited attention to the psychosocial-sexual education of adults. Those working in sex counseling or therapy see a population where dysfunction has already occurred.

Relative to other stages of human development, it is probably adults 50 years old and above who are most handicapped by misinformation, myths, and communication barriers about sexual issues. American society also tends to have a rather ambivalent outlook on sexuality, generally, including sexual expression among older adults. Two trends—ambivalence about aging and ambivalence about adult sexuality—combine and discourage individuals and couples from enjoying a continual

60 process of adjusting and growing as sexual human beings.[2]

Health care professionals can perpetuate this educational need and inadvertently encourage a communication barrier by ignoring the effects of illness, medication, physical, and psychosocial adjustments of aging on sexual expression. By this neglect, old myths are reinforced, and the importance of sex throughout the life cycle is denied. Each individual strives to find a personal standard for intimacy and to form lasting relationships. Sex is the peak physical form of intimacy. Neither age nor infirmity automatically spells the end of sexual activity.

KEY CONCEPTS

There are several key concepts for health care practice regarding sexual activity throughout the life cycle. These are summarized by Woods as follows.

1. There is no arbitrary age in human life at which sexual functioning ceases.
2. Psychosocial demands placed on individuals throughout adult life have the capability of influencing sexual interest, activity, and functional capacity.
3. Sexual activity and interest persist well into old age provided the individual is in relatively good health, and has an interested and interesting partner.
4. Aging is accompanied by changes in sexual anatomy and physiology for both men and women.[3]

The following additional guidelines can assist the individual in maximizing his or her understanding of sexual response at any age.

1. By age 40, 90 percent of males experience at least one erectile failure; this is a normal occurrence and not a sign of a major dysfunction.
2. Most sexual problems are the result of emotional or social, rather than biological or organic, phenomena.
3. Attitude and self-thoughts can influence arousal considerably. The key self-thought is that "sex and pleasure" go together, not "sex and performance."
4. A male does not need an erect penis to satisfy a female. Orgasms achieved through manual or oral stimulation can be just as sexually satisfying.
5. A key element in sexual responsiveness is to become actively involved in the pleasurable and sexually arousing interaction.
6. An important component in learning to feel comfortable with arousal and potency is the ability to make clear, direct, assertive requests of a partner for the type of sexual stimulation one finds most arousing. It is important for partners to learn to verbally and nonverbally guide one another.
7. Myths and misinformation about sexual functioning create anxiety, depression, and a tendency toward overreaction and self-labeling.

SEXUAL ANATOMY AND PHYSIOLOGY

The human sexual response cycle is a highly rational and orderly sequence of physiological events. If the act of sexual intercourse is to be successful, the genital organs of each partner must undergo profound changes in shape and function from their basal state. The changes are not limited to the genital areas, but also include neurologic, vascular, muscular, and hormonal reactions.[4]

The term *biphasic* is used to indicate that sexual response consists of two distinct and relatively independent components: vasocongestion and myotonia. Genital vasocongestion produces penile erection in the male; it produces vaginal lubrication and swelling in the female. Genital vasocongestion is mediated by the parasympathetic division of the autonomic nervous system. The reflex clonic muscular contractions, myotonia, that constitute orgasm in both genders are primarily a sympathetic function.

Because of these physiologic changes that prepare the unaroused individual for coitus, vasocongestion and orgasm are affected in different ways by physical trauma, drugs, and age. Impairment of erection and ejaculation in the male and of lubrication and orgasm in the female results in different clinical syndromes that respond to different treatment procedures. Because the two components of the sexual response cycle are controlled by different parts of the central nervous system, one of these can be inhibited or impaired while functioning in the other remains normal.[5]

Vasocongestion, causing erection in the male and vasodilation and vaginal lubrication in the female, is governed by a reflex mechanism believed to be located in the sacral segments of the spinal cord. Male orgasm has two phases—emission and ejaculation. It is believed that motor nerves of the voluntary motor system control the striated muscles involved in the ejaculatory phases, or expulsion. Thus in contrast to erection, which is governed by a reflex mechanism that usually cannot be brought under voluntary control, most men are able to achieve voluntary control over the ejaculatory reflex, an involuntary reflex mediated by the voluntary nervous system. It is believed that similar mechanisms that provide some level of voluntary control over orgasm operate for females; however, the neurophysiologic and neuroanatomic bases of female orgasm have not been studied yet, and professionals must rely on inferences from the male in this area.[6]

The nervous system is essentially hierarchical, with the "higher" centers exerting control over the "lower" ones. The central nervous system does not discard its primitive structures, but creates higher, more elaborate integrative centers that dominate the original ones. Thus the lower centers for most reflexes, including the sexual responses, are mediated by a more elaborate supersystem of higher centers located in the midbrain and in the limbic cortex and subcortical nuclei. Lower reflex centers are capable of functioning independently, but do not do so in an individual whose nervous system is intact. They receive impulses from a complex system of higher centers and sources of sensory input that have the power to modify, inhibit, and facilitate their functions.[7] Thus it is sometimes said that the most important sex organ is the brain. This accounts for the important role that mood, fatigue, and information can play on sexual response.

Table 1. Voluntary sexual functions of the nervous system

Some degree of voluntary inhibition and facilitation	Usually voluntary and purely autonomic
Urination	Penile erection
Defecation	Vaginal lubrication
Ejaculation	Genital vasocongestion
Orgasm	Vaginal ballooning
	Nipple erection
	Nonsexual reflexes of dilation of pupils, heart rate, blood pressure, gastric secretion

Those reflexes that, by virtue of cortical dominance, can be brought under voluntary control are summarized in Table 1.

Aided by technological advances like radioimmunoassay, nocturnal penile plethysmography, techniques for measuring penile blood pressure and phalloarteriography, researchers are gathering concrete information about the causes of sexual problems. More than ever before clinicians are able to organically evaluate patients to determine neurological and vascular status. Such data suggests that it is time to reestablish and reevaluate the old notion that 90 percent of all sexual problems are psychogenic in origin.

Sexual potency depends upon an intact neurological, vascular, and hormonal system as well as a healthy psyche. Some researchers and clinicians believe that a random study of impotent males might yield a rate as high as 35 percent of undetected endocrine problems. Others quote a figure as high as 40 percent who believe that organic factors cause sexual dysfunction.[8]

Hormones and sex

Sex steroids also appear to have a profound effect on human behavior because of their actions on the brain. They exert organizing effects on the brain of the developing fetus and affect adult behavior. It is believed that androgen enhances the erotic drive of both genders. The psychological state of a person influences androgen level, which tends to fluctuate in response to psychological and sexual variables as well as age.[9]

In particular, there is a complex relationship between the hormones secreted by the hypothalamus, a pituitary gland and the testes. This is known as the hypothalamic-pituitary-gonadal axis. A breakdown in any part of the system can affect testosterone as well as other hormone levels. The hypothalamus, secretes Luteinizing Hormone Releasing Hormone (LHRH); LHRH stimulates the pituitary to secrete Luteinizing Hormone (LH); LH causes Leydig's cells in the testes to produce testosterone. When the hormone level falls, so do libidinal drives; impotence results.[10]

Another hormone that can disrupt the normal functioning of the hypothalamic-pituitary-gonadal axis is prolactin, a pituitary hormone. Its primary purpose appears to be regulating body functions, including milk production in pregnant women. Its function in the male is unclear. Hyperprolactinemia lowers testosterone levels. It is speculated that prolactin levels seem to be regulated by dopamine and that hyperprolactinemia indicates low dopamine levels. Since dopamine appears to be vital to arousal, both general and sexual, low dopamine means low arousal and even impotence.[11]

Four stages of sexual response

As defined initially by Masters and Johnson,[12] there are four stages of sexual response. Katchadourian[13] has summarized some of the changes that occur in each phase. (See Table 2.)

Kaplan enlarged upon the work of Masters and Johnson. This has resulted in what is now called the Triphasic Model of Sexual Response. Kaplan noted that desire was a separate phase in addition to arousal and orgasm. She describes problems of desire—or hypoactive desire—as a distinct area that responds to somewhat different treatment approaches than those of arousal or orgasm.[14] Thus for discussion of sexuality in the later years, this triphasic model will be used, and the following will be addressed: (1) desire, (2) arousal, and (3) orgasm.

SOCIOLOGICAL AND PSYCHOLOGICAL VARIABLES OF AGE

As many complaints are found in later life about sexual incompatibilities between partners as at any other time. Interest on one side and disinterest on the other, passivity, rebuffs, or failure to agree on frequency are not uncommon. Problems also arise when one partner is incapacitated or chronically ill, and the other is healthy.

As many complaints are found in later life about sexual incompatibilities between partners as at any other time.

Table 2. Reactions of sex organs during sexual response cycle

Male	Female
Excitement phase	
Penile erection	Vaginal lubrication
Thickening, elevation of scrotal sac	Thickening of vaginal walls and labia
Partial testicular elevation and increase in size	Expansion of inner $\frac{2}{3}$ of vagina and elevation of cervix and corpus
	Tumescence of clitoris
Plateau phase	
Increase in penile coronal circumference and testicular tumescence	Orgasmic platform in outer $\frac{1}{3}$ of vagina
Full testicular elevation and rotation	Full expansion of $\frac{2}{3}$ of vagina, uterine and cervical elevation
	Withdrawal of clitoris, "sex-skin"; discoloration of minor labia
Orgasmic phase	
Contractions of accessory organs of reproduction; vas deferens, seminal vesicles, ejaculatory duct, prostate	Contractions of uterus from fundus toward lower uterine segment
Contractions of penile urethra at 0.8-second intervals	External rectal sphincter contractions
Anal sphincter contractions	
Resolution phase	
Refractory period with loss of pelvic vasocongestion	Ready return to orgasm with retarded loss of pelvic vasocongestion
Loss of penile erection	Loss of "sex-skin" color and orgasmic platform
	Loss of clitoral tumescence and return to position

64 Certain older people were less interested in sex even as young people. For others sex has been a longstanding focus of emotional conflict—whether in terms of individual psychodynamics or from difficult relations with partners. Other people may stop sex because they have simply grown tired of it, either due to the same partner over time, which has led to dullness, or finding compensation by developing satisfying nonsexual activities. If an individual has made a deliberate decision to share sex only with a particular partner, sex may end when illness or death intervenes. The opportunity to discontinue sex under the socially acceptable guise of "sexless old age" can be a relief for some.

Whatever the reasons, it is possible to live a happy and satisfying life without sex if this is the individual's choice. However those older people who do enjoy sex deserve encouragement, support, and the necessary information and treatment if problems arise. The physical and emotional responsiveness of sexuality goes well beyond the sex urge and the sex act. It offers the opportunity to express not only passion but affection, esteem, and loyalty. It expresses delight in being alive as well as the continuous challenge to grow and change in new directions.[15] By understanding the normal physical changes in sex caused by aging, one can continue to enjoy affirmative evidence in one's body and its functioning.

The human sexual response cycle in older persons has been studied from ages 51 through 89. All four phases of sexual response become slower in aging, but at no point does sexual responsiveness stop. A discussion of the more common sexual changes that occur in males and females as they get older follows. Most of these changes accompany illness (whether temporary or chronic) and some types of injuries. These changes do not necessarily happen at the same time for a given individual; they can occur at different times, and not everyone experiences all of them.

NORMAL PHYSIOLOGICAL AND ANATOMICAL CHANGES IN SEXUALITY WITH AGE

For both males and females, physiological and anatomical changes occur with age in the genitalia. For example, changes in penile blood flow may occur. Often these changes are not identified even though arteriosclerotic changes elsewhere in the body are systemic. In addition to the old mind-body dichotomy, there is also a body-gonadal dichotomy. Only recently have we assumed that changes in vascular and neurological status anywhere in the body could also include the genitalia. As we understand more about the normal changes in sexual anatomy and physiology that occur with age we will adjust without undue alarm or pessimism.

Males

Desire

On the average, frequency of sexual activity declines with advancing age. Serum testosterone decreases over the years. Some men have as much or almost as much sex in their seventies as in their twenties. One study reported that about 15 percent of the people over 65 in the population studied said they were having more sex than ever before.[16] A 1961 study of males with an average age of 71 indicated that 75 percent still had sexual desires, but only 55 percent satisfied them.[17] Widower's Syndrome," the term used by sex therapists to describe psychological and social situations that may lead to temporary impotence, can occur when there is a recent death of a partner or a period of abstinence. In general whatever happens in a relationship at this period in a couple's life depends to a great extent on what has gone on before.

There is no physical menopause in men analogous to that in women because hormone loss in men does not occur precipitously. Decrease in male hormone testosterone takes place gradually as one grows older and there are wide variations from man to man. Distinct psychological symptoms are also rare and can usually be accounted for by other circumstances, such as reactions to retirement, to aging in general, or to other stresses.[18] As noted earlier, behavior is the final common pathway for a variety of variables—the brain can exert the dominant influence on sexual behavior—so the importance of psychological determinants cannot be underestimated.

Excitement

The older the male the more time it takes to attain a full penile erection. More than in younger years direct penile stimulation may be required to achieve erection. If stimuli are removed and erection is lost, it may be more difficult to re-attain. The vasocongestion response of the scrotum is reduced markedly in older males. The testicles elevate later and to a lesser degree. To have a satisfying sexual experience, an older male may have to consider factors he could safely ignore when younger. That is, he can no longer function automatically. Arousal conditions and proper stimulation become crucial.[19]

Plateau

Full penile erection does not always occur until late in this phase, just before ejaculation. In general erections may not be as hard or as full. Some men discussed their erections in terms of percentages of how hard they used to be (i.e., 60 percent or 80 percent). Ejaculatory control, a problem for many younger men, often comes automatically with aging. Not only does orgasm take longer to reach, but many men past 40 years old find that they have no desire to ejaculate every time they have sex. They can maintain an erection for a relatively long time and need not end each experience with ejaculation. Few men see this as a big problem, but can feel surprised and a bit discomforted by it. Acceptance of the fact that orgasm is not necessary for a good sexual experience is needed. An advantage of not ejaculating every time is that the male can have more frequent erections because refractory periods are usually shorter when there is no ejaculation. Vasocongestive increase in the size of the testes rarely occurs in older males, and "sex flush" occurs less frequently.[20,21]

Orgasm

Ejaculation is less powerful. The two-stage process of orgasm is reduced to a one-stage phase in that the sense of ejaculatory inevitability may vanish, and orgasm may feel less intense. Seminal fluid

66 emerges under less pressure and may feel somewhat different than it did before. As noted earlier, the urge to ejaculate with each erection may decrease to every second or third time a man engages in sex. Rectal sphincter contractions during orgasm occur less frequently. Penile contractions may be fewer in number. According to one concept, as the biologic urges lessen with age, older males become more like the traditional stereotype of women in their sexual behavior in that fantasy and ambience become more important in lovemaking, and there is relatively less preoccupation with orgasm.[22]

Resolution

The refractory period between ejaculations may be extended greatly. Masters and Johnson found that many men in their 50s and 60s could not get a full erection for 12 to 24 hours after their last ejaculation,[23] regardless of how much stimulation was applied. Loss of erection after ejaculation occurs extremely rapidly and testicular descent occurs more quickly—even before ejaculation is complete.

Females

Most of the sexual changes in women can be traced to the decline of female hormones following menopause rather than to aging itself. Menopause is a rich source of myths about loss of sexual desire, inevitable depression, and masculinization, among others. In truth 60 percent of all women experience no remarkable physical or emotional symptoms with menopause, and most of those who do, experience only minimal to moderate physical problems. Life stresses can precipitate or exacerbate menopausal symptoms.[24]

Desire

The effect of withdrawal of the female sex steroids is variable. Some women report a decrease of sexual desire; many women actually feel an increase in erotic appetite during the menopausal years and after. As in males the fate of libido seems to depend on a number of factors including physiologic changes, sexual opportunity, and diminution of inhibition. From a purely physiologic standpoint, libido theoretically should increase at menopause because the action of the woman's androgens, which is not materially affected by menopause, is now unopposed by estrogen.[25]

With advancing age a woman may depend on a decreasing number of men for her sexual expression. A woman who has regular sexual opportunity tends to maintain her sexual responsiveness; without such opportunity sexuality declines markedly. Erotic involvements with men and masturbation are not unusual at later ages, and erotic dreams are often reported by women over age 65.[26]

Excitement

Vaginal lubrication produced by congestion of the blood vessels in the vaginal wall is the physiological equivalent of erection in the male. Lubrication of the walls of the vagina takes longer as a women grows older. Due to the atrophy of the vagina there is also a significant reduction in the expansion of the vaginal barrel both in length and width. These changes are related to the loss of estrogen. When this happens intercourse may feel scratchy, rough, or painful. Typically the lining of the vagina begins to thin and can become easily irritated. Intercourse of a long duration or following a long period without sexual contact can result in pain, cracking, or bleeding during and after intercourse.[27]

With the thinning of the vaginal walls and loss of vaginal elasticity, the bladder and urethra are less protected and may become irritated during intercourse. Older women can develop what is sometimes called "honeymoon cystitis," an inflammation of the bladder resulting from bruising and jostling. This tends to be an irritative condition initially, rather than a bacterial infection.

With the loss of estrogen, the usually acid vaginal secretions become less acidic, increasing the possibility of vaginal infection. This condition is variously called estrogen-deficient, steroid deficient, atrophic, or "senile" vaginitis. These conditions are treatable. Treatments with water-soluble lubricants, local applications of vaginal estrogen creams and suppositories, variations in intercourse positions, or steroid replacements are helpful.[28]

Plateau

During the plateau phase the uterus does not elevate into the false pelvis to the same extent that it did when the woman was younger. The labia also do not exhibit the same elevation and skin characteristics as in younger women. Clitoral size may be slightly decreased, but usually not until the woman reaches from 60 to 70 years of age. The clitoral hood atrophies as does the fat pad over the mons. The loss of this fatty tissue may leave the clitoris less protected

and more easily irritated, but it still remains the source of intense sexual sensation and orgasm, as it was in earlier years.[29]

Orgasm

Women in good health who were able to achieve orgasms in younger years can continue having them well into their 80s. In fact some women begin to have orgasms for the first time as they grow older. The orgasmic phase does become shorter in the middle years. Some women experience spasms in the uterus that cause abdominal pain. This is evidence of hormonal insufficiency and can be treated.

In contrast to men elderly women remain capable of enjoying multiple orgasms. Studies have indicated that 25 percent of 70-year-old women still masturbate.[30] Women who have had patterns of regular sexual intercourse once or twice a week over the years seem to experience fewer symptoms of sexual dysfunction than women with infrequent patterns. Regular contractions during intercourse and orgasm maintain vaginal muscle tone and their lubricating capacity continues unimpaired. Contact with the penis also helps preserve the shape and size of the vaginal space.[31]

Resolution

As with males the resolution phase occurs much more rapidly as the body recovers to its preexcitement phase.

Fear of failure

With both males and females there is generally no way to overemphasize the

68

> *There is generally no way to overemphasize the importance that "fear of failure" plays in withdrawal from sexual performance.*

importance that "fear of failure" plays in withdrawal from sexual performance. Problems arise when a male asks the question: "Can I finish what I start?" He is then less likely to try. Knowledge about the normal physiological changes that occur during aging can greatly enhance adjustment and enjoyment of sexual expression. Learning new patterns of lovemaking to adjust to changes is not difficult. Sex education and supportive intervention can aid the individual in making the behavioral adjustments as well as the psychological adjustments necessary to continue sexual enjoyment. It also can aid in discriminating between drug effects, illness effects, and the expected range of sexual expression. Without adequate information the message comes through that "sex is not for you."

EFFECTS OF ILLNESS AND DRUGS ON SEXUAL RESPONSE

Because of the increased incidence of illness and use of medication during the aging process the effects of medication on the sexual response cycle should be discussed. As noted earlier despite some organic disability, it is still very possible for individuals and couples to enjoy sexual experiences. Understanding the effects of drugs and illness can minimize overreactions and destructive assumptions.

A disturbing example is a client who recently sought psychotherapy for depression subsequent to his decision to divorce his wife after 25 years of marriage. A major complaint was his decreased libido and inability to maintain an erection during sex with his wife for the last five years. He attributed these problems to problems in their relationship. A detailed history revealed that this man had been put on medication for hypertension by his physician five years earlier and was not informed that probable side effects included decreased libido and erectile problems. A subsequent consultation with his physician resulted in the lowering of his antihypertensive medication, with noted improvement in sexual responsiveness. Knowledge of the drug's effect and brief sex therapy intervention resulted in major improvements in the couple's sexual relationship.

A CONCEPTUAL SCHEME FOR INTERVENTION

Nurses can support the quality of sexual adjustment by willingness to convey information and support. Annon provides a conceptual scheme for the behavioral treatment of sexual issues that can serve as a guideline for a nursing approach.[32]

Annon's model is referred to as the P-LI-SS-IT model. The model provides for four levels of approach, and each letter or pair of letters designates a suggested method for uncovering and resolving sexual concerns. The four levels are: (1) Permission, (2) Limited Information, (3) Specific Suggestions, and (4) Intensive Therapy. This model allows the nurse to gear the approach to a client's particular level of competence and supplies the nurse with a plan that aids in determining when referral elsewhere is appropriate.

Level I. Permission

As the first level of treatment, the client is "permitted" to communicate about sexual issues. This is an opportunity for the nurse to open up the topic for discussion and to convey a humanistic, pleasure-oriented view of sexuality rather than a performance-oriented view. By including a discussion of sexual matters along with other aspects of health and illness, the nurse conveys the assumption that sex is an expression of the self. As part of the health assessment, a psychosexual assessment is included in order to develop a comprehensive nursing plan.

The guidelines below may be helpful for the assessment. Some of these are suggested by Annon as an adjunct to his model.[33]

1. Conduct several interviews or discussions to complete the history of the client and initiate his or her sexual education.
2. Ensure privacy and confidentiality.
3. Proceed from "less" sensitive to "more" sensitive areas of discussion; from general to specific.
4. Do not reinforce defenses or take sides. Anxiety will be present in several forms, including jokes, silence, testing, distortions, or trying to please.
5. Clarify vocabulary in order to share meaning. Try to use the same words the client does to convey respect and reassurance. Words are a powerful way to convey a value system.
6. Help the client describe his or her

sexual life accurately. Be careful not to overgeneralize or oversimplify.
7. Use an interviewing style that assumes most people have experienced the phenomenon to be introduced. Use of the "ubiquity" question discourages yes or no responses (For example, "When did you first hear about ...", or "Many people experience .... What has been your experience ... ?").
8. Maintain a strong awareness of the client's sense of comfort and value system. It is possible for a nurse to give the nonverbal communication that she or he would prefer not to hear the answers to his or her questions. Role-playing a sexual history with a colleague can be helpful in producing more ease and skill.

Level II. Limited information

Providing limited information is a preventive measure as well as a treatment technique. Limited information is usually given in conjunction with permission giving. By limiting information to the patient's concerns, the nurse can dispel myths and provide key information. This is an opportunity for the nurse to share knowledge of sexual anatomy and physiology and the normal changes that occur in aging.

Level III. Specific suggestions

Active steps that the client can follow to change his or her sexual behavior and that can be given to an individual alone or to a couple include specific readings, self-stimulation procedures, graded sexual responses, and alternative sexual positions or

70

activities. Here a more detailed sexual problem history is needed as well as greater expertise on the part of the nurse.

Level IV. Intensive therapy

Intensive therapy involves a referral to a qualified sex therapist. In each of the earlier levels of intervention, the nurse has the opportunity to share knowledge or to choose to refer the client to another professional with specific training in sex therapy. More nurses should consider getting certified as sex educators, counselors, and therapists. Interest in this process can be pursued by contacting the American Association of Sex Educators, Counselors, and Therapists in Washington, DC.

The nurse must give herself or himself permission not to have to be an expert on all issues. Rather he or she serves as a patient advocate and assists the client in maximizing his or her health potential by taking the appropriate nursing action. The nurse can undertake each level of intervention or make the necessary referral.

SEXUAL HEALTH

The role of health care providers is to provide comprehensive health care for all clients. Because sexuality is critically important to the client's self-image and to feelings of self-worth and accomplishment, the tasks of health care providers include: (1) assessment of sexual health functioning; (2) provision of sexual education; and (3) inclusion of treatment for sexual dysfunctions as part of the concept of rehabilitation.

Key to the concept of rehabilitation is the notion of assisting the individual to achieve maximal level of functioning. By their willingness to move into a largely ignored aspect of human functioning, nurses can take a central role as client advocates in their efforts to improve the quality of life in health and in illness.

REFERENCES

1. Roberts, E.J. and Holt, S.A. "Parent-Child Communication about Sexuality." *SIECUS Report* 8 (March 1980) p. 2.
2. McCarthy, B.W., Ryan, M., and Johnson, F.A. *Sexual Awareness: A Practical Approach* (San Francisco: Scrimshaw Press and Boyd and Fraser 1975) p. 165-178.
3. Woods, N.F. *Human Sexuality in Health and Illness* (Saint Louis: The C.V. Mosby Co. 1979) p. 69-70.
4. Kaplan, H.S. *The New Sex Therapy* (New York: Brunner/Mazel Publishers 1974) p. 5.
5. Ibid. p. 5-33.
6. Ibid.
7. Ibid. p. 34-45.
8. "A Blueprint for the Medical Evaluation of Impotence." *Sexual Medicine Today* 4:10 (October 1980) p. 4.
9. Ibid. p. 46-61.
10. "A Blueprint" p. 5-6.
11. Ibid. p. 7-8.
12. Masters, W. and Johnson, V. *Human Sexual Response* (Boston: Little, Brown and Co. 1966).
13. Katchadourian, H.A. and Lunde, D.T. *Fundamentals of Human Sexuality* (New York: Holt, Rinehart, and Winston 1972) p. 78.
14. Kaplan, H.S. *Disorders of Sexual Desire* (New York: Simon and Schuster 1979).
15. Butler, R. and Lewis, M. *Love and Sex After Sixty* (New York: Harper & Row 1976) p. 1-9.
16. Zilbergeld, B. *Male Sexuality* (New York: Bantam Books 1978) p. 334.
17. Kaplan, H.S. *The New Sex Therapy.* p. 104-116.
18. Butler and Lewis. *Love and Sex After Sixty.* p. 23.
19. Zilbergeld. *Male Sexuality.* p. 332-334.
20. Ibid.
21. Butler and Lewis. *Love and Sex After Sixty.* p. 192-194.
22. Zilbergeld. *Male Sexuality.* p. 332-334.
23. Masters and Johnson. *Human Sexual Response.* p. 248-270.

24. Butler and Lewis. *Love and Sex After Sixty.* p. 12.
25. Kaplan. *The New Sex Therapy.* p. 111.
26. Ibid. p. 112.
27. Butler and Lewis. *Love and Sex After Sixty.* p. 12-13.
28. Ibid. p. 13-14.
29. Ibid.

30. Kaplan. *The New Sex Therapy.* p. 112.
31. Butler and Lewis. *Love and Sex After Sixty.* p. 15.
32. Annon, J.S. *Behavioral Treatment of Sexual Problems* (Hagerstown, Md.: Harper & Row 1976) p. 43-47.
33. Ibid. p. 38-39.

Chronic Care and the Elderly: Impact on the Client, the Family, and the Nurse

Charlotte Eliopoulos, RNC, MPH
Director of Nursing
Levindale Geriatric
  Center and Hospital
Baltimore, Maryland

DURING THE PAST SEVERAL DE-CADES tremendous strides in health and medical care have been witnessed. Congenital defects that once guaranteed early mortality can now be improved or corrected through modern medical technology. Diseases, such as diabetes, which were once synonymous with severe disability and death, need not rob today's generation of full lives. New medications, modern surgical procedures, and other interventions help significant numbers of people survive and function with a permanent health problem that requires long-term management—that is, a chronic disease. In the United States alone, more than 23.3 million people have a chronic illness[1] and, with increasing numbers of people enjoying a longer life expectancy, the number of chronically ill people in the general population continues to grow.

Some individuals advance to old age with chronic conditions that were congenital or acquired in their younger years.

Table 1. Number of selected chronic conditions in persons aged 65 years and over in community and institutional settings

Chronic condition	Noninstitutionalized elderly	Institutionalized elderly
Arthritis	1,691,000	259,000
Arteriosclerosis	338,000	453,000
Cerebrovascular diseases	376,000	183,000
Diabetes	354,000	88,000
Heart disease	1,628,000	285,000
Mental and nervous disorders	241,000	445,000

Source: U.S. Department of Health, Education, and Welfare. "Chronic Conditions and Impairments of Nursing Home Residents: U.S. 1969." Vital and Health Statistics Series 12, No. 22 (December 1973) p. 4.

Table 2. Number of institutionalized persons aged 65 years and over with multiple chronic conditions—by sex

Multiple chronic conditions	Males	Females	Multiple chronic conditions	Males	Females
Heart trouble, stroke	13,579	29,063	Arteriosclerosis, heart trouble, stroke	11,278	24,205
Heart trouble, arteriosclerosis	60,824	157,663	Arteriosclerosis, heart trouble, diabetes	7,710	21,822
Heart trouble, diabetes	10,105	29,838	Arteriosclerosis, heart trouble, arthritis-rheumatism	23,259	74,955
Heart trouble, senility (including advanced)	31,002	134,518	Arteriosclerosis, heart trouble, senility (including advanced)	43,737	113,253
Heart trouble, arthritis-rheumatism	27,548	90,464	Arteriosclerosis, stroke, diabetes	2,026	6,263
Stroke, arteriosclerosis	21,880	48,199	Arteriosclerosis, arthritis-rheumatism, stroke	7,723	20,431
Stroke, diabetes	3,633	8,944	Arteriosclerosis, senility (including advanced), stroke	16,374	38,540
Stroke, senility (including advanced)	21,118	49,121	Heart trouble, stroke, diabetes	1,646	4,584
Stroke, arthritis-rheumatism	9,487	24,831	Heart trouble, stroke, arthritis-rheumatism	5,118	11,572
Arteriosclerosis, diabetes	14,504	39,266	Arteriosclerosis, heart trouble, stroke, senility (including advanced)	8,804	19,352
Arteriosclerosis, senility (including advanced)	89,325	237,616	Arteriosclerosis, heart trouble, stroke, arthritis-rheumatism	4,717	10,476
Arteriosclerosis, arthritis-rheumatism	45,358	145,685			
Diabetes, senility (including advanced)	13,544	36,835			
Diabetes, arthritis-rheumatism	6,024	23,562			
Senility (including advanced), arthritis-rheumatism	41,163	130,944			

Source: U.S. Department of Health, Education, and Welfare. "Chronic Conditions and Impairments of Nursing Home Residents: U.S. 1969." Vital and Health Statistics Series 12, No. 22 (December 1973) p. 25.

However, for many, chronic illness is a new problem in their later years, resulting from age-related changes that increase the body's vulnerability to certain pathologies. Among the population age 65 years and older, 80 percent have at least one chronic disease:[2] more often than not, several chronic conditions exist simultaneously within an older individual. (See Tables 1 and 2.) Almost one-half of the elderly have some impairment in their ability to participate in their daily activities, ranging from the inability to button clothing to the inability to sit up independently. (See Table 3.) To prevent additional impairment and promote the highest possible level of health and function, close attention must be paid to the management of a chronic condition.

Management of a health problem has its share of challenges and frustrations for any individual; when the problem requires long-term management and the affected individual is aged, the situation becomes more complex and difficult. After the medical evaluation has determined the nature and scope of the diagnosis, the task is to help the individual function with the chronic illness. Long-term management involves maintaining and promoting self-care capacity while overseeing and directing a specific plan of care.

Consideration must be given to the altering condition and capacity of the individual resulting from changes in physical, emotional, and social factors, as well as the illness itself. Interventions must be planned to meet temporary and permanent needs. These and many other components of chronic care frequently and appropriately are managed by nurses. Their broad knowledge base in the biological, psycho-

Table 3. Number and percentage of persons aged 65 years and over with activity limitations resulting from chronic conditions

	Number	Percentage
No activity limitation	11,230,000	54.1
Any type of activity limitation	9,511,000	45.9
Limited but not in major activity	1,365,000	6.6
Limited in amount or kind of major activity	4,594,000	22.1
Unable to carry on major activity	3,552,000	17.1

Source: U.S. Department of Health, Education, and Welfare. "Health Characteristics of Persons with Chronic Activity Limitation: U.S. 1974." *Vital and Health Statistics* Series 10, No. 112 (October 1976) p. 11.

logical, and social sciences; their theoretical and clinical insight into pathophysiology; and their practical experience in delivering direct care enable nurses to assume a leadership role in chronic care. Along with this potential leadership role, however, comes the responsibility for nurses to understand the dynamics of chronicity.

GOALS OF CHRONIC CARE

A majority of today's nurses were trained to care for patients with acute illnesses; specific courses in chronic care and clinical experiences in long-term care settings were minimal at best. Goals in acute care involve diagnosing, treating, and curing persons of their illness. Care efforts are aimed at curing; clients' progress is determined by how well they

76 are approaching cure; and providers' successes are judged by whether or not cures are achieved.

Chronic care poses a dilemma for nurses. The nature of a chronic disease is such that it will remain with the client for life; cure is not possible. The direction of care, the evaluation of the client's progress, and the provider's reward system differ from those in acute illness cases. To provide realistic, effective chronic care, nurses must learn to operate under a set of goals that does not aim at curing the client. These goals pertain to helping the client:

- improve function;
- manage existing illness;
- prevent secondary complications;
- delay deterioration and disability; and
- die with peace, comfort, and dignity.

Table 4 gives examples of activities related to each goal. Chronic care goals are no less important or complex than acute care goals, but they do indicate that the success of the plan of care and the progress of clients must be evaluated in a different manner. For instance the disease may be growing more severe, but if the client can prevent secondary complications and continue to manage the illness satisfactorily, the plan of care and progress is successful. The internalization of chronic care goals can be difficult for nurses because it requires a resocialization of care norms and the recognition of a different reward system.

Progress in chronic care is not judged by how successful the staff and client have been in achieving cure: *in chronic care a standstill, even regression, can imply tremendous progress.* Instead of feeling ineffective and frustrated that a client's condition has not improved for years, nurses must appreciate that it could have been significantly worse without their intervention. This shift in thinking is essential if nurses are to be realistic in the expectations of clients and themselves, and if they are to achieve satisfaction from working with the chronically ill.

Table 4. Examples of chronic care goals

Goal	Example
Improve function	Teaching an individual who is disabled from arthritis to use special utensils and self-care devices
Manage existing illness	Supervising the self-care activities of client with diabetes
Prevent secondary complications	Encouraging a person with a chronic respiratory disease to eat properly, perform breathing exercises, and identify sputum changes
Delay deterioration and disability	Helping a family to maintain maximum orientation and self-care ability in their relative possessing a chronic brain syndrome
Die with peace, comfort, and dignity	Protecting the client's stated desires as to terminal care

DELIVERING CHRONIC CARE

Regardless of the specific chronic disease, there are basic steps in the process of caring for the chronically ill. This process is not foreign to nursing, as Figure 1 illustrates. The existence of a chronic illness does not necessarily imply a need

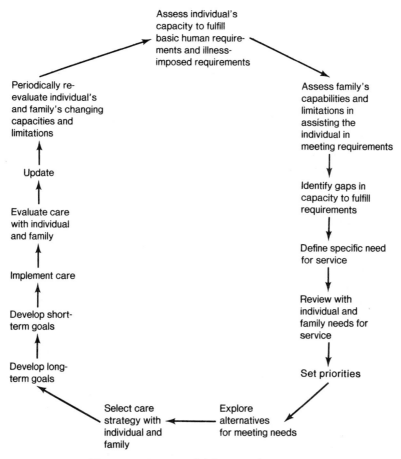

Figure 1. Process of delivering chronic care.

for nursing services. Many individuals and their families manage and cope with chronic illness amazingly well. To maximize chronically ill persons' potential and avoid undue dependency, nursing services should fill the gaps that clients and their families have in meeting care requirements. Astute assessments, therefore, are crucial. It is essential to review how well basic human requirements (i.e., respiration, nutrition, excretion, activity, rest, and safety) are fulfilled, and the degree to which illness-imposed requirements (i.e., medication administration, dietary adjustments, dressing changes, and special therapies) are being met.

Consideration must be given to how well the family as a whole is coping with and managing the chronic illness. Freeman has discussed this point in depth, and her position that *the family is the patient* is worth reinforcing.[3] Chronically ill individuals with multiple needs may not require nursing assistance if their families are compensating for their deficits, whereas nursing intervention may be essential if the affected individuals are coping and managing admirably well, but their family units are disrupted as a result of the illness.

Assessing needs

For both basic human needs and illness-imposed therapeutic needs to be fulfilled several factors must exist:

1. *The physical, mental, and socioeconomic capabilities to fulfill the needs.* For clients to follow their medication orders they must be capable of travelling to a pharmacy, having the financial means of paying for the prescription, remembering when and how to administer the medication, opening a medication container, and handling and swallowing the medication.

2. *The knowledge, skills, and experiences associated with fulfilling the requirement.* Clients may be able to afford insulin, remember when to administer it, and have the dexterity to manipulate a syringe, but unfamiliarity and inexperience with the injection technique interfere with insulin administration.

3. *The motivation and disposition to fulfill the requirement.* Although clients may be fully capable of administering medication, they may choose not to do so for a variety of reasons.

The specific factor responsible for a need not being fulfilled must be identified as part of the assessment. For example identifying that a client does not ingest ample amounts of vegetables is an incomplete assessment; it is more productive to note: "insufficient finances to purchase vegetables," "low vegetable intake due to painful gums," or "no kitchen facilities to store and prepare vegetables." More effective and less costly care can be rendered if services based on specific needs can be provided.

Once defined the need for services is reviewed with the client and family so that priorities can be determined. Consideration is given not only to what the most important needs are, but also what risks or losses are associated with placing certain items low in priority. Nurses employed in rehabilitation facilities can appreciate what it means when they receive clients from acute-care hospitals where the major focus of the care provided was on meeting immediate versus long-range needs. By

---

More effective and less costly care can be rendered if services based on specific needs can be provided.

---

having had rehabilitative measures placed low on the priority list (e.g., not beginning range of motion exercises early or not arranging intervention from physical, occupational, or speech therapists), clients may require longer periods of hospitalization in a rehabilitation facility or suffer an irreversible loss of a portion of their functional ability.

Offering alternatives

Presenting several alternatives to helping the client and the family meet their needs may prove to be beneficial in establishing individualized services with which there will be greater likelihood of compliance. For instance an elderly woman who is unable to prepare her own meals and in need of good nutrition to improve her health status may have the following options offered:

1. Meals on Wheels;
2. a daily visit from a home health aide who would prepare meals;
3. having meals prepared a week in advance by her daughter and keeping them in the freezer until ready for use; or
4. having a neighbor-friend visit daily and prepare meals.

Many health care providers would suggest, and perhaps argue, the use of option 1. However the client above may object to eating meals that are planned and prepared by persons who do not understand her preferences and may not want neighbors to observe the meal delivery and realize her dependency. She may not want an "outsider," such as an aide, coming to her home daily, nor may she want to burden her daughter with meal preparation. Because she has had a long friendship with her neighbor, who visits daily anyhow and who is delighted to provide this service, option 4 is preferred by the client. How often are options other than those of routinely used official agencies overlooked when services are planned?

Establishing goals

An important component of planning and delivering care for chronically ill persons is the establishment of long- and short-term goals. Goal setting offers the nurse an opportunity to assess clients' views of their condition and expectations and indicates how clients will participate in the care program. Long-term goals may consist of (1) preventive health maintenance, (2) restorative care, or (3) support.

In caring for an older man recovering from a stroke, the nurse may assume that the goal of care is restoration to maximum independent functioning. However the client may not want the nurse to instruct him in self-care but rather to have the nurse visit him so that he knows "someone is there." This conflict in goals tells the nurse a great deal about the client's self-concept, motivation, understanding of his problem, and likely compliance with a plan of care. Other interventions may be necessary before the client will agree to work toward the goal of restorative care; if the client chooses not to make restorative care his goal despite interventions offered, the nurse may need to readjust plans.

In addition to long-term goals that provide an understanding of the projected course and outcome of care, short-term goals also are important to develop. Short-term goals can be set weekly or daily, depending on the frequency of the nurse-client encounter. These goals guide actions, serve as a means of evaluation of care, provide an opportunity for the client to note progress, and offer hope that, although cure may not be achieved, some accomplishment may be realized.

A contract between the nurse and chronically ill client can be extremely beneficial. Such a contract, developed as early in the relationship as possible, specifies the time, dates, location, and fees for care; the expected length of the relationship; and the obligations and expectations of both the nurse and the client. This arrangement clearly defines the relationship and establishes a mechanism for accountability.

80

ADVANCED AGE AND CHRONIC CARE

Nurses may deliver care more realistically and effectively if they anticipate and compensate for certain factors. Although these factors are not exclusive to the elderly, they are more likely to have a major influence on the course of chronic care for this population.

More time for care

Specific physiological and psychological changes associated with the aging process will slow the pace of activities and necessitate more frequent or longer periods of nursing time. An initial interview that can be completed in one hour for a middle-aged adult can take several hours, and consequently several visits to complete, with an older person. Slower movements and the reduced ability to manage physiological stress may demand that more time be provided for the performance of care activities and that more rest periods be allowed.

Poorer short-term memory, shorter attention span (especially if some degree of organic brain syndrome exists), and additional time required for impulses to travel throughout the nervous system command more time for health education. Nurses may find it especially important to plan several shorter teaching periods instead of fewer longer ones; provide extra time for additional reinforcement and feedback; and use memory aids, written instructions, and family resources to provide more effective learning by older persons.

Different priorities

Individual priorities can determine clients' expectations and the degree to which they will invest themselves in single episodes of care, as well as the entire care plan associated with the management of their chronic illness. An elderly man may reject a prescribed plan for portable oxygen therapy because he prefers a life style in which his independence and image are unaltered to one that may bring more comfort and longer life but will demonstrate his limitation to others. An older, wheelchair-bound woman may insist that the visiting nurse assist her in a tub bath rather than spend the time teaching her about her new medications. An elderly couple may refuse to obtain the vision and hearing examination that they both require because they would rather use that money for the badly needed repairs to their home. Desires for life styles unhampered by the management of a chronic illness, interests in having basic physical needs met, and concerns for fulfilling life demands other than health management often slide health care low on the elderly's priority list. Nurses can spare themselves considerable frustration by identifying and incorporating clients' priorities rather than proceeding with a plan because it is "professionally sound."

Age-related changes

Some demands imposed by illness may be difficult for older individuals to fulfill due to changes associated with the aging process. Decreased coordination of fine muscle movements and stiff joints can interfere with the ability to manipulate a syringe or change a dressing. Problems in differentiating blue and green shades due to yellowing of the lens can create a problem for older diabetics who may need to use urine testing kits that require the differentiation of these shades. Changes in the taste buds can alter the flavor of certain foods and compound difficulties the elderly may have in adhering to a special diet. Medications and other therapeutic routines may be omitted as a result of poor memory. Astute assessment can help nurses identify age-related factors that can interfere with clients' abilities to comply with and meet therapeutic needs.

Family surrogate

There are various reasons for older chronically ill persons to desire that the nurse serve as a family surrogate. There may be no family, or the family may have a poor relationship with the client or may live too far away to offer ongoing support. The aged individual may not want to be a burden or be dependent on the family. The family may not be able to accept or cope with the illness due to their own physical, emotional, or socioeconomic limitations. Being the surrogate daughter who "lectures" the client about ambulating more, the surrogate son who accepts the hand-knitted tie, and the surrogate spouse who listens patiently to the joys and disappointments of life can be therapeutic and helpful roles for the nurse to fill.

Multiple resources

In addition to the various problems stemming from illness, features of the aging process may result in the demand for multiple services. For instance the nurse may recognize that the woman being visited for diabetes supervision is having a difficult time coping with widowhood. Arranging for this woman to attend a widows' group or referring her for counseling services may prove advantageous to her total well-being. Likewise a hypertensive individual may express anxiety about a rent increase. Assisting this person in seeking financial aid can result in multiple benefits, not the least of which is to reduce a stress that could interfere with hypertension control. Although the chronic illness may be the original or allegedly only reason for nursing intervention, the nurse must be aware of other problems, such as those associated with retirement, altered body image, housing relocation, and death, and utilize the many resources available to help the elderly with their complex needs.

Impact on the family

Frequently nurses will promote care goals that may be optimal for the client but devastating for the family unit. Take for example the care of an aged man who has terminal cancer. This man, like most individuals, prefers his own home to an institutional setting; thus the nurse develops a plan to maintain him in his home and to allow him to die in familiar surroundings. His wife and child are instructed in medication administration, skin care, lifting techniques, and other activities. This appears to be an ideal situation: institutionalization is avoided and the family can spend the remainder of this man's lifetime in intimate contact with him.

Closer scrutiny however may reveal

82

many difficulties with this arrangement. The wife and child may be physically exhausted from trying to provide 24-hour supervision and care. (It should be remembered that 20 percent of all aged individuals have children who are 65 years of age or older themselves—thus the "child" depended on to care for an aged parent also may be an aged individual.)[4] It may be emotionally draining to cope with this man's reactions to dying and their own reactions to his decline. The physical, emotional, and social well-being of other family members can suffer as a result of following the ideal plan for the client.

Nurses must seek an approach to chronic care that can achieve optimum

---

Nurses must seek an approach to chronic care that can achieve optimum results for the client at the least physical, emotional, and social expense to the total family unit.

---

results for the client at the least physical, emotional, and social expense to the total family unit. It must be recognized that the most appropriate plan for the family unit may not necessarily be the most ideal plan for management of the chronic illness. Compromises are essential.

REACTIONS TO CHRONIC ILLNESS

There are times when nurses will perceive the flow of care being interrupted by specific behaviors of the chronically ill. These behaviors may be interpreted as illogical and inappropriate unless nurses understand them to be reactions to the serious and continuous responsibility of managing and coping with a chronic illness. Reactions commonly observed by persons working with the chronically ill include the following.

Anger

The demands imposed by a chronic illness and the subsequent changes in life style that may result give understandable reason for feelings of bitterness, resentment, and anger. Chronic illness may compound the multiple losses that the aged person may normally experience. It is not unusual for this anger to be displaced on nurses, evidenced by excessive criticism and hostile outbursts.

Depression

Anyone who has been temporarily incapacitated, whether by a minor injury or a serious illness, can recall how disheartening and demoralizing it was to be unable to function perfectly, to forfeit social invitations, or to depend on others for assistance. Knowing that the incapacitation and associated inconveniences will be present for the remainder of one's life and could potentially worsen with time can lead to depression in the older chronically ill person. At times this depression may cause the client to lack the motivation to engage in care and can even promote suicidal thoughts.

Denial

When confronted by the nurse with queries as to why a regime was not adhered to, clients may deny ever being informed of the procedure. "No one told me to watch for changes in my sputum"; "How was I to know to count my pulse before taking my digitalis?"; "No one ever mentioned to me that I have cancer." Such reactions can cause the nurse to question the practices of previous care givers or the honesty of the client. The nurse should understand that selective listening and acceptance of information may be taking place in these situations. Clients often will accept only what they have the capacity to handle and block information that is too threatening or stressful to deal with.

Manipulation

When an individual is in a vulnerable position and ego strength is threatened, dependency on and the security of a stronger person may be sought. Clients frequently see the nurse as a potential source of this strength and may manipulate the relationship in a manner that maintains the nurse's good graces and consequently ensures ongoing support from the nurse. Flattery, gift giving, and such statements as "I don't know what I'd do without you" are examples of manipulation.

Projection

"I can deal well with my emphysema but I know that my wife worries that I may have lung cancer." This may be a valid perception, but this man may also be projecting his own concerns about his illness. Seeing below the surface of such statements is essential in understanding clients' concerns and reactions to their chronic illness.

Rationalization

Occasionally the real cause of clients' or their families' actions may be too painful to accept, and more tolerable and acceptable explanations for these actions may be developed. For instance it may be less difficult for proud elderly persons to say that they do not like meats than to admit that they cannot afford them. Likewise a lack of children's concern for their parent may be more tolerable if the parent excuses the children because they have busy lives and too many demands already.

Regression

The sometimes overwhelming demands imposed by chronic illness can create stresses which the aged person is not able to manage. In an effort simply to cope, some aged persons may retreat to a more comfortable, earlier stage. An older diabetic man may be able to manage his basic diet successfully. However he may have difficulty comprehending exchange lists and advanced information related to his diabetic management. To deal with this situation he may reject the new information and function solely within the basic framework established when he was initially diagnosed.

Reminiscing

Aged persons may wish to share descriptions of their life experiences. These stories may seem irrelevant to the management of the health problem at hand unless the therapeutic value of reminiscing is appreciated.[5] By using past experiences as a point of reference, aged persons are better able to maintain their self-esteem in light

84

of changes resulting from aging and chronic illness.

These reactions may be unconscious and occur in combinations; they are among the defense mechanisms employed by chronically ill aged persons to cope with the multiple problems they face. By assessing defense mechanisms, nurses can determine the aged individual's ego strength and plan appropriate interventions. For example more may be accomplished by helping regressed persons achieve security and comfort at their present level than by convincing them that they are able to perform on previously achieved higher levels.

PROVIDER PROBLEMS

Different criteria

Profound, dramatic results, such as are common among the young or the acutely ill, are infrequent in the chronically ill aged individual. The nature of a chronic illness makes for a slow achievement of goals; this is compounded by declines associated with the aging process. This is not to say that progress and accomplishments are absent—they must merely be evaluated differently. Maintaining a stable status can be a marked accomplishment for the chronically ill. Even when unavoidable declines occur, retarding the decline can be significant. Also the importance of providing comfort, happiness, and hope in the lives of chronically ill persons should not be underestimated. Discouragement and frustration may be avoided if nurses use different criteria to measure their accomplishments in chronic care and derive their ego rewards from these.

Overinvolvement

Loss of objectivity can result from an ongoing nurse-client relationship. There is the risk that the warmth and fondness developed from a long-term relationship could cause nurses to assume more responsibility for clients than is necessary (e.g., calling the social worker for the clients when they are able to make calls independently), become involved in family affairs (e.g., arguing with the children for not paying more attention to their parent), and deny the reality of the illness (e.g., telling terminally ill clients that they will get better), to mention a few behaviors. Nurses cannot always avoid becoming emotionally involved with their clients. However they should promptly identify loss of objectivity in the relationship and seek the assistance of a colleague who can offer insight into nontherapeutic behaviors and intervene if necessary.

Burnout syndrome

When demands are great and ego rewards limited, emotional "wear and tear" on the provider is not unusual. Nurses may notice that their attitude toward their clients and coworkers becomes negative, they experience vague symptoms, they are unpleasant with their families, and their once meaningful work becomes an eight-hour burden that they reluctantly tolerate. This situation is not unique to nurses; the "burnout syndrome" has been identified in many occupations. Increased attention is being paid to the risk of burnout among nurses, and it is particularly useful for nurses to become familiar with the dynamics of this problem.[6,7] Nurses must appreciate that the physical and emotional burdens of chronic care can be as draining as the stresses in intensive care and coronary care units.

The management of chronic illness in older persons is a difficult process, requiring a careful blend of patience, sensitivity, and skill. Chronic illness may exaggerate the multiple losses experienced by elderly persons and threaten the independence and comfort of their limited years. By understanding the unique features of chronic illness in elderly persons, recognizing potential reactions to chronicity, and being realistic in expectations of clients and themselves, nurses can enhance maximum function, comfort, and health in an older chronically ill person, and add dignity and meaning to precious remaining years.

REFERENCES

1. U.S. Department of Health, Education, and Welfare. *Vital and Health Statistics: Prevalence of Chronic Conditions of the Genitourinary, Nervous, Endocrine, Metabolic and Blood and Blood-Forming Systems and of Other Selected Chronic Conditions U.S. 1973* Series 10, No. 109 DHEW Pub. No. 77-1536 (Rockville, Md.: March 1977) p. 3.

2. Butler, R. and Lewis, M. *Aging and Mental Health* (St. Louis: C.V. Mosby Co. 1977) p. 21.

3. Freeman, R. *Family Coping Index* Developed by the Johns Hopkins University School of Hygiene and Public Health and the Richmond Instructive Visiting Nurses Association. (Baltimore: Johns Hopkins University School of Hygiene and Public Health, Community Health Nursing Division 19, 1969).

4. Butler, R. and Lewis, M. *Aging and Mental Health* (St. Louis: C.V. Mosby Co. 1977) p. 21.

5. Ebersole, P. "Reminiscing." *American Journal of Nursing* 76:8 (August 1976) p. 1304-1305.

6. Pines, A. and Maslach, C. "Characteristics of Staff Burnout in Mental Health Settings." *Hospital and Community Psychiatry* 29:4 (April 1978) p. 233-237.

7. Storlie, F.J. "Burnout: The Elaboration of a Concept." *American Journal of Nursing* 79:12 (December 1979) p. 2108-2111.

Aspects of Aging in Planned Communities

Barbara Hornum, PhD
Assistant Professor of Anthropology
Drexel University
Philadelphia, Pennsylvania

IT IS IMPORTANT to consider the interaction between elements of the macroculture, such as the world view and perception of values, and the microculture, such as the development of local-level agencies to deal with sociocultural problems including care of the elderly. Without an adequate assessment of both levels of the culture program, implementation seems likely to fail. It will fail either because the client population will reject the plans as not meeting their needs or because of conflict between the local-level agencies, which lack a common core of values, thereby preventing coherent, integrated delivery of services.

Increased longevity has become a reality in the urban-industrialized societies of Europe and North America. As a result of changes in the composition of the population the social institutions of these societies have to respond to the demand for increasing services to the elderly.[1] This is particularly important as it is these very same social systems that also have experi-

88 enced social and geographic mobility with resultant population relocations. In turn this has accelerated the attenuation of family contracts. Therefore the society as a whole, rather than the small mobile, and often fragile nuclear family, must play a larger service role in dealing with the older individual.

BACKGROUND

The British New Towns, planned communities working with various county and regional councils, local housing authorities, district social services, and health boards, seem to offer opportunities for implementing long-range as well as interim programs. Experimental dwellings, day care facilities, sheltered housing schemes, as well as the more traditional "Old Person's Home" are found in all the New Towns. This provides an ideal research opportunity to assess the reactions of the residents to varied types of housing and service provisions within a relatively compact area. It should be noted that the income and rent subsidies available in Great Britain essentially mean that all alternatives are available across different socioeconomic levels. Thus no one can be excluded from any type of designated accommodation for the elderly on the basis of income, nor are the home care services out of reach of people on small fixed incomes.

Data were gathered during four trips in 1972, 1974, 1978, and 1979. Thamesmead, a "New Town-In-Town" built by the Greater London Council on the banks of the Thames, was seen in 1972. In the summer of 1974 the towns of Cwmbran and Newtown in Wales, Glenrothes and Cumbernauld in Scotland, and Runcorn, Peterlee, Aycliffe, Harlow, and Hemel Hempstead in England were visited. The English New Towns of Crawley, Basildon, Bracknell, Milton Keynes, Northhampton, Stevenage, and Welwyn Garden City were visited in the summer of 1978, followed by Irvine New Town on the west coast of Scotland and Glenrothes again in 1979.

Interviews were held with several social service workers, health care personnel, development corporation officials, directors of facilities in the different towns, and some of the elderly themselves. While each town is quite distinctive in character the facilities for the older individual have a number of common denominators, thereby making it possible to generalize descriptions of housing and services. Furthermore, it must be recognized that the elderly are an extremely diverse population in terms of backgrounds, interests, personalities, health, sex, and age. Thus the needs of the "young elderly," for example, which are technically those between 55 and 70 years of age may be quite different from the "old elderly," those from 70 to 95 years of age.

NEW TOWN DEVELOPMENT

In the 1940s the British government promulgated a New Towns policy. The desire to control random suburban sprawl led to the establishment of a "green belt" around London in which no new development would be permitted. There was also a need to deal with the problem of continued growth and congestion within London itself. The thinking of Ebenezer Howard, influential in the founding of earlier "garden cities," became relevant.[2]

The New Towns Act of 1946 gave power to the minister of housing and local government, which is now held by the secretary of state for the environment, to designate New Towns throughout Great Britain and to appoint development corporations to plan, construct, and administer them.

The boards of each corporation, consisting of a chairperson and up to 12 members, are appointed by the secretary of state. The executive staff is composed of a general manager and a team of chief officers for Architecture and Planning, Civil Engineering, Estates Management, Finance, Law, and Social Development.

Funds for acquiring land and financing building projects are made available by the central government. These funds are in the form of loans repayable at a low interest rate and on an annuity basis over a period of 60 years. The development corporation builds and leases residential, commercial, and industrial properties. Housing may be purchased in ratios to leased housing, but this varies according to the policies of the political administration in Great Britain.

The development corporation is not a town council. It exists alongside and cooperates with county, regional, and district councils, which are responsible for education, police, fire, water, public transport, social work, public health, libraries, and many other social and civic needs.

Since the earliest "overspill" New Towns others have been established to meet a wider variety of conditions. Some were designated to help support the development of a particular industry and to alleviate unemployment. Others were established to aid in the coordination of the development or redevelopment of rela-

tively large urban areas that may encompass a number of existing towns and villages. Still other New Towns were designated to help halt depopulation of an area.

As of 1979 the New Towns were in varying stages of development and were inhabited by more than 600,000 people. A New Towns Commission has been established by the central government, and development corporations are being phased out in several of the older, established New Towns. Recently it was decided that rental housing and related assets shall be transferred to local housing authorities in the "old" New Towns, and the social development responsibilities will then be completely carried by local government.

In the "newer" New Towns the population is composed of newcomers and the original, indigenous inhabitants of the area. Most newcomers are young married couples with small children who have assured jobs in the new environment. But the older relatives of New Town residents are also a priority category. Government regulation additionally specifies that some housing provision be made in specially built accommodations for those over 65. The indigenous population is typically representative of a small, rural community whose ancestors have lived in the area for a long time. This population may indeed contain a high proportion of people above age 65. Therefore even in the newest New Towns there will be an older segment of the population for whom provision must be made.

In the more established New Towns second- and even third-generation residents are heavily represented in the popu-

90 lation. They have aged along with the town. Many of these people, who first arrived in the late 1940s and early 1950s, have chosen to remain in the New Town upon retirement and to shift from one type of residence to "purpose-built" housing. In fact the rate of out-migration from New Towns is only about five percent annually.

GENERAL FACILITIES FOR THE ELDERLY

The major thrust of the facilities for "seniors" established in the New Towns and by the local authorities is to enable older persons to live the life they prefer as much as possible. There are different types of specialized accommodation, including the "Old Person's Dwelling."

Old person's dwellings

An Old Person's Dwelling is generally a one-bedroom bungalow house, sometimes mixed with other types of family houses, often at the end of a row of two- or three-storied houses. These bungalows are often referred to as "Granny Flats." The interior design, particularly with the newer housing, has an open floor plan with no door frames to interfere with the use of wheelchairs or crutches. Light sockets are placed at waist level to eliminate bending. Bathrooms and kitchens have safety features. The population of a particular section with these ungrouped Old Person's Dwellings is mixed by age.

Some of the older residents find the noise and traffic patterns of young children and adolescents upsetting. As a result older residents prefer grouped Old Person's Dwellings—rows of bungalows attached, with a house for a warden at one end. Often these are next to a common room so that there can be some shared leisure activities. Outside each of these grouped houses is a light that can be turned on by an interior switch. If lit it indicates that someone is in difficulty and anyone passing by should notify the warden. These are often the most popular because they give some assurance that others can be reached quickly if aid is needed. Additionally the grouped houses are quieter than those that are scattered among non-specialized housing. In both types of Old Person's Dwellings people can maintain living patterns that are not radically different from those in earlier years. They also can keep many if not all of their most important possessions with them. People most comfortable in Old Person's Dwellings seem to be those with good health and physical mobility.

Sheltered housing accommodations

"Sheltered Housing Accommodations" consist of specially adapted, unfurnished flats, each independent of the others but under the supervision of a resident warden. Intercom systems link each elderly person's flat to the warden and can be used in case of emergency. In Milton Keynes, the newest New Town, the most recently built Sheltered Housing was fully enclosed and had covered sidewalks so that people could move comfortably outside their own flats even in inclement weather. The doors opening to the covered streets had access for chairs so that neighbors could sit outside and chat. There were common laundry facilities, a common leisure activity room with its own small kitchen, and two guest suites that could be used for overnight guests. All of the flats had the standard, specialized light sockets and guardrails in the bathrooms. Some were fully equipped to accommodate the handicapped with stoves and sinks in the kitchens placed at wheelchair height. Along with small individual garden units there was a common garden for general use. The warden in Sheltered Housing was a trained geriatric nurse; a warm person who in less than a month had helped to establish a real sense of community among people who were previously strangers.

"Old person's homes"

Some older people are in frail health and find that even minimal daily basic chores are difficult. These people are apt to seek residence in an "Old Person's Home," a residential facility where people live in either a single or double furnished room, have all their meals prepared and served in a common dining room, receive assistance in daily washing, and have a resident staff on the premises day and night with an on-premises medical room and daily visits by a physician. Those who select this option are generally mobility-impaired and need the reassurance of regular resident care. Residents here are not in need of sustained hospital treatment, although many do have chronic health problems.

As a rule people are encouraged to spend a week as a live-in guest before deciding whether to enter an Old Person's Home, and if coming from Sheltered Housing or Old Person's Dwellings, these will be held open for an agreed-upon period so that individuals may change their minds if necessary. There is a shortage of both Old Person's Homes that meet council standards and full-scale nursing homes for those who need more intensive medical care. Attempts are being made to fill in these gaps. It is standard procedure for Old Person's Homes in New Towns to have some rooms available for short vacation stays. This is primarily done to benefit the older person living with children, allowing all a chance to be temporarily apart.

Accommodations however are only half of the story. The services available to enable older people to exercise options are equally impressive.

Other services for the elderly

First there are Home Help and Home Aides—trained workers who may visit from one to five times a week depending on need and who perform basic services, such as bathing the old person, light housekeeping, marketing, and chatting to mitigate isolation. Their efforts may be augmented by "Good Neighbors," local residents who receive a small stipend or rate-free telephone in exchange for contacting a few older residents on a daily basis. Meals delivery programs similar to the Meals on Wheels program in the United States are also available.

Medical treatment may be given at home by Health Services Department personnel, such as visiting nurses. Other health services, such as physiotherapy and chiropody, may be provided at the day hospitals. Older people who need transport are taken on a weekly basis for such care. Some of the older New Towns have

92

geriatric day hospitals that can meet the needs of people who were either recently released from a hospital stay or who need sufficient services to avoid a residential hospital admission. A stated aim of the Health Services and Social Services Departments is to help those older individuals who have lost some aspects of their independence to live as long and successfully as possible in their own homes.

Day centers are also part of the caring arrangements established to meet some of the nonmedical needs of elderly persons. Ideally there are several of these centers scattered throughout the larger New Towns so that transport is not prolonged. However there are really only three or four such centers to take care of hundreds of older people on a rotating basis. At some day centers scheduled and unscheduled activities are encouraged, from private conversations to bingo games. A hot lunch is served and there are facilities for people to fix tea or coffee. A volunteer hairdresser comes twice a week and is in great demand because the charges are about equivalent to 50 cents in American money for a wash and set. Day centers are primarily intended to serve as bases for social activities and interpersonal interaction. The participants are encouraged to take an active role in the planning and running of the centers. Paid staff is usually quite small.

Intersecting with the New Town and local authority services are many private groups, such as Age Concern, who are aware of the need to increase the facilities available to people between the ages of 55 and 95 and who recognize that there is likely to be an increasing number of such people in the years ahead. The interest in

The interest in social services is doubly intriguing because older people constitute a relatively small, if growing, percentage of New Town residents.

such social services is doubly intriguing because older people constitute a relatively small, if growing, percentage of New Town residents.

GLENROTHES NEW TOWN

Glenrothes, Scotland, in the Region of Fife, was designated as a New Town in 1948. Its location, originally selected because of its proximity to coal reserves, has placed it far enough away from Edinburgh to prevent it from becoming a "bedroom" subject. It has had to become a community on its own. Due to a growth spurt many noticeable changes occurred in the town between 1974 and 1979. Glenrothes House, which is the location of the Glenrothes Development Corporation, is new, as is the town center.

In particular there has been an increase in the facilities and services for the elderly. For example in Woodside, one of the earlier residential sections, the development corporation has had to introduce bungalows in the last few years. Initially they had not needed them as their housing was planned for families. As these families have gone through a natural life cycle many of the children have moved to other areas or to other sections of Glenrothes. The parents, now newly retired, are in homes that are large and frequently difficult to manage. The new, purpose-built accommodations provide an alternative that enables them to stay near friends and in familiar surroundings. These houses have the additional benefit of keeping the larger ones available to new young families, thus maintaining age desegregation in Woodside.

Glenrothes has just built its first Sheltered Housing. In addition a geriatric hospital should be completed in 1981. Services, such as social and civic clubs, are encouraged as a way of facilitating the older people's continued involvement in the daily affairs of Glenrothes.

A high percentage of the elderly in Glenrothes are the young old because of the age and patterns of development of the town itself. Statistics in 1977 indicated that 2.4 percent of the residents were between 65 and 69. At that time there were 5.9 percent who were between 55 and 64 years of age; so almost 2.5 percent of the people in this group have now passed their 65th birthdays. Seniors, age 70 and over, constituted 3.0 percent of the 1977 population breakdown. Therefore there is a growing segment of the population in Glenrothes with a vital interest in matters pertaining to the life style of "pensioners." Certainly a core of seniors seems to interact with both the official and unofficial organizations of the town. These people are concerned, visible, and know how to work within the system.

The Edelweiss Club is a group of seniors who have been learning German for the past several years. This club has also become a social network because the members maintain contacts outside of the regular meetings. It is also part of the larger interlocking networking pattern of Glenrothes as many of the participants are active in other organizations, such as Age Concern and similar outreach volunteer groups.

Members of the Edelweiss Club enjoy New Town living. Most of them have lived in Glenrothes for more than 15 years, but some are relatively new, having moved to the town after retirement elsewhere to be closer to children who work for one of the industries in Glenrothes. When interviewed their primary complaint was about the transportation system. It was felt that service should be more frequent, should connect the various estates directly, and should continue later into the evening. However they also recognized that transit problems were a general problem in the Region of Fife. Another concern was the behavior of juveniles, whose use of walkways for skate-boarding was felt to pose some physical dangers to the older pedestrian. Nonetheless the people of the group had positive outlooks on their being able to influence change.

Age concern

A rent-free ground floor flat is provided to Age Concern by the Glenrothes Development Corporation. This is located in the high-rise apartment house close to the town center. When interviewed, the chairperson of Age Concern, its organizer, a board member, and a local justice of the peace stressed that the interest in helping the elderly is part of a natural concern for a segment of the population and should not be considered charity. The organization began in November 1959 to build up a volunteer set of services for the elderly because little existed in Glenrothes at that time. It was felt that this was an advantage in that "the field was green" and there

94 would be no base of traditional behaviors to hold plans back.

Interest was expressed in seeing that life for the elderly was as pleasant and meaningful as possible, with independence. The staff of Age Concern see their role as providing the background and facilities for elderly people to do things for themselves but not to foster dependency by taking charge and doing the setup and operations for them. The Glenrothes Development Corporation, the district council, the trade unions, and the factories were all seen as providing assistance to foster the aims of the Age Concern. Whenever the organization came up with an idea they were able to look to individuals and groups connected with the New Town for such things as money.

In mid-1974 Age Concern in Glenrothes was able to gain the services of a paid organizer, the only one appointed to a voluntary association in Scotland. She was able to get out and reach a wider number of the old people. Thus there is a feeling that Age Concern became more aware of the personal problems and needs of the elderly and could plan for services accordingly. This woman also has been able to gain the support of the health service, the churches, the social workers, and the local authority people as these groups began to see increased ability for Age Concern to help their aims. The professional image of Glenrothes Age Concern has therefore been enhanced. Among the many services provided is a weekly bus that goes through the town and picks up old people, takes them to the sports center for the day, then returns them to their homes.

There are approximately 70 regular volunteer workers who can visit through-out the community. This is seen as a great boon to the housebound elderly. In each area of the town there is a small "cell" of visitors with a senior volunteer. There is a planned outreach program, and the volunteers are trained so that they can be comfortable in what they are doing. In these instances they see themselves as taking the role of substitute family and filling in in areas where there are no statutory provisions. For example they will find temporary homes for pets of people who may have to go into the hospital or provide "budgies" (small, canary-like birds) for other lonely people.

They also encourage the older people to reach out in turn and to transmit the skills and knowledge they have to teenagers who might otherwise have little contact across the generations. An additional general function is to foster two-way communication between the individual and the various organizations in the town and to act as temporary liaison. The chairman stated that the purpose of Age Concern could be summed up as "Help for Self-Help." He also expressed concern that a nonbureaucratic, personal touch be maintained no matter how large the organization becomes. He and the rest of the organization want to keep the focus on the needs of the old people as *people*. To do this they will work as a pressure group to lobby for such facilities as Sheltered Housing. But it was reiterated that this is because people matter and such housing gives them a third alternative, in addition to living alone or being in an institution.

Housing

The new Sheltered Housing, while not as elaborate in layout as those built at

Milton Keynes, nonetheless provides all necessary amenities. The accommodation was built in 1978. It is a well set up and comfortable facility, and most residents seem extremely pleased to have been able to get in. (There is a waiting list and similar housing is planned, sponsored by the British Legion.) In an interview Mrs. C., an 81-year-old widow, stated that she was happier than she had been in years because she felt secure and protected with the alarm-intercom system. Her flat was cheerful and bright and basically comprised a large bed-sitting room, kitchen, bath, and walk-in storage closet. Two people qualify for a one bedroom flat if they wish. Should one member of the couple die the other may remain. But an incoming individual may only apply for the "bed-sitter."

Just across the green, a distance of about 200 yards, a row of bungalows was built at about the same time as the Sheltered Housing. These are generally occupied by couples and are designed for maximum space and minimal care. There are front and rear entrances and provision for small rear gardens. During an interview Mr. and Mrs. P. stated that they enjoyed the privacy but also indicated that the proximity of the Sheltered Housing with its common rooms gave them more chance for social contacts. The warden from the Sheltered Housing does a visual scan of the exterior emergency light twice daily in addition to primary shelter responsibilities. Home Help and Meals on Wheels are available to those residents who need these services. Every attempt is made to provide the necessary auxiliary services that would enable the older person to stay as independent as possible.

Old Person's Homes are not only in short supply but are backlogged with elderly whom staff feel should properly be in geriatric hospitals. Because this facility is absent in Glenrothes and those in Kirkcaldy and Dundee are crowded, movement is not possible on a when-needed basis. As a result there are more feeble elderly in the Old Person's Homes than originally intended, and a few in the Sheltered Housing who ought to be moving on to the facilities. The Glenrothes Development Corporation housing welfare officer feels that the lack of bed space at the geriatric hospital is creating a "downward shift," so that the other facilities are not being used for the populations that they were originally intended to service.

A visit to the Old Person's Home in Glenrothes substantiated many of the housing welfare officer's statements. The facilities were certainly bright and cheerful. The staff seemed well trained and caring. Yet the average age of the residents was 90, and many of them clearly required more regular and ongoing medical supervision than is possible in an Old Person's Home.

Nurses at one of the larger New Town health centers also discussed the lack of geriatric beds. They seemed pessimistic about the planned facility, feeling that it will be too small to meet what they perceive as a growing need. These nurses and the home visitor were experiencing an increasing caseload. Yet the cooperation between these different individuals as well as the local authorities they represent is facilitated by open channels of communication. Even if existing services are not always in adequate supply it was felt that few older people were likely to remain at risk because their needs would be noted

96

by someone. At the very least substitute coverage could be supplied within the person's home on an almost full-time basis until they could be shifted to a purpose-built accommodation.

Of all the "help-agents" observed in Glenrothes the physicians in the health Center appeared to be the least concerned with either the present or future needs of the elderly. Their general reaction was that other groups had greater health priorities. They also stated that regular screening for potential problems could not be done because of monetary and time costs. Rather wryly however they did admit that pressure from Age Concern volunteers, social workers, housing welfare officers, and nurses (in other words, the other parts of the network) brought them into frequent contact with the medical needs of the older individual. The interlocking of service delivery in Glenrothes, as in all of the New Towns, tends to cut across some bureaucratic regulations and speeds the recognition of the needs of the population to be served.

IRVINE NEW TOWN

Irvine, located on the West Coast of Scotland not far from Prestwick, is the only coastal New Town in Great Britain. It was officially designated as the fifth Scottish New Town in 1966. Because of its location and history Irvine is potentially the largest New Town in Scotland and already has a population of over 58,000.

The forces leading to Irvine's designation included industrial decline and large scale unemployment. Because it is not a "greenfield" site it incorporates the old

towns of Irvine and Kilwinning and a number of smaller, established communities. This has provided the town with an indigenous population base. It has also meant that the Irvine Development Corporation (IDC) is concerned not only with creating new housing but with coordinating redevelopment of the older areas. In the older areas upgrading of facilities is combined with an interest in historic preservation.

The concept of integrating the old with

The concept of integration is carried over from the architectural designs to the type of housing provided for the elderly.

---

the new is strong. Thus the town center combines a modern new facility with the narrow winding main street of Irvine Burgh. The IDC has available grants to help in housing modernization. Local authority aid can be received for the renovation of commercial buildings. The concept of integration is carried over from the architectural designs to the type of housing provided for the elderly.

Irvine housing

It should be noted that, because of the large population, Irvine has more of the older elderly than would generally be found in other New Towns. The housing and facilities for the older people are juxtaposed with family houses, area town centers, and community centers. Thus there are no long rows of bungalows, but the Granny Flat is prevalent. This is a one-bedroom bungalow, that either sits at the end of a row of mixed-purpose housing or is mixed into the row itself. The purpose-built, interior design of the flat has equipment that can make mobility easier for either an older or handicapped person. But it is assumed that most older people will want to take an active part in the general life of the community.

Responsibilities are shared by the IDC and the authorities of Cunninghame District and Strathclyde Region. The IDC is responsible for establishing area community centers within the New Town. The IDC also built the extremely impressive £3 million Magnum Leisure Centre. The local authorities take care of the Old People's Homes and the Sheltered Housing.

Killand linked housing

Off to the side of the town center and within walking distance of it is Killand Linked Housing. This type of facility for the elderly combines a Part Four Accommodation, or Old Person's Home with Sheltered Housing. There were 16 rooms in the Old Person's Home section and 28 flats in the Sheltered Housing. The whole complex is tied together by its square shape and open central patio-atrium. A dining room and several common rooms are also available for use by all of the residents. However where full meal service is given to those in the Old Person's Home, only the midday meal can be taken there by those who live in flats with kitchens. Nonetheless those people living in the Sheltered Housing who need additional meal help can receive it via Meals on Wheels or Home Help service. The warden who supervises the total linked complex is also aware of any special health

needs of the flat residents and will immediately call for needed services.

The average age of the residents in the Sheltered Housing flats is 70, while the average age of those in the Old Person's Home is 90. As a result the medical needs of the latter group tend to be higher. A lack of geriatric beds has tended to hold some people in the Old Person's Home who require more extensive medical or psychiatric supervision. This has prevented the natural flow of people from one type of accommodation to the other, which was originally envisioned as a major reason for Linked Housing.

Initially it was expected that some of those in the flats of the Sheltered Housing section would move, as increased age and health required, to a room in the Old Person's Home. Because of familiarity with the dining room, lounges, and staff such a move was expected to be less disruptive to the life style of the individual. Some moves of this type do occur but not as many as were originally hoped. Irvine Development Corporation personnel are less directly involved in the Sheltered Housing or Old Person's Homes than they were in Glenrothes. This seems to be due to the fact that in Glenrothes the Sheltered Housing that exists was built by the Glenrothes Development Corporation, whereas in Irvine it is the responsibility of local authorities. Nonetheless the flow of information between the different agencies seemed open, and frequent contacts were attempted.

Conversations with IDC staff, Linked Housing staff, and the Area Chief Social Worker highlighted their concern that older people be given the same options to select a life style as other age groups.

98

There was some discussion of the fact that the newcomers of *all* ages tended to use the social services more readily, while the residents of the older mining villages tended to back off except for the local community centers. Thus for these people the programs and staff in the community centers were the main links with the network of Irvine New Town.

CONCLUSION

Researchers have found that most older adults link self-esteem with being able to maintain independent residence.[3,4] Yet they are frequently threatened by loss of financial and physical independence. It is thus necessary to explore what social mechanisms can help people feel self-sufficient but not isolated.

Where institutionalization is necessary it would be to the advantage of the older person to be able to maintain some sense of self-determination even if over minor areas. The right to choose how one will live is seen as a reasonable expectation within the context of the New Towns. The total social system is geared to help support as wide a range of choice as possible. Thus there are rate subsidies for rentals. No older persons in the New Towns who otherwise qualify for housing have to worry about whether they can afford it. In one Irvine Old Person's Home only one resident was paying the full rate. The rest paid on a sliding scale and the Strathclyde Region paid the difference. This was viewed by the majority of staff, residents, and outsiders as a right and not a gift.

Those elderly who prefer to maintain either a flat or a bungalow are encouraged to do so. The provision of auxiliary care helps to increase their options for self-maintenance. It seems reasonable that the provision of a number of feasible alternatives allows a necessary perception of autonomy. This wide range of alternatives seems to lead to better adjustment, irrespective of the actual decision. With deft handling, most attempts to help the elderly in the New Towns appear designed to reduce the sense of external intrusion in decision making. Most of the older individuals interviewed perceived people in authority as working for them. This perspective was also held by a majority of the authority figures.

Clearly the macrocultural and microcultural levels are working together in increasing the options available to older people within the New Towns. Formal and informal organizations seem able to provide continuing socialization, helping older people learn to work competently with new statuses and roles. Generally people treated as a valuable resource will be more able to give freely of their knowledge and skill.

The reciprocal patterns of social exchange supported by the system within the New Towns require further research. In these instances the development corporations and the local authorities may become mediators in the exchange, thereby creating Good Neighbors who check on area elderly and in return receive rate-free telephones. Such arrangements are sustained by the type of networking found in most of the New Towns that were visited.

The life style of the elderly and the

delivery of services to them in the New Towns provide a striking contrast to the situation for the majority of the elderly in the United States, where restructuring of the values of society regarding aging has been taking place during the past decade. It is interesting to speculate on whether the United States is moving closer to or farther away from a system like the British New Towns.

REFERENCES

1. Shanas, E. "Measuring the Home Health Needs of the Aged in Five Countries." *Journal of Gerontology* 26: (1971) p. 37–40.
2. Howard, E. *Garden Cities of Tomorrow* (Cambridge, Mass.: MIT Press, 1965).
3. Clark, M. "The Anthropology of Aging, a New Area for Studies of Culture and Personality." *Gerontologist* 7: (1967) p. 55–64.
4. Clark, M. and Anderson, B. *Culture and Aging* (Springfield, Ill.: Charles C Thomas 1967).

Is Health Education for the Middle-Aged and Elderly a Waste of Time?

Sir W. Ferguson Anderson, M.D., F.R.C.P.
Emeritus Professor of Geriatric Medicine
University of Glasgow
Consultant Physician
Geriatric Medicine
Stobhill General Hospital
Glasgow, Scotland

THE IDEA OF PLANNING health care services is a relatively recent one. Those individuals given this task have been faced with a changing age structure of the population in their own lifetimes. Brotherston noted in 1969 that the comparatively young society produced by the large Victorian birthrate has given way to one with a more normal proportion of elderly, the so-called aging society, and that this still seems to surprise many people.[1] Another challenge has been presented by the massive increase in the number of very elderly persons, mainly women, age 80 and over. This is occurring all over the world, but will have more far-reaching effects in those countries that already have a high proportion of elderly.

The village life of small communities is generally disappearing because of the global population shifts from rural areas into cities. In many countries like the United Kingdom, these phenomena have been associated with a fall in the propor-

102   tion of men age 65 years and over in the work force and an often marked increase of working married women. This affects the care of elderly individuals.

In 1963 the World Health Organization suggested a new classification for older persons: *middle-aged* from 45 to 59 years, *elderly* from 60 to 74 years, *old* from 75 to 89 years, and *very old* from 90 years on. The needs of the elderly were said to be occupation, interest, use of acquired skills, and knowledge. These needs differed from those of the old, who required many kinds of help, care, and services.[2]

ILLNESS IN THE ELDERLY

Physicians caring for the elderly have recently been interested in studying the disabilities and illnesses that occur in older people living in their own homes in the community. The conditions found by Andrews and colleagues[3] in a random sample of people age 65 and over in a small town near Glasgow were cardiac failure, anemia, urinary problems, and problems with vision and hearing. Nearly all the individuals with these complaints could be helped, and many were cured.

In another random sample of a similar age group, researchers found that major disability (defined as the inability to lead an independent existence) increased dramatically with age. By age 85, approximately 80% of the people suffered from such disabilities and were unable to live an independent life in their own homes without some kind of help. When the cause of the disability was considered, many individuals had more than one clinical diagnosis (382 diagnoses were found

in 227 disabled individuals). The prevalence of disability increased from 12% for persons age 65 to 69 to greater than 80% for persons over age 85. In 48% of the 227 disabled individuals a disorder of the central nervous system contributed to the disability, 22% had a functional psychiatric disorder, 38% had a cardiorespiratory diagnosis, 24% had joint disease, 16% were obese, and 11% had visual impairment. Only 3% were persistently incontinent. When the women age 75 years and over in the organic neuropsychiatric disorder group were examined, the two great problems were nonvascular dementia and disorders of balance.[4] Thus it is not surprising to find that the incidence of fatal home accidents from falls increases greatly in elderly individuals.

In such samples, about 20% to 30% of those approached refused to participate, but studies have revealed that the physical and mental health of those who refused to take part in the survey was similar to that of those who had agreed.[5,6]

In 1964, Williamson and colleagues demonstrated that with certain complaints (painful feet, difficulty in walking, trouble with micturition, anemia, and dementia), the elderly individual frequently did not seek medical advice. The symptoms were attributed to aging and not to disease. This may be due to the fatalism of the elderly or their relatives, or the fear of the elderly that they may be admitted to a hospital or institution, or because many elderly individuals are mentally impaired and thus cannot seek medical advice. Williamson and colleagues called this phenomenon "the iceberg of unreported illness."[7] There is an enormous pool of tolerated illness in

> *There is an enormous pool of tolerated illness in the population at any one time, which has been ignored, normalized, or left to develop.*

the population at any one time, which has been ignored, normalized, or left to develop.[8] Hicks felt that chronic sickness is concentrated in the aged. Chronic conditions gradually become incorporated as an essential part of the person and thus part of the definition of that person's normal health.[9]

DIAGNOSIS

As certain attributes alter with age, early diagnosis becomes difficult. In some elderly persons the sensation of pain seems in clinical practice to be diminished (ie, the pain threshold is raised). Postural control is also upset while the appreciation of ambient temperature appears to be diminished, and the response by fever to disease is impaired in some elderly people. In the elderly the sensation of thirst is not as demanding as in younger persons. In addition, the occurrence of multiple pathology, the onset of illness in an insidious way, and the frequent atypical presentation of illness increases the problem of accurate diagnosis or, more commonly, the list of diagnoses.

However, diagnosis is essential. Many physicians working in hospitals have found that elderly persons are seen by them at a late stage in their illness and that much more could have been done if the patients had been referred to hospitals earlier.

Many elderly individuals with an impaired reserve of mental capacity become confused whereas younger individuals would not suffer from this symptom. Fecal impaction, urinary retention, anemia, infectious illness, dehydration, cardiac failure, uremia, and the administration of drugs are common causes of such confusion. Metabolic disorders such as diabetes mellitus, hypothyroidism, and hyperthyroidism may present with mental upset, and rarely potassium deficiency among the elderly may produce depression, apathy, weakness, paranoid ideas, and disturbances of sleep rhythm.[10]

Andrews and colleagues recorded the incidence of mental illness in the age 65 and over group as 22.5% of men and 39% of women.[3] In 1975 Stenbäck reported a high incidence of depression (around 30%) in the elderly in the community.[11] The coexistence in the same person of physical and mental disorders tends to be discovered more frequently than can be explained by chance. A high proportion (60% to 80%) of cases of depression in elderly persons appear to have been precipitated by incidents such as acute physical stress (eg, surgery, acute illness, or exacerbation of chronic disorders).[12]

A constant danger to the physical and mental health of elderly individuals today is the amount of drugs prescribed for them. Drug-induced mental confusion is common, accounting for approximately 10% of admissions to psychogeriatric units.

In regard to social condition, Busse noted that social and economic levels affect the frequency of depressive epi-

104 sodes. A low-income group of elderly individuals had a considerably greater incidence of depression than groups with higher income. Social activity appears to be an excellent technique for preventing depressive reactions, but the maintenance of such physical capacity depends on other factors such as good physical health, stability, and control of the living situation.[13]

This close relationship between physical, mental, and social health means that a comprehensive assessment of the elderly in their own homes is essential for accurate diagnosis.

PREVENTIVE MEASURES

The first preventive measure in attempting to keep people healthy as they age is health education of the public. In 1978 Mehighan recorded that in a 500-bed teaching hospital in Dublin, 35% of the beds were occupied by patients suffering from diseases caused by cigarette smoking, and 25% more were used for the treatment of diseases caused by the use of alcohol or drugs, accidents, obesity, or faulty dietary habits. He called this massive group of illnesses lifestyle diseases.[14] The situation was highlighted by McKeown,[15] who declared that a moderate to heavy smoker would probably live longer by giving up smoking and physicians than by retaining both. He continued, "in developed countries an individual's health is unhappily in his own hands. Smoking, consumption of refined foods and sedentary living are all profound departures from the conditions under which man can operate."[15]

Exercise

Exercise is essential, especially for the elderly. Leaf has reported, as a result of visiting places in the world where individuals are supposed to live a long time, that nearly all the very old people were self-employed and had continued to work in difficult circumstances that required much exercise.[16]

It is common knowledge that as people grow older they tend to take less exercise. Yet the elderly have a special need for continued mobility. Joints become stiff and limited in their range of movement unless used to the full extent. Neuromuscular coordination deteriorates with age, and loss of muscle strength is particularly serious. Adequate muscle power is essential in maintaining balance and posture and, if allowed to diminish, precipitates accidents. Increased levels of physical activity may reduce the risk of hypothermia, and regular exercise may lead to a small, persistent increase in resting heat production. Muscle power, tendon strength, and cardiovascular reserves can be restored and maintained with exercise. Elderly persons who take regular exercise can continue to cope with life at home and to face safely sudden demands for exertion required in daily living.[17]

In homes for the elderly in Japan, it is usual for the elderly to assemble just before lunch and, under supervision, to perform exercises with a large ball.

Nutrition

Individuals are at risk of malnutrition at age 70 and over, when the socioeconomic factors of retirement are felt more strongly, physical health may be deteriorating, and bereavement or some other strain on mental status may also be evident. With advancing age the effects of disease and resultant disability become more marked. Malnutrition, shown by obesity and undernutrition, must be watched for by health care professionals.

In England, ignorance of basic facts of nutrition is prevalent, especially among elderly women.[18] The bereaved man may be in an even worse state. As anticipated, daily intake is better in elderly individuals who eat with others, while those individuals who are isolated lose interest in food. Physical difficulty, mental disturbances, poverty, malabsorption, alcoholism, and physician-induced dietary deficiencies are important factors.[19] Only by random and accurate sampling of the food intake of the elderly in a particular community can estimates be made of the risk of dietary deficiency. The socially isolated (especially the housebound), those with physical disabilities, the recently bereaved, those with mental disorders, and very old men living alone are especially in danger.

Routine visiting of people 70 years old and over seems the only way to detect dietary deficiency at an early stage. Advice can be given, not only on correcting any deficiency discovered, but, if necessary, in encouraging the older person to join clubs. If these simple suggestions fail, then food supplementation may be necessary.

The dangers of obesity are evident. Observation of obese women in geriatric units demonstrates the problem of nursing, while osteoarthritis, diabetes mellitus, and heart disease are a few of the complications brought on by being overweight. Every effort must be made to discourage women in particular from becoming obese with advancing age.

Motivation

Society today does not seem to have a life-satisfying place for older individuals who tend to be discarded and isolated. Efforts will need to be made to stimulate and improve the mental health of the

Efforts will need to be made to stimulate and improve the mental health of older people.

elderly. Motivation is essential to encourage elderly people to stay healthy and to help them lose weight.

Mental health is especially important as retirement approaches. The experience of providing part-time paid employment to the elderly has demonstrated how anxious many elderly individuals are to give various services. The elderly need to feel useful and to help others. More than chance accounts for alcoholism being the second most frequent cause of admitting elderly patients to a psychiatric facility in the United States.[20]

Health education of the elderly

Education is important to prevent illness in the elderly. This has been undertaken in Glasgow, Scotland, by activities such as preretirement training, education

106 in retirement, and part-time reemployment in retirement.

Recently, in the British House of Lords, Lady MacLeod drew attention to the great problems of loneliness encountered by widows. She also pointed out that many women have never been educated to undertake minor household repairs. This is one of the basic lessons given in preretirement training courses for both men and women.

Preretirement training

Since 1959 preretirement training courses have been held in Glasgow. Men and women are sent 1 day per week from their place of employment for 7 weeks; full pay is received for this day. Ideally, individuals should attend the courses within 3 to 5 years of retirement. Such a time interval gives individuals the opportunity to consider a positive approach and to prepare to adjust to a new life. In practice most of the individuals who attend for training are within 2 years of retirement.

The courses cover a wide variety of subjects, including health in retirement, retirement and money, balancing the budget, and retirement and mental health. Demonstrations are arranged to encourage developing hobbies (eg, fishing, gardening, and appreciation of music and literature). Visits to museums and theaters are included. There are lectures on home safety, accident prevention; do-it-yourself exhibitions are included. For men, instruction on nutrition and advice on cooking, especially for those who are not accustomed to preparing meals, is invaluable. The classes meet in new technical colleges for higher education. The older students have the opportunity of mixing with younger students attending such colleges. No fees are charged for the course, but there is a moderate charge for lunch, morning coffee, and afternoon tea. The chairpersons for each session are usually men and women who have passed through such preretirement courses some years ago and have returned to offer their help. All lectures are given voluntarily, and no fees are paid to speakers.

Approximately 10,000 persons have now passed through such training programs. It is the intention now to proceed with a proper research evaluation of the work.

Education in retirement

Opportunity for preretirement training can be given to relatively few. A new type of group education called "Living in Retirement Courses" has begun for retired persons. If a group of more than 15 retired individuals wish to learn almost any subject, a lecturer can be obtained from the local education authority funded by the community, and a course of instruction will be started. In this way individuals in a local area who have not known one another previously will become acquainted and will take an interest in one another. Once a group is formed, group members usually wish to continue and become the focus of a new club.

Reemployment of the elderly

In continuation of the idea that mental health is extremely important for the elderly, in 1967 an office was opened in

Glasgow to commence a part-time employment bureau for the elderly. This office is open every afternoon during the week and staffed by retired voluntary workers who are experts in finding employment for retired persons. Approximately 7,000 men and women have applied to be registered, including men and women with professional qualifications as well as tradespeople and the so-called unskilled workers. All persons who seek this type of part-time paid employment indicate that they do not wish any more responsibility. Since 1967 over 2,300 retired men and 400 retired women have obtained part-time employment, even in an area of high unemployment. Positions have been obtained in clerical work, yard work, domestic work, and bookkeeping.

Hobbies and crafts centers have also been set up in former school buildings. A successful senior citizens' orchestra has been formed, and in many clubs throughout the city of Glasgow, old-time dancing has become extremely popular. This type of activity provides continued essential motivation for the elderly.

ASCERTAINMENT SERVICES

The finding that many older people did not report their illness to the physician prompted the initiation of ascertainment services (a seeking out of illness at an early stage). In the area around Stobhill General Hospital in Glasgow, where the geriatric unit is situated, general practitioners have been encouraged to send a member of their health care team, namely, a health visitor (community nurse),

who is a fully trained state registered nurse who also has had additional education in accident prevention and health maintenance. This person visits all individuals 70 years of age and over in their own homes in the district. The physicians in practice are responsible for people of all ages who have registered with them as patients. They are paid slightly more per year for looking after the elderly. They keep an age-sex register so it is possible for them to obtain the names and addresses of people in this age group. Experience has shown that the health visitor is able to detect physical, psychiatric, and social ill health.

During or after the home visit, the health visitor completes a structured proforma and reports the findings to the elderly individual's general practitioner. The physician and the health visitor, along with the other members of the health care team and social work team as required, can then plan a future health program for each elderly individual. Health visitors are exceptionally good at this type of work because they have learned that by informing a person of some minor deviation from normal, they can make individuals aware of minor illnesses.[21]

Health education (eg, accident prevention, dietetic advice, diagnosis of physical illness, psychological aid, and improvement in social living standards) can be achieved by the use of health visitors.

Health education can be achieved by the use of health visitors.

108 Referral to a social worker at an early stage, if necessary, and provision of household services (eg, domestic help or structural alterations in a kitchen or bathroom) can help to keep elderly people in their own homes. Foot care must be stressed and provided if necessary in the individual's own home because the need for this is so commonly found in housebound individuals.

This technique of ascertainment—seeking out of physical, mental, and social disease—is, of course, applicable to individuals throughout the complete age range and particularly the total care of families with problems.

CONTINUITY OF CARE

Work with the elderly has shown that continuous supervision of some individuals is also necessary. Such supervision is required, either following an illness treated at home by the physician or, more particularly, following discharge from the hospital. This is to ensure that not only does the elderly patient continue to take the prescribed therapy, but also that communication has been established between the hospital and the caring physician. This is done at Stobhill General Hospital by district nurses provided by the community. Such nurses make hospital ward visits with the physicians; these nurses then visit elderly clients who have been discharged to their own homes. The result of such visits is reported to each client's general practitioner and to the hospital physician, thus ensuring continuity of communication and care. Without continuity of care, repeated episodic hospital admissions can occur and no coordinated home care plan is possible.

Vision and hearing

Problems with vision and hearing are common among the elderly, and it is essential that elderly individuals have regular eye examinations, especially after age 50. In this way the onset of glaucoma or cataracts can be detected. Although these particular illnesses can be recognized by patients, they may fail to report symptoms to their physicians because of fear that nothing can be done.

A recent survey of over 2,600 individuals age 65 and over found that if changes in prescription lenses are considered normal, 90% of the people examined had normal vision. It was only after age 85 that vision started to fail. Thus if routine eye examination is undertaken, the chances of going blind are minimal.[22]

The elderly also require advice concerning their hearing. A certain number of elderly, approximately 8%, are hard of hearing because of wax blocking their ear canal and require the wax to be removed.[23] However, the vast majority of elderly who become deaf cannot hear the higher tones. This means that they are unable to recognize their friends' voices and that listening to a group of people may become embarrassing. Modern electronic hearing devices are excellent, but elderly persons require training in their use, as all the sounds are amplified.

CONCLUSION

To preserve the health of the elderly it is essential to educate those involved in their care. The establishment of 13 chairs of geriatric medicine at universities in the United Kingdom has enabled much progress to be made in the teaching of undergraduate and postgraduate medical students. Instruction in geriatric medicine is a compulsory and accepted part of the medical curriculum in most medical schools.

Training of nurses in geriatric medicine has now become routine, and courses of instruction are offered to social workers, physiotherapists, and to all branches of the caring professions. Paid organizers of voluntary workers inside and outside of hospitals have also contributed to the well-being of the elderly.

The marked increase in the number of very old individuals is the reward for better housing, improved sanitation, efficient medical and nursing services. These new years of life must be regarded as a prize, and society must be prepared to provide the amount of help required by senior citizens to keep them healthy.

REFERENCES

1. Brotherston JHF: Change and the national health service. *Scottish Med J* 14:130–144, April 1969.
2. World Health Organization, Regional Office for Europe. Report of seminar on the health protection of the elderly and the aged and the prevention of premature ageing, Copenhagen, May 14–22, 1963.
3. Andrews GR, Cowan NR, Anderson WF: The practice of geriatric medicine in the community, in McLachlan G (ed): *Problems and Progress in Medical Care.* London, Oxford University Press, 1971, pp 58–86.
4. Akhtar AJ, Broe GA, Crombie A, et al: Disability and dependance. *Age Ageing* 2:102–111, May 1973.
5. Akhtar AJ: Refusal to participate in a survey of the elderly. *Gerontol Clin* 14:205–211, 1972.
6. Milne JS, Maule M, Williamson J: Method of sampling in a study of older people with a comparison of respondents and non-respondents. *Br J Prev Soc Med* 25:37–41, February 1971.
7. Williamson J, Stokoe IH, Gray S, et al: Old people at home: Their unreported needs. *Lancet* 1:1117–1120, May 23, 1964.
8. Johnson ML: Patients: Receivers or participants, in Barnard KA, Lee K (eds): *Provisions, Patients and Politics: Conflict in the National Health Service.* London, Croom Helm, 1977, pp 72–98.
9. Hicks D: *Primary Health Care: A Review.* London, Her Majesty's Stationery Office, 1976.
10. Judge TG: The milieu interieur and ageing, in Brocklehurst JC (ed): *Textbook of Geriatric Medicine and Gerontology,* ed 2. Edinburgh, Churchill Livingstone, 1973, pp 120–121.
11. Stenbäck A. Psychosomatic states, in Howells JG (ed): *Modern Perspectives in the Psychiatry of Old Age.* New York, Brunner/Mazel, 1975, pp 269–289.
12. Post F: The relationship to physical health of the affective illnesses in the elderly, in *Proceedings of the 8th international congress of gerontology.* Washington, DC, Federation of American Societies for Experimental Biology, 1969, pp 198–201.
13. Busse ER: Psychophysiological reactions and psychoneurotic disorders related to physical changes in the elderly, in *Proceedings of the 8th international congress of gerontology.* Washington, DC, Federation of American Societies for Experimental Biology, 1969, pp 195–197.
14. Mehighan JA: The doctor's lifestyle. *Irish Med J* 71:174–178, April 21, 1978.
15. McKeown T: The determinants of human health: Behaviour, environment and therapy, in Gibson WC (ed): *Health Care Teaching and Research.* Vancouver, University of British Columbia Alumni Association and Faculty of Medicine, 1975, pp 58–77.
16. Leaf A: Every day is a gift when you are over 100. *Nat Geog Mag* 143:93–119, January 19, 1973.
17. Fentem PH, Bassey EJ: *The Case for Exercise.* Sports Council research working paper no 8. London, Sports Council, 1979.
18. Exton-Smith AN, Stanton BR: *Report of an Investigation into the Dietary Habits of Elderly Women Living Alone.* London, King Edward's Hospital Fund, 1965.
19. Exton-Smith AN, Overstall PW: *Geriatrics.* Lancaster, England, MTP Press Limited, 1979.
20. US National Academy of Sciences. *Aging and Medical Education.* Report of a study by a committee of

110   the Institute of Medicine. Pub 10M–78–04. Washington, DC, NAS 1978.

21. Anderson F: The effect of screening on the quality of life after seventy. *J R Coll Physicians* 10:161–169, January 1976.

22. McWilliam RJ: Vision in the elderly. *Health Bull* 36:69–71, March 1978.

23. Anderson F: *Practical Management of the Elderly,* ed 3. Oxford, Blackwell Scientific Publications, 1976.

Health Care Maintenance for the Elderly

Susan Krauss Whitbourne, Ph.D.
*Associate Professor of Education and
    Psychology
University of Rochester
Rochester, New York*

David J. Sperbeck, Ph.D.
*Veterans Administration Center
Bath, New York*

SENSITIVE AND facilitative health care provision to the elderly is a goal that can be achieved only through an awareness of their needs and capabilities. Misconceptions regarding the elderly and the aging process far too frequently stand in the way of the health care professional being maximally effective. On the one hand, some of the popular beliefs about the elderly as repositories of knowledge and experience can lead to overevaluation of an elderly person's competence. On the other hand, the more frequently expressed negative statements about the elderly as incapable of change, new learning, or self-care can result in underutilization of the elderly adult's potential. Stereotypes, defined as socially held overgeneralizations regarding people who share some external characteristic, are potentially destructive to any health care professional–client relationship.

There is nothing unique about the need for the elderly to be evaluated and offered services individually. However, there is a

112 substantial body of knowledge available on the aging process that health care professionals can and should take advantage of to improve their interactions with the elderly. Familiarity with the ways in which learning abilities can be facilitated among the elderly is a first step toward reducing stereotypic beliefs and stimulating the health care provider to design new and innovative educational strategies that consider the needs and capacities of the elderly.

OPTIMIZATION OF THE LEARNING PROCESS

Any summary of the research on changes in learning during the later years of adulthood must begin with three critically important qualifying statements. First, there are wide individual differences in learning ability among the elderly. Second, the findings of current research may be potentially misleading to the extent that differences associated with generational differences in educational and other relevant experiences are confounded with differences due to age when age groups are compared on learning tasks. Changes with age may be confounded with historical changes when individuals are studied over time. Third, the practical significance, in terms of the effects on the elderly individual's life, of any changes in learning ability must be considered when evaluating a particular research finding that may be only minimally related to learning tasks in which the elderly engage daily. With these qualifications the following discussion will provide a general orientation for health care professionals to use in approaching ways of optimizing learning in elderly adults. For the specifics regarding research methodology, the reader can refer to the excellent reviews in the *Handbook on the Psychology of Aging*.[1]

FUNDAMENTALS OF THE LEARNING PROCESS

Learning is defined here as the acquisition of information, rules, knowledge, and skills. To be learned, information must be selectively attended to, perceived, stored in short-term memory, rehearsed, and ultimately integrated with material learned earlier. Learning studied in a laboratory setting is generally quantified by counting the number of study trials (exposure to information) the person requires to achieve some criterion of performance, the number of errors the learner makes in a standard number of study trials, or the number of errors and number of trials when the person is given the opportunity to learn a criterion.

Memory is by necessity an essential counterpart of learning. Based on research on memory, the initial acquisition stage of the memory process (when material is introduced into the memory system for long-term storage) appears to be less efficient in the elderly. Therefore

Once information is acquired by older learners, their memory for that information can be as accurate as that of younger persons, even over relatively long periods of time.

the information presented here focuses on the initial acquisition of information through learning rather than its subsequent recall. Moreover, there is reason to believe that once information is acquired by older learners, their memory for that information can be as accurate as that of younger persons, even over relatively long intervals of time.[2]

To study the learning process, most researchers design experiments that will bear structural similarities to the learning in which people engage in the real world. While the materials themselves may be fairly common units of speech or numbers, the way in which they are to be combined are unique to the experiment and may seem unfamiliar or strange to the learner. This method enables the researcher to manipulate and structure the learning task to meet experimental specifications that are not possible to achieve with ordinary learning methods or tasks.

Research on the learning process may be divided into that which deals with studying the *conditions* under which learning takes place and that which deals with the factors within the *learner* that affect the learning process. While these two general sets of variables must of necessity interact, research on learning in the elderly can be usefully categorized according to this distinction.

CONDITIONS OF LEARNING

The conditions of learning that have been studied with respect to age differences in adulthood include: (1) the *pacing* or rate of presentation of information; (2) the type of *instructions* learners are given when attempting to acquire new information; (3) the amount of negative *interference* or possible competition between learning tasks; (4) the amount of positive *facilitation* or transfer from one task to another; (5) the general positive effects of *practice;* and (6) the general negative effects on learning of *fatigue.*

Pace

The elderly appear to learn more efficiently (need fewer trials and make fewer errors) when they are allowed to determine their own pace of studying the material[3-5] or for preparing their response.[6] If the rate of learning must be predetermined by the instructor, the elderly should be given more time to acquire the material than would be given to younger individuals. The educator should informally experiment with varying rates of presentation to determine which result in maximum efficiency of learning.

Instruction

It is not sufficient, however, to allow the elderly more time to look at or hear the material they are to learn. First, the material must be presented in a way that will make it perceptible to the elderly individual who may have various sensory limitations. Thus visually presented material should be of sufficient size, at a moderate distance from the learner (to overcome presbyopia), with sufficient light but no glare, and, if colors are used, these should not be in the green to violet range of the spectrum.

114   Auditorily presented material should be low-pitched, free from noise interference, distinctly spoken, and of normal loudness. Second, when presenting new material to be learned, instructions should take advantage of the specific nature of the material or at least provide opportunities and suggestions for ways the learner may structure the material. For example, with concrete words and sentences, the elderly can benefit from instructions to form mental visual images that dramatize the information pictorially.[7] It is not necessary, and may be somewhat detrimental, to provide pictures or images for the learner to accompany the verbal material. It is sufficient and probably more advantageous to make the learner aware that idiosyncratic visual associations can be used to connect otherwise unrelated material.

There is some indication that the elderly are less willing or able to use or report the use of visual imagery as a learning tool.[8] Therefore encouragement must be given to allow them to take advantage of this potentially powerful tool. With more abstract material that does not lend itself to visual imagery, suggestions to use verbal associations will be as effective as imagery is for concrete material. These suggestions should fully exploit the more natural tendency of the elderly to use words or phrases as mediators or cues for encoding new information.[9]

Interference

The terms *negative interference* and *positive transfer* refer to the contrasting effects of learning one set of materials on the acquisition of another set of materials. Both effects may operate in two directions: (1) retroactive—learning a second set of materials affects what was already acquired from a first set of materials; and (2) proactive—the learning of a second set of materials is affected by what has been previously learned. There has been considerable controversy over whether elderly individuals are more subject to the negative effects of interference, but the current view is that there is little reason to attribute learning or memory deficits to interference.[10,11] Nevertheless educators wishing to maximize the amount of information that the elderly acquire from exposure to more than one set of learning materials should consider the potential for these sets of materials to either impair or optimize abilities.

Any material that can potentially alter in a negative way the learning of material presented prior or subsequent to its learning should be distinctly separated (in time or mode of presentation), with the differences between the sets of material clearly and concretely emphasized. Thus items that are easily confused because of semantic or auditory similarities (see boxed material on p. 15 should not be presented in a sequence, but should be clearly separated according to the basis for their similarity.

Discrimination learning can be used to reinforce responses that correctly differentiate items to be included in one set of materials from items in the other. Because interference can be reduced in the elderly when the individual sets of material are learned completely,[12] the health care provider should ensure that

EXAMPLES OF SIMILAR ITEMS CAPABLE OF INTERFERING WITH PREVIOUS OR SUBSEQUENT LEARNING OF EACH OTHER

Semantically similar	*Auditorily similar*
Atherosclerosis vs. arteriosclerosis	Dietetic vs. diabetic (diuretic)
Immunization vs. inoculation	Estrogen vs. progesterone
Fructose vs. glucose	ECG vs. EEG
Cardiac fibrillation vs. flutter	Hemostasis vs. homeostasis
Antibodies vs. antigens	Diastolic vs. systolic
Psychogenic vs. psychosomatic	Ingestion vs. digestion
Pneumonia vs. bronchitis	Gastritis vs. gastroenteritis

the learner demonstrates thorough understanding of each set of material presented in a sequence as defined by specific objective performance criteria. Moreover, attempts should be made to structure a sequence of learning tasks so that each complements and enhances the other rather than requiring competing responses from the learner.

Facilitation

The educator should take advantage of the ways in which one set of materials can help in the learning of another through the generalization of specific information from one set to the other. Such generalization can be promoted by using concept learning involving reinforcement for the responses that correctly identify the concept connecting two instances. Research on discrimination learning[13] and concept learning[14] suggests that the elderly may require some assistance in determining the conceptual basis for distinctions or similarities among and within related items. Therefore providing instructions would benefit the elderly by enabling them to take advantage of

concepts that form the basis for discriminating and generalizing material when interference or facilitation is potentially involved in a series of learning tasks. For example, the ability to learn proper nutritional habits may be facilitated by teaching the elderly the relationship between different food groups and their effects on different bodily functions.

Practice and fatigue

The aforementioned considerations apply to specific relationships among sets of items presented in a sequence. However, in learning a series of materials, more general effects are also potentially present and must be considered by educators. These effects include gaining familiarity with the type of task required to learn the material (practice) and the exhaustion of mental facilities through repeated presentations of material (fatigue).

The potential balancing effects of practice and fatigue must be continually weighed by the educator. Sensitivity to the verbal and nonverbal cues given by the elderly is a sine qua non of successful education. Consideration of what is a

116 reasonable amount of time for someone to spend in dealing with health care information must always be given priority, especially when working with the elderly. Moreover, educators must be aware of the possible reluctance of the elderly to admit to fatigue and also their discouragement early in the process before the positive effects of practice have been made evident.[15]

Acknowledgment that it is acceptable for people to become tired as they progress through a series of learning tasks will facilitate the signaling by the elderly individual that fatigue is setting in. The identification of ways to promote practice through the structuring of related tasks in sequence can also increase the amount of time the individual can spend in learning before experiencing fatigue. In every task that educators prepare for elderly individuals, the conditions present in the learning situation must be analyzed. The factors within individuals that affect the learning process must be combined with factors present in the conditions to develop the optimal situation for learning.

Conditions that are applicable to one type of learner may not be appropriate for another if there are profound differences in their physical, cognitive, or emotional characteristics. Clearly a depressed and

> *Conditions that are applicable to one type of learner may not be appropriate for another if there are profound differences in their physical, cognitive, or emotional characteristics.*

visually handicapped elderly person living in an institutional setting requires a different set of learning conditions than does a healthy and highly motivated elderly person living in the community.

FACTORS WITHIN THE LEARNER

The factors within the learner that can influence the learning process can be summarized as follows: (1) the past experience with the learning materials and amount of familiarity with the type of information being presented; (2) the strategy used by the individual in dealing with different types of information; (3) the individual's level of cognitive development; and (4) the individual's emotional state in the context of the learning situation.

Familiarity

The greater the familiarity with learning materials, the better the learner's performance will be, a point related to the previous discussion regarding practice. Because many studies of learning deliberately make use of nonmeaningful information or artificial conditions, the elderly individual's learning abilities may be underestimated. Practice or familiarity in the job setting is one factor that works to the advantage of elderly people, whose response speed or ability to learn new material quickly may be somewhat impaired relative to younger adults.[16]

However, when the learning task is such that elderly learners have no experience to draw on, the quality of their performances will be reduced to the degree that it reflects response speed alone. Although this point does not directly pertain to the practitioner working with the elderly, in an applied setting, it is mentioned here to sensitize the consumer of research findings reported in professional and lay journals to the potentially biased picture that may be obtained from reading studies involving materials and techniques unfamiliar to the elderly.

Given that familiarity with the material can work to the elderly person's advantage, educators should survey their clients to determine, before presenting new information, the learners' knowledge of that area of health care. Where individuals indicate that they have some familiarity, the educators should attempt to draw on that information and relate the new material to it in direct and concrete ways.

Even more important, perhaps, will be the differentiation between the new material and the former knowledge where changes in practices contradict previous methods. In such cases educators should be exceptionally careful not to downgrade the learners' knowledge as obsolete and inaccurate but should point out in a positive way that changes have occurred as a result of recent research and technology. This approach can be varied according to the nature of the specific information. For example, a common but inaccurate approach to handling cardiac patients was to drastically restrict their exercise and activity levels. A positive approach to handling an elderly person who believes in this practice might include a thorough discussion of the relationship between exercise, strength, and stress tolerance.

Strategy

117

The learner's strategy in approaching a learning task is particularly relevant when the task involves the use of problem-solving skills. In this situation the learner must not only retain new information but must discover solutions that can be used in future situations. Research on problem solving indicates that the elderly may have difficulty in adopting logical strategies and in particular may not be able to select the most useful strategy for the task.[17] However, the elderly can initiate relevant and useful strategies with proper encouragement[18] and can determine the relevant structure of even complicated learning material.[19]

Prior familiarity with a task can facilitate the use of appropriate strategies. However, if this background leads the individual to adopt an inflexible strategy and to fixate on one dimension of the problem, then it is essential for the educator to provide structured learning tasks that demonstrate the effectiveness of alternative strategies. The strategy itself rather than the specific content of the information may be the desirable objective for the particular learning material. Attempts should be made to provide as many varied and concretely different content areas as are feasible to allow for generalization and discrimination of appropriate strategies.

Cognitive development

Health and physiologic functioning are factors within the learner that can potentially be affected by the aging process and that influence intellectual ability learning

118 performance.[12,20] To the extent that physiologic changes have occurred to affect the overall integrity of the nervous system, the processing of information at the higher cortical levels may be impaired, reducing the amount of integration and organization of information that can occur during perception, preparation of responses, and the storage of information in long-term memory.

A more precise way of characterizing the way the individual structures and mentally represents information is through knowledge of the individual's cognitive stage of development. Piaget has described the process of cognitive development in childhood and adolescence, and others have applied his theory to adults.[21] The major point is that the three levels of cognitive development described by Piaget can characterize the elderly individual approaching a learning task.

Most adults are assumed to have achieved the stage of formal operations where they have at their disposal the use of abstract symbolization and reasoning based on formal logic. However, this level of functioning may not always be available to the elderly adult if the task is unfamiliar[22] or if it is not appropriate to the task. Adults also may use concrete operations (the second most advanced level) involving logical reasoning with materials that can be seen, heard, or felt. They may also use sensorimotor processes (the most basic level) that involve the mental representation of objects, events, and people through actions rather than verbalizations.

Knowledge of these three levels of cognitive development can allow the educator to assess the learner's abilities and to structure the learning task so that it begins at the learner's level and advances from there. For example, individuals at the concrete level of thinking may need extensive practice with actual materials before it is possible for them to progress to abstract representation of the principles involved in what is being taught. However, regardless of the present level of cognitive development, all learners can benefit in being progressed from action representation to concrete demonstration and finally to abstract symbolization in the form of general principles.

Creative educators will find ways to structure the learning sequence so that it parallels the sequence of cognitive development within individuals. For example, in teaching the self-application of a hearing aid, an educator might begin by having the elderly person hold and examine the device (sensorimotor). After this initial orientation, proper application might be demonstrated by applying the device to the learner and eventually having him or her practice until mastering the technique (concrete operations). Finally a conceptual understanding could be facilitated by describing the device mechanically and functionally with the use of a chart or diagram (abstract reasoning).

Emotional state

The fourth and final learner-related factor affecting the learning process is the individual's state of emotional arousal during the time that learning is to occur. Ample evidence demonstrates that elderly persons are uncomfortable in situations where their learning abilities are being evaluated.[23,24] Anxiety can depress the individual's awareness of external phenomena and impair the accuracy of responses. It can also lead the learner into focusing or fixating on unsuccessful strategies to acquire new information or solutions to problems.

Unfamiliarity with the task, present in many learning studies, can have the opposite effect on arousal by reducing it to the point where the individual does not sufficiently exert himself or herself to take advantage of instructional strategies. The educator must be aware of the individual's feelings and take precautions to reassure the individual about his or her learning performance. At the same time the educator must structure the learning situation so that it is interesting and meaningful. Sensitivity to the background and knowledge of the individual learner will further convey to the elderly person a feeling of confidence in his or her abilities. This will reduce anxiety and make the task more interesting so that optimal arousal can ultimately be achieved.

Given that there are many individual differences in learning abilities and gaps in the research literature, and also that the type of learning tasks that have been used in laboratory experiments are not particularly meaningful to the elderly, it is nevertheless safer to assume that the elderly learner can potentially benefit from the procedures described here. Perhaps the most important point is that educators must be alert and attentive to

The educator must keep respect for, acknowledgment of, and capitalization on the experience and knowledge of elderly individuals as a foremost priority.

the special needs, both cognitive and emotional, of elderly learners.

Educators must keep respect for, acknowledgment of, and capitalization on the experience and knowledge of elderly individuals as a foremost priority. It is too easy to discount the potential of the elderly to participate in the health care process. Recognition of past and present skills is the first step toward making it possible for the elderly to participate in the treatment and preventive aspects of health care.

CAPITALIZING ON POTENTIAL: THE NEED FOR ACCURATE PERSON PERCEPTION

The process of assessing the capacity of the elderly for learning the principles of health maintenance and contributing to their own preventive and treatment programs requires accurate perceptions of abilities and objective evaluations of the factors that can inhibit or promote health maintenance behaviors. However, the nature of the situation in which an elderly person seeks health care assistance or consultation may preclude the health care professional's accurate evaluation of the elderly adult.

Health care professionals possess information the elderly do not have access to,

120 such as medical treatment alternatives, hospital and community services, technologic innovations, and other related knowledge. In a health care setting, such information is often exchanged in case conferences attended by elderly individuals, relatives, or both. The various health care professionals may inadvertently disregard the elderly individual's potential contribution to the decision-making process because the professionals have access to greater factual information.

Although anyone receiving services in such a situation is likely to appear and feel helpless when confronted with the "experts,"[25] the devaluation of the client by health care professionals can be greater when they have preexisting negative attitudes toward the elderly.[26] The failure of many elderly persons to comply with prescribed programs of health maintenance is probably the direct result of their self-perceptions being lowered by the kind of situation just described. Such failures can contribute further to the devaluation of the potential of elderly patients by health care professionals, and a vicious cycle may ensue.

Greater insight into the factors that could be manipulated to offset the negative regard of the elderly client by health care professionals comes from the framework of social psychology. The area of person perception has been receiving heightened attention because of its broad applicability to a variety of theoretical and applied disciplines.

Attribution

One facet of the person perception process that has received extensive treatment is the process through which persons observing the behaviors of others make judgments about the causes of behavior. The process of inferring causality regarding behavior is called *attribution*. Various theories have been developed to account for the factors that influence the attribution process.[27] In general, these factors may be categorized into two groups: factors within the person (dispositional factors) and factors within the situation in which the behavior is performed (situational factors).

Attribution theories predict which configurations of behaviors and settings will indicate that a person's behavior was caused by dispositional or situational factors. Although such predictions are based on the premise that observers objectively weigh the possible contribution of person and situation factors, an accumulating body of evidence shows that observers are not completely objective or rational.[28] Instead observers tend to favor attributing the behavior of other people to dispositional factors, even when the setting is such that almost everyone would exhibit the same behavior, regardless of actual dispositional tendencies. This bias is called the fundamental attribution error.[29] It also includes the relative tendency of people to attribute their own behavior to situational rather than dispositional factors.

Overattribution

In applying the attribution process to the perception of the elderly, it is clear that overattributing behavioral limitations exhibited by an elderly person to biological and irreversible processes will contribute to the relative devaluations of elderly clients by health care professionals. Treatment plans that would be considered appropriate for a younger client would be dismissed as useless if it was believed that the older individual was suffering from strictly internal and unavoidable losses.[30]

In terms of the health care professional–client interaction, when the elderly person appears incapable to the health care professional, the attribution error can enhance that professional's esteem at the expense of the client's. In such a case the attribution error results from the failure of observers and the elderly participant to recognize and acknowledge that the professional holds an advantage by virtue of his or her access to information that the client does not have. If the roles were reversed, the client would be able to provide the needed information.

Thus the situational constraints or restrictions on the elderly person's ability to appear knowledgeable are ignored, and the apparent lack of information is over-attributed to dispositional factors. Devaluation of the elderly person would be expected to be even greater if the health care professional held negative attitudes toward the elderly in general.

Need for sensitivity

Sensitivity to the elderly is imperative if the health care professional is to capitalize on the elderly person's learning potential. Awareness of situational factors that can constrain the elderly person's behavior in this setting can reduce the magnitude of the attribution error. Moreover, health care professionals, by examining their own attitudes, motivations, and behaviors regarding the elderly, can contribute to accurate perception of the elderly.

By incorporating some of the strategies to optimize the learning process into the health care setting, professionals increase the potential contribution of the elderly to their health maintenance. The positive outcome of such learning strategies will show health care professionals that the elderly are capable of learning. This can further redirect the attitudes of health care professionals in a positive manner.

THE TRANSACTIONAL MODEL: COMPENSATING FOR AGE-RELATED CHANGES

The transactional model is an approach to understanding the relationship between the older individual and his or her environment that is gaining increasing acceptance among gerontologists. The transactional model assumes that individuals affect their environments and that environments affect the individuals within them in an ongoing, interactive, mutual, and reciprocal process.[21,31,32] Aging is viewed as resulting from changes within the individual interacting with changes within the individual's environment. Losses within the individual associated with the aging process can be augmented by a failure of the environment to provide proper supports for the individual.

Conversely, support from the environment can offset or at least minimize losses within the individual. However, even without supports from the environment,

122 many elderly persons use coping or adaptive strategies to deal with age-related losses.[33] The fact that these strategies are initiated by the elderly should indicate their potential to contribute to their own health maintenance programs. Moreover, knowledge of what the elderly actually do to maintain their own functioning can be useful to health care professionals who wish to optimize the learning process by capitalizing on the abilities of the elderly.

COMPENSATING FOR CHANGES IN APPEARANCE

Older men and women who appear and feel attractive (not necessarily "youthful") take advantage of ways to enhance physical functioning and the appropriate use of dress and cosmetics. Although economic limitations can make unaccessible the expensive "health" foods, spas, fashionable clothing, and cosmetics, elderly persons with restricted incomes nevertheless can adapt to changes in their physical features.

One such adaptation is attention to principles of personal hygiene and grooming.[34] While high-fashion clothes may be beyond their means, to maintain their appearance the elderly can select clothes that provide freedom of movement, consist of flattering colors and styles, and are appropriate to the weather and occasion. A balanced use of cosmetics and hair-grooming aids can complement their facial features. Walking, simple exercises, and monitoring of eating habits can prevent physical changes caused by poor nutrition and inactivity.

COMPENSATING FOR CHANGES IN HEALTH AND PHYSICAL FUNCTIONING

Older individuals make many adaptations to the changes occurring in various bodily systems, including some fairly obvious measures such as restricting or avoiding tobacco and alcohol. Less apparent but also helpful is the management of diet by including foods with high fiber content to help regulate digestive processes and avoid dependence on laxatives.

Other measures include voluntary restriction of high-cholesterol foods, salt, and sugar. To avoid problems caused by malnutrition, a regular schedule can be followed for meals composed of a balance of the basic nutritional requirements. Constructive coupon clipping, selective shopping for groceries, and communal eating arrangements further stretch a limited food budget. Such adaptations would not be new for those who experienced similar financial problems during the Depression.

Sexual functioning can also be maintained by persons who are aware of normal changes that occur in later years. Masters and Johnson have given many useful suggestions regarding the personal adaptations that older men and women can make in this realm of functioning.[35] If both partners in an intimate relationship recognize that slower arousal patterns and decreased pressure for ejaculatory release in men often occur in the elderly, concern over loss of virility or sexual attractiveness to the partner will not be a factor and will thus decrease the probability of secondary impotence.

Reduced estrogen production, which can have deleterious effects on sexual functioning in postmenopausal women, can be offset by regular sexual activity as much as by drug therapy. Communication between partners regarding sources of sexual pleasure and displeasure, a crucial element to sexual adjustment throughout adulthood, becomes especially critical in old age and can help the elderly adapt to sexual changes. Of course if the elderly (usually women) find themselves without sexual partners, they will need to find other outlets for sexual feelings that will be personally acceptable. Reassurance by health care professionals can be especially helpful in this area.

COMPENSATING FOR SENSORY CHANGES

If the elderly can afford sensory prostheses, such as hearing aids and bifocals, and can wear them without feeling overly self-conscious, then they will be able to compensate for losses that can be overcome by these devices. However, other means of adaptation to sensory changes are available, such as using other sensory modalities as alternatives or supplements to those that do not operate as efficiently. Persons with hearing losses may start to read lips and those who have visual problems may use kinesthetic or auditory cues to maintain their mobility in the home and on the street.

One consequence of reduced sensory skills that is often difficult to overcome is the inability to drive an automobile. Without adequate public transportation people who cannot drive are forced into isolation, a reluctant dependence on relatives, or possibly institutionalization. There is no simple solution to this situation without some form of outside aid. However, cooperative arrangements may here again help the elderly compensate for personal losses without requiring actual "help," that is, direct intervention by health care providers or governmental agencies. Moreover, groups of elderly can exchange services; for example, the elderly woman can drive her visually impaired friend on errands and, in turn, receive companionship.

Changes in sensory functioning often interact with changes in physical mobility. An elderly man may not exercise sufficiently through walking because he is unsure of his ability to see when there is too much glare from bright sunshine or too little light on a cloudy day. Inability to distinguish street noises may make him fearful of walking where there is traffic. In his home he may experience problems in seeing the stairs, finding his way around the kitchen, or avoiding obstacles in the hallways. Yet isolation or institutionalization is not a necessary consequence of such changes.

A careful home inventory can be taken with the objective of providing proper levels of illumination, placing objects within accessible reach, removing unnecessary or unused furniture or other belongings, and in general structuring each room and connection between rooms to permit the greatest mobility and range of convenience. Outdoors the elderly person can ask a friend or relative to identify routes to the nearest services and

124

places of interest that can be easily reached on foot without undue physical threats. Learning these routes and taking action to correct sensory limitations through prostheses (even those as simple as nonglare sunglasses) can heighten the elderly person's confidence to successfully negotiate a previously dangerous environment.

COMPENSATING FOR COGNITIVE CHANGES

Although the elderly may have more difficulty acquiring new information than younger persons, learning deficits can be compensated for by proper instruction. However, the elderly may originate their own strategies. Awareness of a declining long-term memory may stimulate the individual to use simple aids, such as lists, notes, self-enforced rehearsal, and idiosyncratic mnemonic devices to register material that will be needed later. The person may also seek out the opportunity to regularly practice these skills, avoiding the otherwise debilitating effects of sensory and cognitive deprivation.

Slower response speed is automatically adjusted for in many elderly by reliance on previous experience when a task must be performed quickly and accurately. Self-monitoring can enable the elderly individual to avoid errors due to anxiety or lack of an organized strategy. Practice can further increase familiarity with a task that demands both speed and accuracy.

Many of the compensations already discussed involve some form of new learning. The fact that individuals make these compensations on their own indicates that learning is possible at any age.

In particular the ability to view a situation from a different vantage point is often required for continued functioning in familiar surroundings. Imagination and creative solutions are most likely to come from the individual who must deal with the problem. However, the incentives must also be present if the necessary effort is to be expended. This is a role in which the alert and sensitive health care professional can be of great value.

COMPENSATING FOR PERSONALITY AND EMOTIONAL CHANGES

One of the more frequently noted and disturbing changes experienced by the elderly is the onset of depression. This can be a concomitant cause or result of what Erikson has termed "despair," the unfavorable resolution of the critical developmental issue facing all older persons.[36] "Ego integrity," the favorable resolution of confrontation with mortality, is partly achieved through a process called *life review*.[37] Life review is a form of reminiscence in which an elderly person relives and reworks previous events, experiences, and interactions that may have been incompletely resolved or not dealt with at the time they occurred.

On their own many elderly progress through the life review and ultimately an acceptance of their past actions, present self, and future death. Moreover, they retain emotional involvement with family and friends, substituting personal attachments and meaningful activities from earlier periods of life that are no longer available with others that are personally rewarding and supportive. Despite physical and cognitive changes, they maintain a positive self-concept and accept, but do not become discouraged by, the limitations they experience.

One of the major limiting factors to well-being and life satisfaction among the elderly is the perception of poor health.[38] With proper support and education, the elderly can maintain satisfactory health. This maintenance in itself facilitates positive emotional adjustment which, in turn, allows for a more complete use of potential and compensation for other changes.

COMPENSATING FOR CHANGES IN SOCIAL ROLES

The elderly can overcome restrictions in social roles by creating definitions of their various roles and developing these roles to maximize the advantages potentially inherent in each. For example, the role of "over 65" can have some positive features if individuals use discounts offered in certain stores and for certain services. There are groups to which the elderly belong that have social, legal, and financial privileges attached. At a more personal level, many elderly cite the greater personal freedom that comes from having fewer normative role expectations constraining their behavior. They can speak their minds without fear of reprimand or rejection because there are fewer persons to whom they must answer. The positive use of leisure time can promote satisfaction. The widow can experience a sense of personal growth when she finds herself becoming more independent and autonomous than she ever thought possible. Grandparenting is a source of emotional gratification with less of the practical obligations entailed in parenting.

Despite the outward loss of social functioning and integration, the elderly can successfully create innovative and flexible forms of social participation in their families, neighborhoods, communities, and within the broader levels of society. The term *senior citizen,* often abbreviated as *senior,* which has come to describe the elderly, has been deliberately avoided by the authors.

Originally this term probably was meant to convey the experience and "seniority" that the elderly possess in comparison to their younger counterparts. However, it appears that the use of this term has not had its intended effects, and health care professionals should probably refrain from using it (unless the elderly individual specifically prefers it). The same can be said for the use of first names in addressing the elderly. Health care professionals who would be offended by being called by their first names by their clients should respect the status of their elders and abide by their wishes for how to be addressed.

Social roles for the elderly are still being defined, as the presence of a large proportion of the elderly in the population is still a relatively recent phenomenon. However, as the elderly define and originate their own roles, expectations for these roles, and the ensuing responsibilities and privileges, they deserve support and recognition for a task often made difficult by unfavorable stereotypes.

126 SUMMARY

In attempting to achieve the objectives of orienting health care professionals to the abilities, social regard, and potential of the elderly, a broad range of topics within the field of gerontology has been covered. The main goal has been to alert and sensitize health care professionals to the need to optimize the learning situation, accurately evaluate the older individual, and take advantage of the potential that older people already possess to learn new coping mechanisms.

The maintenance of good health is both a goal and a starting point. With good health, or at least the minimization of potential losses, the individual is psychologically advantaged in confronting the tasks of learning to cope with age-related changes. The successful completion of those tasks further enhances the individual's functional health status. Health care professionals are of most value when their involvement is facilitative rather than intrusive or overly directive. This involvement is as much an attitude as a didactic skill. It can best be communicated to the elderly when health care professionals convince themselves that, unlike children, the elderly do not need to be taught how or what to learn regarding health maintenance. Instead they need to be given the opportunity to draw on what they already are doing and what they already know in restructuring their interactions with their environments.

REFERENCES

1. Birren JE, Schaie KW: *Handbook of the Psychology of Aging.* New York, Van Nostrand Reinhold, 1977.
2. Hulicka IM, Weiss R: Age differences in retention as a function of learning. *J Consult Psychol* 29:125–129, 1965.
3. Arenberg D: Age differences in retroaction. *J Gerontol* 22:88–91, 1967.
4. Hulicka IM, Sterns H, Grossman J: Age-group comparisons of paired-associate learning as a function of paced and self-paced association and response time. *J Gerontol* 22:274–280, 1967.
5. Monge R, Hultsch D: Paired associate learning as a function of adult age and length of anticipation and inspection intervals. *J Gerontol* 26:157–162, 1971.
6. Canestrari RE: Paced and self-paced learning in young and elderly adults. *J Gerontol* 18:165–168, 1963.
7. Hulicka IM, Grossman JL: Age group comparisons for the use of mediators in paired-associate learning. *J Gerontol* 22:46–57, 1967.
8. Whitbourne SK, Slevin AE: Imagery and sentence retention in elderly and young adults. *J Genet Psychol* 133:287–298, 1978.
9. Rowe EJ, Schnore MM: Item concreteness and reported strategies in paired-associate learning as a function of age. *J Gerontol* 26:470–475, 1971.
10. Arenberg D, Robertson-Tchabo EA: Learning and aging, in Birren JE, Schaie KW (eds): *Handbook of the Psychology of Aging.* New York, Van Nostrand Reinhold, 1977, pp 421–445.
11. Craik FIM: Age differences in human memory, in Birren JE, Schaie KW (eds): *Handbook of the Psychology of Aging.* New York, Van Nostrand Reinhold, 1977, pp 384–414.
12. Hulicka IM: Short-term learning and memory efficiency as a function of age and health. *J Geriat Soc* 15:285–294, 1967.
13. Nehrke MF: Age and sex differences in discrimination learning and transfer of training. *J Gerontol* 28:320–327, 1973.
14. Arenberg D: Concept problem solving in young and old adults. *J Gerontol* 23:279–283, 1968.
15. Hultsch DF: Learning to learn in adulthood. *J Gerontol* 29:302–308, 1974.
16. Sheppard HL: Work and retirement, in Binstock RH, Shanas E (eds): *Handbook of Aging and the Social Sciences.* New York, Van Nostrand Reinhold, 1977, pp 286–309.
17. Arenberg D: A longitudinal study of problem solving in adults. *J Gerontol* 29:650–658, 1974.
18. Labouvie-Vief G, Gonda JN: Cognitive strategy

training and intellectual performance in the elderly. *J Gerontol* 31:327–332, 1976.

19. Gordon (Whitbourne) SK: Organization and recall of related sentences in elderly and young adults. *Exp Aging Res* 1:71–80, 1975.

20. Wilkie F, Eisdorfer C: Terminal changes in intelligence, in Palmore E (ed): *Normal Aging II.* Durham, NC, Duke University Press, 1974.

21. Whitbourne SK, Weinstock CS: *Adult Development: The Differentiation of Experience.* New York, Holt, Rinehart and Winston, 1979.

22. Hornblum JN, Overton WF: Area and volume conservation among the elderly: Assessment and training. *Dev Psychol* 12:68–74, 1976.

23. Ross E: Effects of challenging and supportive instructions on verbal learning in older persons. *J Educ Psychol* 59:261–266, 1968.

24. Whitbourne SK: Test anxiety in elderly and young adults. *Int J Aging Hum Dev* 7:201–210, 1976.

25. Ross LD, Amabile TM, Steinmetz JL: Social roles, social control, and biases in social perception processes. *J Pers Soc Psychol* 35:485–494, 1977.

26. McTavish DG: Perceptions of old people: A review of research methodologies and findings. *Gerontol* 11:90–101, 1971.

27. Schneider DJ, Hastorf AH, Ellsworth PC: *Person Perception.* Reading, Mass, Addison-Wesley, 1979.

28. Jones EE: The rocky road from acts to dispositions. *Am Psychol* 34:107–117, 1979.

29. Ross L: The intuitive psychologist and his shortcomings: Distortions in the attribution process, in Berkowitz L (ed): *Advances in Experimental Social Psychology.* New York, Academic Press, 1977.

30. Rodin J: Somatophysics and attribution. *Pers Soc Psychol Bull* 4:531–540, 1978.

31. Glenwick DS, Whitbourne SK: Beyond despair and disengagement: A transactional model of personality development in later life. *Int J Aging Hum Dev* 6:261–267, 1977–1978.

32. Schwartz AN, Peterson JA: *Introduction to Gerontology.* New York, Holt, Rinehart and Winston, 1979.

33. Whitbourne SK: Psychological adaptation in old age. *Long Term Care Health Serv Admin Q* 1978, pp 145–151.

34. Krauss TC: Feminine beauty in maturity. *J Am Geriatr Soc* 11:466–471, 1963.

35. Masters WH, Johnson VE: *Human Sexual Inadequacy.* Boston, Little, Brown & Co, 1970.

36. Erikson EH: *Childhood and Society,* ed 2. New York, WW Norton, 1963.

37. Butler RN: The life review: An interpretation of reminiscing in the aged, in Neugarten G (ed): *Middle Age and Aging.* Chicago, University of Chicago Press, 1968.

38. Larsen R: Thirty years of research on the subjective well-being of older Americans. *J Gerontol* 33:109–125, 1978.

Is Health Promotion Affordable for the Elderly?

Amasa B. Ford, M.D.
*Professor of Community Health
and Family Medicine
Case Western Reserve University
School of Medicine
Cleveland, Ohio*

THE TWIN SPECTERS of illness and poverty haunt the elderly. These are not imaginary ghosts but foreshadowings of reality. Despite an unprecedented financial outlay, mainly through Medicare, with more than half of public personal health care expenditures and 29% of all such expenditures going for the care of the elderly, only two thirds of their health care expenses were paid for by the government. The average elderly individual was left with annual out-of-pocket health expenses of $613 in 1977, equivalent to 11% of income. [1] Therefore both to the individual and to American society the present operating costs of meeting emergencies, providing treatment for episodic and acute illness, nursing home care, and minimal preventive services are already a major economic burden, apparently leaving little room for increased investment in health maintenance and health promotion "at the margin."

Not only is the present burden of paying for the health care of the elderly

130

great, but it is rapidly increasing because the number of elderly is increasing.

In 1900, 1 in every 25 Americans was age 65 or older; today 1 in 9 Americans is age 65 or older. In 40 years, when the peak of the post–World War II baby boom reaches geriatric age, 1 in 7 will be age 65 or older. Among the elderly, 38% are now over age 75, and this proportion will rise to 43% by the year 2000.[2]

The characteristics and needs of the elderly cannot be projected from present and past experience. The elderly of the next two decades will be considerably better educated, less likely to be foreign-born, and more likely to live in cities than their present-day counterparts.[3] Their attitudes toward health promotion will probably be different, and their overall need for health care will certainly increase.

RISING HEALTH CARE COSTS

The impact of an expanding elderly population on overall health care costs will be magnified by the fact that even at present the elderly, who constitute 11% of the population, account for 22% of physicians' charges, 28% of hospital costs, and 84% of nursing home costs.[1] These three elements, which make up more than 75% of total personal health care costs, can therefore be expected to increase at a more rapid rate than would be predicted based on total population changes. Considering population projections alone, if age-specific health care costs remained at 1977 levels, by the year 2000 the total bill for ages 0 to 19 years would decrease 4%, for ages 19 to 64 would increase 23%, and for those age 65 and over would increase 27% or $11.2 billion annually.

Rising health care costs also hit the elderly harder as individuals because of their fixed or diminishing incomes. More than half the recent increase in health care costs can be attributed to general inflation, while about a third is due to increased "intensity" (more use of specialized and technical services), a phenomenon that is no more under the control of the elderly person than is inflation itself. Other factors contributing to increased cost are duplication, inefficiency, waste, and fraud. The magnitude of these leaks in the system is hard to estimate. There is evidence that even though Medicaid abuse may not be as extensive as some newspaper accounts suggest, the elderly are especially vulnerable to quackery, fraudulent insurance schemes, and other forms of exploitation related to health care. Among the elderly the poor are likely to receive disproportionately less from such apparently equitable federal programs as Medicare, probably because of inadequacies in access, information, and "knowing how to use the system."[4]

PAYING FOR BASIC HEALTH CARE SERVICES

If the task of continuing to pay for current health care services in spite of an aging population, inflation, expanding technology, and other drains seems formidable, how much more so will it become if attempts are made to meet presently unmet needs by providing basic services to the elderly who are not now receiving them? The U.S. General Accounting Office (GAO), to estimate the magnitude of this problem as a basis for future legislation, interviewed a large representative sample (1,609) of all elderly persons in Cleveland, Ohio, in 1975 and again in 1976.[5] Using specified measures of six kinds of help (medical treatment; compensatory, such as home-making; financial; social-recreational; caregiving; and developmental, such as education), the investigators found that "65 percent of the older people in our sample needed one or more of the kinds of help we measured. Only 8 percent received all the help needed; the other 57 percent needed additional help."[5(p15)]

A crude estimate of the national cost of meeting all the needs identified is $34 billion, without correcting for inflation, increased unpaid services by friends and family, or improved health resulting from increased services. Of this total, 6.8%, or $2.3 billion, would pay for presently unmet needs for medical treatment of conditions such as arthritis, heart disease, and mental illness. This would be equivalent to an increase of approximately 1.5% in the annual personal health care budget—not to mention the competing claims on the public purse of the larger costs of responding to unmet needs for compensatory and financial help.

Another trend that will inevitably aggravate the problem of paying for basic health care services for the future elderly is the predictable decrease in the numbers of the younger working population relative to the mainly dependent population age 65 and over. At the same time that demands for retirement and health care benefits for the elderly will be rising, the tax base of productive workers will be stable or shrinking, with the result that tax money to meet the needs of the elderly will be harder to raise. An indirect effect of these demographic changes will be to reduce the size of the pool of potential health care workers, which may, in turn, cause pressure for increased fees and wages.

Because hospital and nursing home care together account for 51.4% of expenditures for the care of the elderly, much interest centers on the possibility of substituting less costly day care or home care for institutional care. These hopes have recently suffered a setback with the publication of a report of a randomized trial of the effects of adult day care and homemaker services in a Medicare-eligible population. Total costs increased 71% for the day care and 60% for the homemaker experimental groups, which suggests that these services (paid for by Medicare under the special conditions of the study) were used as additional benefits rather than as substitutes for nursing home care.[6]

Can an affluent society afford to meet these predictably increasing health care costs for an inevitably increasing elderly

---

Can an affluent society afford to meet predictably increasing health care costs for an inevitably increasing elderly population and *meet the added costs of new programs of health promotion and maintenance?*

132 population *and* meet the added costs of new programs of health promotion and maintenance? Before attempting to answer this question, some benefit-cost implications of preventive medicine and health maintenance must first be examined. Then the issue of paying for health services in the larger framework of health and social services in competition with other national priorities must be faced.

THE FAILURES OF SUCCESS

The social costs of advancing science and technology are proving to be higher than anticipated: the release of energy for industrial and domestic use leads to exhaustion of resources and injurious environmental pollution; a dramatic reduction in infant mortality has resulted in a population explosion; and the powerful preventive and therapeutic methods already introduced in modern medicine are introducing new difficulties, some of them potentially greater than the problems they originally addressed.[7]

Effects of advances in medical care

In a challenging article entitled "The Failures of Success," Gruenberg advances the proposition that "in assessing the effect of our technical advances in the past four decades . . . the net contribution of our successes has actually been to worsen the people's health."[8] This startling state of affairs, he reasons, has been brought about by the effect of advances in medical care that enable the victims of chronic disabilities and illnesses to survive infections and other previously fatal complications, thereby prolonging their individual conditions and adding to the total disease and disability in the general population.

Several major conditions, he estimates, have actually shown increasing prevalence over the past 30 years, including senile brain disease, arteriosclerotic heart and brain disease, hypertension, schizophrenia, and diabetes. This has happened mainly because persons with these conditions no longer die as early as in the past, during epidemics of influenza and pneumonia, or because of intercurrent individual infections, and instead survive as high consumers of health care services.

In some ways more disturbing is the fact that certain disabling congenital conditions, including severe mental retardation, spina bifida, and Down syndrome, which have always been associated with high early mortality, are now treatable by medical and surgical means so that these unfortunate children may live prolonged lives. Plans for the geriatric population may soon need to include provisions for elderly persons with Down syndrome—a possibility that would have been unthinkable 40 years ago. For some genetically determined diseases, the burden of disease in the population may be increased, not only by the prolonged survival of affected individuals, but also by the increased likelihood of their being able to reproduce.

Gruenberg's thesis suggests that the increased prevalence of chronic disease and disability in the population leads to greater costs, but he does not attempt to compute the bill. The GAO, in projecting costs of the care of the elderly, takes a more optimistic view: "our projections for the 65 to 69 age group over the next 20 years show that, if medical treatment were expanded to all in need, total medical costs over the 20 years would decrease slightly."[5] Thus there is at least a theoretical possibility that prolonged survival will not entail increased costs if adequate treatment of existing conditions can be effectively introduced to prevent secondary complications.

Benefits and costs of prevention

A different effort to assess the benefit-cost equation has been made by economists Gori and Richter.[9] They used an econometric model to predict the effects of introducing "high-yield" preventive measures, such as favorable changes in smoking, dietary habits, occupational hazards, and alcohol consumption, over the next few years. Taking into account secondary effects on the general economy of eliminating preventable causes of death, they conclude:

Prevention of some significant fraction of current causes of morbidity and mortality in the United States appears possible, with the potential of extending useful and healthy longevity. It is by no means clear that prevention of what are now the major causes of morbidity can reduce the costs of disease care, because a surge of competing causes is likely as the population becomes older.

It seems hard to escape the conclusion that not even the addition of effective primary and secondary prevention to the present health care system will prevent major increases in costs.

CAN COSTS BE CONTROLLED?

An argument commonly advanced for health promotion among the elderly is that more healthful lifestyles and the exercise of greater personal responsibility for health will be less expensive than the present system. Kristein et al, for example, present estimates of favorable benefit-cost ratios of 2 to 1 for smoking cessation and alcohol abuse programs. They also give examples of demonstration programs of health screening and preventive intervention among children, programs that are now being extended to adults.[10] These authors state that "a preliminary result of our studies indicates that generally prevention can be cost-effective, particularly managerial primary prevention [ie, control of environmental factors], individual primary prevention (healthful life style), and selective screening and appropriate early therapy."[10(p461)]

Education

In spite of the plausibility and appeal of such assertions, there is little firm evidence that educational programs actually reduce health care costs. Programs intended to modify health-related behavior will constitute an added cost that must be met before any savings can be achieved. Furthermore, studies of compliance with the advice and prescription of physicians show, with considerable consistency, that only half of the medication prescribed is actually taken by patients, and that direct educational efforts do not increase compliance.[11]

134 Further research will probably be needed before programs of education in salutary behavior, which are proven to be effective and ultimately to reduce costs, can be recommended.

Regulation

If it is not currently possible to be sure of abating costs by advocating healthier lifestyles and health maintenance, what alternatives are available? Most proposals for controlling the health care costs advocate regulation, incentives, or some combination of the two. Without attempting to analyze the many complex issues this question touches on, it may nevertheless be observed that the continued resistance of the American political system to national health insurance for nearly 50 years indicates a strong desire to avoid central regulation.

Some partial regulatory programs have been adopted but usually with such cautious checks and balances that there are few results. For example, it remains to be proved that physician self-regulation (professional standard review organizations) or community-based restraints on hospital construction (health systems agencies) have had any retarding effect on escalating health care costs. Neither the limited degree of federal regulation included in Medicare nor the uneven and inequitable state-by-state control of Medicaid has prevented the rise in cost of health care for the elderly, disabled, and poor.

Economic incentives

Efforts to change economic incentives are somewhat more acceptable, but even when successful they have not been widely adopted. Shifting the economic responsibility for health care, so that the providers share in the risk and thereby become motivated to help control costs, seems to hold some promise.[12] Probably the most consistently successful effort at cost control has been exemplified by the Kaiser-Permanente system, which uses a combination of prepayment and whole-system management to minimize high-cost components.[13]

Technology

The Office of Health Economics (London) provides a recent commentary on the worldwide problem of meeting health care costs with scarce resources.[14] It describes the continual introduction of new technology into the health care field as a principal cause of rising costs and an ever-present destabilizing force. New technology, especially that which entails high per capita costs, virtually guarantees that, no matter how wealthy a country may be, it will continue to face serious problems of inequitable allocation of resources that cannot be solved with additional personnel or money. In its view, all countries face the necessity of rationing health care, with choices restricted mainly to whether rationing will be according to market forces (a dominant pattern in the United States), by bureaucratic control, or, as suggested by Cochrane, by science (only tested forms of treatment to be paid for).[15]

Rationing

The concept that health care services are rationed by price and accessibility, if not by government regulations, certainly describes the situation of the elderly, who must often do without if they do not fit a certain prescribed entitlement formula or if they do not have money to spare. The increase in use of health care services by the elderly which was observed after Medicare came into effect and after documentation by the GAO of persisting unmet needs for health care among the elderly, indicates that there has been significant rationing of such services in the past and that the elderly have been and still are disadvantaged by the existing system of rationing.

The picture so far looks rather gloomy: high and rising costs, increasing numbers of elderly, unmet needs, dubious cost-effectiveness of preventive and health maintenance programs, and urgent pressure for cost control with low priority for the elderly. What chance is there that society can afford health promotion—or even continuation of the present imperfect services?

RESOURCES FOR HEALTH PROMOTION IN THE UNITED STATES

After observing the social security programs of France, Germany, Sweden, and the United Kingdom in the spring of 1979, the former US Commissioner of Social Security, Stanford G. Ross, offered sober appraisal and some hopeful ideas for the evolution of the US system. All the industrialized countries he visited are facing similar general problems. None is immune to unfavorable demographic developments, payroll taxes

pushed beyond previously acceptable limits, limited economic growth, and the need for austerity in governmental budgets. He summarized the worldwide issues: "The optimistic expansionist philosophy that underlay social security planning ever since World War II has now changed to one of guarded hope that the best of the past can be preserved while the considerable needs of the future are addressed."[16(p3)]

Potential financial resources

However, compared with the countries of Western Europe, Ross finds the United States relatively fortunate. Over the past 50 years social benefits and services have

---

Social benefits and services have not expanded as rapidly in the United States as elsewhere, leaving more room for future development.

---

not expanded as rapidly in the United States as elsewhere, leaving more room for future development. Whereas the United States allocates 11.9% of gross national product to social security, Canada spends 13.2%, the United Kingdom spends 14.2%, West Germany spends 22.5%, and Sweden spends 24.5%.[16] The rate of employer-employee payroll taxes in the United States exceeds that of Canada, Japan, and Switzerland, but is lower than that of Belgium, France, and West Germany, and only half or less in proportion to that of Austria, Sweden,

136 Italy, and the Netherlands. The argument that increased taxes and benefits for social security will damage the American economy is not supported by these data: economic growth in many of these countries equals or exceeds that of the United States.

Another potential resource for funding future social security benefits is the possibility of a value-added tax. This tax is widely used in Europe for such purposes, but is being considered seriously for the first time in the United States.

Other possible changes

More than new sources of money will be needed. Ross calls for a broad-based planning effort so that social security can be integrated into overall national policies.[16] There is a need to analyze and make choices among increased federal financing, the encouragement of savings and private pension plans, and such new ideas as tax incentives to encourage earnings among the elderly and reinforcement of the large but presently unrecognized contribution made by families and friends to the care of the elderly.

The elderly can participate in solving their own problems. The stereotype of aging as a bleak period of incapacity starting at age 65 is finally beginning to be questioned. There are many vigorous and capable elderly persons who want to be active and productive—often in careers different from their previous ones.

Old age is usually only a partial handicap and one with which many individuals can cope well. The elderly are becoming better organized politically and have already succeeded in raising the mandatory retirement age through state and national legislation. The consequences of this action for employment, the labor market, and the economy in general may be considerable and will have to be dealt with soon. For example, to balance the economic trends predicted by their econometric model, Gori and Richter found it necessary to posit increased transfer (social security) payments and to *restrict* the labor force to ages 16 to 65.[9] Here is a real and immediate dilemma; most significantly, it is one brought about by political action generated by the elderly themselves.

Other kinds of change expected to be introduced by and for the elderly could have more favorable economic implications. For example, a vigorous movement to establish hospices for the care of the dying in this country is moving in the direction of home care rather than institutionalization, and early studies indicate that this may be a less costly as well as a more humane form of treatment.[17] Unemployment among retired persons seems to have stopped increasing, and the elderly may become more economically productive in the next two decades.

More broadly, there are hopeful prospects in current trends to develop family medicine and other forms of primary care and to alter the organization of health care and its financing so as to encourage the use of ambulatory and home care over hospitalization and institutionalization. The pattern of care toward which these changes seem to be leading is one well suited to the elderly. The general practitioner; office visits; possibly occasional home visits rather than hospitalization; recognition of social, psychological, and economic as well as biomedical needs; and an opportunity to participate in decisions about treatment, life, and death are all characteristics of a health care system that many elderly remember and would like to have available again.

Such a program need not be excessively expensive—certainly not in comparison with organ transplantation and cardiovascular bypass surgery. If well planned, it could offer many opportunities for employment of the elderly in rendering services at a pace and of a type that they find attractive. The possibility of continuing a useful life, with diminished fear of illness-induced poverty, and with the assurance of a humane system of health and human services available in case of need, would go far toward improving the motivation of elderly individuals to accept and participate in health promotion. Without this motivation, the question of financing may be irrelevant.

CONCLUSIONS

The cost of care of the elderly is certainly increasing. With a faltering economy and a less populous younger generation, serious trouble meeting the bill can be expected, even without adding new expenses. However, not all the possibilities for solving these problems have been explored. More and different tax sources can be tapped, and the example of other industrialized nations shows that a more generous social security program is consistent with economic stability and progress. Health and human services can certainly be made more appropriate to the needs of the elderly and not necessarily more expensive. The elderly may become more productive, more actively employed in providing services for their contemporaries, and more engaged in maintaining health in order to live out a more interesting life. Health promotion is probably affordable for the elderly, but it will take some compromises and much hard work.

REFERENCES

1. Gibson RM, Fisher CR: Age differences in health care spending, fiscal year 1977. *Soc Security Bull* 42: 3–16, January 1979.

2. US Department of Commerce, Bureau of the Census: *Population Estimates and Projections.* Current population reports, series P-25, no 704. Washington, DC, US Government Printing Office, 1977.

3. Uhlenberg P: Changing structure of the older population of the USA during the twentieth century. *Gerontologist* 17: 197–202, June 1977.

4. Davis K: *National Health Insurance: Benefits, Costs, and Consequences.* Washington, DC, Brookings Institution, 1975.

5. US General Accounting Office: *Conditions of Older People: National Information System Needed.* Pub no HRD 79-925. Washington, DC, US Government Printing Office, 1979.

6. Weissert WG, Wan TTH, Livieratos BB: *Effects and Costs of Day Care and Homemaker Services for the Chronically Ill: A Randomized Experiment.* NCHSR Research Summary Series, DHEW Pub no (PHS) 79-3250. Springfield, Va, National Technical Information Service, 1979.

7. Ford AB: Casualties of our time. *Sci* 167: 256–263, January 16, 1970.

8. Gruenberg EM: The failures of success. *Milbank Mem Fund Q* 55: 3–24, Winter 1977.

9. Gori GB, Richter BJ: Macroeconomics of disease

138

prevention in the United States. *Sci* 200: 1124–1130, June 9, 1978.

10. Kristein MM, Arnold CB, Wynder EL: Health economics and preventive cares. *Sci* 195: 457–462, February 4, 1977.

11. Sackett DL, Haynes RB: *Compliance with Therapeutic Regimens.* Baltimore, Johns Hopkins University Press, 1976.

12. Egdahl RH: Foundations for medical care. *N Eng J Med* 288: 491–498, March 8, 1973.

13. Somers AR (ed): *The Kaiser-Permanente Medical Care Program: A Symposium.* New York, The Commonwealth Fund, 1971.

14. Office of Health Economics (London): Scarce resources in health care. Special report. *Milbank Mem Fund Q* 57: 265–287, Spring 1979.

15. Cochrane AL: *Effectiveness and Efficiency: Random Reflections on the National Health Service.* London, Nuffield Provincial Hospitals Trust, 1971.

16. Ross SG: Social Security: A worldwide issue. *Soc Security Bull* 42: 3–10, 1979.

17. Metropolitan Health Planning Corporation: *A Plan for a Hospice System of Care.* Cleveland, Ohio: Metropolitan Health Planning Corporation, 1979.

Family Support of the Elderly

Jean R. Miller, R.N., Ph.D.
Associate Dean of Research and
  Development
College of Nursing
University of Utah
Salt Lake City, Utah

FAMILY SUPPORT of the elderly is becoming increasingly important in promoting health and preventing disease. The influence of families on their elderly members is a relatively new area of study because past generations did not live as long as people do today. In 1900 there were only 13 Americans age 60 and over for every 100 adults age 20 through 59; by 1975 there were 29; and projections by the US Bureau of the Census suggest that 44 of every 100 Americans will be age 60 and over by the year 2030.[1] The family serves as a resource for the growing number of elderly citizens who seek emotional and social support, crisis care, and a link to bureaucracies. For many elderly on fixed incomes the family also serves as an economic resource as inflation continues to escalate.

PRESENT FAMILY SUPPORT

The widespread belief in American society that the elderly are alienated from

140

their families is based on several unfounded ideas. Many people believe that the high degree of geographic mobility has resulted in the elderly living at great distances from their children. Some people think the generation gap between the old and the young has resulted in the elderly rarely seeing their children. Still others believe that the predominance of the nuclear family has resulted in the elderly not seeing other relatives. Furthermore, the existence and availability of human service bureaucracies have made it appear as though the elderly are well cared for and do not need their families. Nothing could be further from the truth.[2(p6)]

Surveys have shown that most elderly and their families are not alienated from one another. There has been a decline in the percentage of elderly who live with an adult child (36% in 1957 compared with 18% in 1975), but there has been a rise in the proportion of elderly who live near an adult child.[3] In 1975, 3 of every 4 elderly persons with children either lived in the same household as an adult child or within a half hour distance from a child. A survey of 4,553 persons age 65 and over with surviving children showed that the majority of elderly saw their children or their siblings at least once a week.[4] A report of the survey indicated that more than half of the elderly sampled saw one of their children either the day they were interviewed for the survey or the day before the interview; and 3 of every 4 elderly persons saw an adult child within the week preceding the interview. Among elderly persons who did not see a child during the week preceding the interview, 4 of 10 saw a sibling or other relative.

There also are indications that families are providing long-term care for the elderly rather than taking elderly family members to institutions. When Medicare and Medicaid are readily available, there are nearly twice the number of elderly being cared for in their homes rather than in institutions.[2(p8)] The majority of American families apparently are involved in the care of their elderly members, but the quality of family relationships with the elderly needs broader investigation.

FAMILY RELATIONSHIPS

The quality of family relationships plays a large role in the degree to which elderly members maintain their independence. In families where members relate to one another in healthy ways, there is interdependence that allows members to love and care for one another while simultaneously developing and engaging in individual activities. These patterns are established early in the development of the family and continue after children leave the family of origin to establish homes of their own. Interdependence among family members allows elderly parents to live in their own dwellings and manage their own lives, but interdependence also permits them to accept and give assistance as needed. Interdependence can be maintained even when

Interdependence allows family members to love and care for one another while simultaneously developing and engaging in individual activities.

elderly persons live in the same dwelling as an adult child. When the ability of elderly persons to care for themselves becomes limited, interdependence is expressed more by sentiment and verbal communication than by physical actions.

Family structure

The degree of involvement family members have in one another's lives has been described through the use of a disengagement-enmeshment continuum.[5] Placement on the continuum is based on

boundaries that resemble rules specifying how closely involved family members should be in one another's lives. The clarity of these invisible boundaries guides the degree of interaction among members.

Families with clear boundaries

Families with clear boundaries among members maintain a transactional style that is neither too involved nor too distant. A diagram of a family with clear boundaries is shown in family structure 1 in Fig 1.

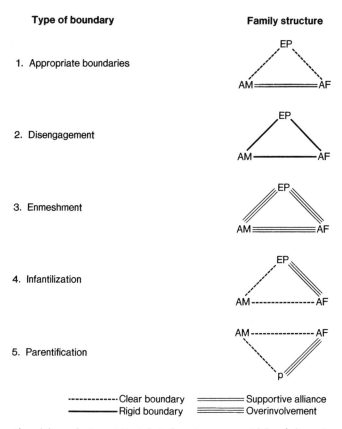

Fig 1. Family generational boundaries. AF, Adult female spouse; AM, adult male spouse; EP, elderly parent of adult woman. (Adapted from Minuchin S: *Families and Family Therapy.* Cambridge, Mass, Harvard University Press, 1974, p 53.)

142   *Disengaged families*

Disengaged families at the extreme end of the disengagement-enmeshment continuum have rigid boundaries that inhibit communication among family members. Elderly members in such families tend to be emotionally isolated from children and siblings. Members are so independent from one another that they seldom, if ever, request or respond to needs for help unless there is extreme stress. Even in stressful circumstances, members of disengaged families share few of their thoughts and feelings (see family structure 2 in Fig 1).

Enmeshed families

Enmeshed families, at the other end of the continuum, are so close, with such a strong sense of belonging, that members lose a sense of their own autonomy and mastery of skills. This excessive concern and involvement produces intense overreaction, especially in times of stress. It is difficult to learn and grow from stressful experiences in this type of family because individuals are not given the opportunity to solve problems in their own way and in their own time. The elderly in these families no doubt have their physical needs met by members in the family, but at the expense of self-worth and individualization (see family structure 3 in Fig 1).

Subsystems

Sometimes there are enmeshed relations within subsystems of the family. Subsystems usually are dyads or triads that evolve according to sex, generations, age, or interests. Typical examples include the spouse, parental (parent-child), and sibling subsystems. Because family members are members of several subsystems, overinvolvement in one subsystem hinders relations in other subsystems.

Parent-child subsystems exist for life, but the nature of the boundaries changes, particularly in childhood. Early intense parent-child bonds must be resolved so that the child can separate from the parents and gain a developmentally appropriate sense of self. This enables the child to function autonomously and to become involved in relations outside the family and eventually in a long-term relationship with a spouse. Most children marry, but not all who marry have adequately separated themselves from their parents. The bond between spouses is weakened by alliances between adult children and parents. Their overinvolvement threatens integrated family functioning. Pathologic patterns occur when a parent forms a coalition with an adult child against the child's spouse. This relationship breaches generational boundaries with serious consequences for the adult and the spouse subsystems.

Infantilization

One consequence for adult children who have not matured in the parent-child subsystem is infantilization of the adult child. Adult children who have inadequately separated from parents may function adequately in most situations, but in the presence of their parents they regress to former childlike states. A middle-aged child may be unable to make decisions without consulting the elderly parent who provides constant support and approval. This usurps the role of the spouse and weakens relations in the spouse subsystem.

Parentification

Conversely, adult children may inappropriately act as parents to elderly parents when generational boundaries are not clearly defined (see family structure 5 in Fig 1). As a result, adult children strip parents of independence and responsibility for self-maintenance. Instead of differentiating the areas that the elderly can manage by themselves, adult children assume that they know what is best for their parents without allowing mutual participation in the decision-making process. Such behavior encourages parents to become dependent and to act as children of their children. Neither parent nor child can be comfortable in this type of relationship for long periods because breaching of generational boundaries again impairs self-integration, ranging from identity and boundary confusion to delusional beliefs about self in relation to others.

In both infantilization and parentification, cross-generational bonds are maintained at the expense of the spouse subsystem. These pathologic boundaries function to support the tenuous equilibrium of the extended family system, but at a cost to all members. The dependency needs of elderly parents and their adult children are met; however, the needs are met in an identity distorting manner that prevents the investment of energies into individual and spouse subsystem development.[6]

Family losses

The time when elderly members need increased support from extended family is also the time when adult children are experiencing losses of their own. It is the life stage when the children of the middle-aged adults leave home to establish separate homes. If the mother has mainly cared for her children with few outside roles, she is likely to experience a sense of loss when her role with the children is terminated. Similarly, the husband experiences feelings of loss when he retires from active occupational life. It is a period of stress as spouses adjust their desires to preserve the past and reestablish meaningful relationships with one another. Not all couples successfully adjust to their losses and to the increasing demands of elderly parents.

Middle-aged adults respond to their losses by dealing with their feelings or by externalizing their hurt. Middle-aged parents may feel hurt because their children seem too busy to care about them any longer. The husband may feel inadequate because his services are no longer needed by his boss or subordinates. Misunderstanding of one another's feelings precipitates tension, which deteriorates the relation between them. A negative way of dealing with the hurt is to place responsibility for the stress on someone else. This person becomes a scapegoat who assumes blame for the stressful situation while the scapegoater goes free.[7]

144 Scapegoating

The elderly can easily become a scapegoat for everything that is wrong in the family. This is commonly the time when the elderly have increased problems that place new demands on the extended family and that place the elderly in a weakened position. The target for frustrated feelings usually is within the family system because it is difficult to link persons outside the family to the frustration felt within the family. The elderly are ready targets to whom family members can transfer stressful feelings. Transfer of conflicting feelings to the elderly relieves the scapegoater of stressful symptoms and helps build the scapegoater's self-esteem. Once this process is started, it is difficult to stop.

Nonacceptance of the role of scapegoat is especially difficult for the elderly when they are physically ill and depend on the extended family for assistance. As the elderly are continually reminded in verbal and nonverbal ways that they are the cause of stressful feelings in the family, they gradually accept the label of being the cause of all the problems the family is experiencing. In their weakened states the elderly lose their ability to evaluate themselves in relation to the total situation and consequently they give in to the pressures and relinquish their responsibility to escape the situation.

Continuous scapegoating behavior further separates the elderly from their extended families to the point where they may become isolated and act in unusual ways. Isolation perpetuates the debilitation and weakened state, which further alienates the scapegoat from the rest of the family. This alienation reinforces the elderly in their belief that they, rather than other family members, are sick.

Role of health care professionals

The health care professional's response to alienated elderly patients can further isolate the elderly person unless the entire family is assessed and treated. Caring only for the elderly person's symptoms may provide temporary relief, but long-lasting results require internal changes by all family members. Family members need to recognize and express their feelings to one another. As they evaluate their personal response to their stressors, they become more open to listening to other family members' feelings. Listening increases understanding of problems, which in turn helps families to develop new patterns of behavior. The man who has retired and lost his role in the work world needs to express his feelings of loss and the value of the job to him. He needs to preserve those memories while reestablishing meaningful relationships in his new life. Health care professionals can aid families in this process, but both health care professionals and families must be motivated to accept this type of treatment.

Surveys suggest that most families are in contact with their elderly members, but the nature of most family relationships is unknown when extended family members are with one another. Despite frequent family visits with the elderly, stressful family relations are highly likely to precede and prolong illness in the elderly. Health care professionals need to be alert to signs of structural family problems and scapegoating when the elderly seek care for chronic illnesses and health care needs commonly associated with old age.

Social support

Theoretical explanations have been suggested to explain why social support is so important in the etiology and course of disease. It can be generalized from the social support research that family support, a form of social support, also has a profound effect on preventing disease in the elderly. Family members enforce preventive health behavior and assist one another in coping with disease by influencing one another to behave in ways

---

When the elderly cannot meet the standards for acceptable health behavior themselves, family members can assist them with services and emotional support.

---

that will maintain health. For example, when an elderly person is not eating proper foods, the family usually is the first to note the poor eating habits and to ask about the problem. If the problem is one that the elderly individual cannot manage alone, families provide ways to maintain the norms of proper eating. Other health practices that are influenced by family norms include exercise, social activity, health checkups, medications, immunizations, and home safety.[8] Families provide standards for acceptable health behavior. When the elderly cannot meet these standards by themselves,

family members can assist the elderly with services and emotional support.

Family members also support one another in coping with disease and life changes. Families modify the stress of illness by eliminating or changing the conditions that gave rise to the problem, by controlling the meaning of the problem so that the problem is not perceived as stressful, and by keeping the emotional consequences of the problem within manageable limits.[9] Families are presently a great source of support to the elderly; however, changing times will affect the support families will be able to provide in the future.

CHANGING FAMILY INVOLVEMENT

Reasons for change

A number of factors suggest that the nature of family involvement in the nurturance and care of the elderly will change over the coming years.[10] First, there are proportionately fewer young persons to old persons in this generation versus a generation ago. This means there will be fewer descendants to care for elderly parents in the future. The effect on the elderly will be less resources on which to draw for all types of family support. This also will result in a greater strain on adult children who will not be able to share the responsibilities for elderly parents with as many siblings as in past years.

Second, most elderly individuals will not be able to use economic controls to influence their offspring to care for them in times of need. Younger generations no

146 longer depend on the transfer of parental wealth in exchange for their support of elderly parents. It now is more likely that inflation will absorb much of the elderly person's fixed income, leaving few, if any, resources for descendants. Adult-child or filial responsibilities increasingly will be based on emotional bonds rather than economic coercion by elderly parents. The desire for affection and parental approval will affect adult-child compliance to care for elderly parents in the future, rather than economic control by the parents as was true in some families in past years.

Third, the role of women in society is changing. This creates problems as to who will care for the noninstitutionalized elderly in the future. It has been the role of adult women to care for the elderly through such activities as running errands, transporting the aged, providing custodial care, and visiting the elderly. Proportionately more women are now working outside the home than in past years, and they are not, therefore, as readily available to care for ailing parents as previously. If women are willing to leave their children in the hands of baby-sitters and daycare workers to pursue a job, it is doubtful that many women will be willing or financially able to relinquish their jobs to care for elderly parents in the future.

Fourth, the elderly are living longer, which means that those in greatest need of care and support have adult children who also are older and are experiencing diminishing energy, health problems, and financial difficulties of their own. It seems clear that changes in these four factors—diminished number of descendants, decreased economic incentives, changing women's roles, and increasing life spans—contribute to the need to explore new ways to care for the elderly in the future.

New methods of support

Definition of family

The definition of family will need to be broadened in the future. A family is usually viewed as persons who are linked to one another through blood relationships or the law (ie, marriage and adoption) and who feel an emotional bond that spans a lifetime. This definition, however, is limiting when the elderly are isolated geographically and emotionally from their families, when there are no or few descendants, or when the family is deceased. In such cases, friends, neighbors, and groups can become the family of the elderly.

Emotional bonds can develop between the elderly and persons outside the family who are willing to reach out to others. For such relationships to be sustaining, the elderly must give as well as receive in these broadened social relationships. Dissatisfaction with current narcissistic values may provide the stimulus to become more involved in the needs of neighbors.

Regardless of definition, the family is and will continue to be the major support system of the elderly, especially in times of illness. Support can be offered in many ways, including regular communications, home maintenance, food preparation, transportation, physical care, financial resources, and affection. It is important,

It is important that the elderly be given opportunities to both give and receive in tasks that are adjusted to their abilities and desires.

however, that the elderly be given opportunities to both give and receive in roles and tasks that are adjusted to their abilities and desires. The elderly must feel they are an important part of the family system, even when they do not live within the same household. They also need to be active in the interaction patterns, whether to share information or feelings.

Role changes

Old age is so often viewed as a period when roles are lost and the person is seen as a nonproductive member of society. Roles are shifted in old age. The elderly give to society and to their families in ways that differ from their younger years, depending on the abilities of the elderly and on the willingness of the younger generation to assume complementary roles.

The elderly vacate their roles, leaving their positions open to younger persons, thus freeing the elderly to assume new roles that complement the roles of the young. For example, the elderly give up many of the provider roles and take on more activities associated with consuming goods and services. They vacate occupational roles and assume new or expanded roles in the family. Societal biases regard such changes as moving from socially productive behavior to restricted and devalued behavior. These attitudes are

not realistic in terms of what the elderly can contribute to family life.

Adult children and grandchildren can profit from the elderly family member's increased time to share affection and past experiences and to help around the home. The roles of the aged are not lost—the roles are merely changed to include new activities that can have value to the family. When the elderly are no longer capable of interacting or performing certain roles and activities, they often continue as integral members of the family system because younger members remember the elderly person's past contributions and feelings of cohesiveness.

Assistance

Families will undoubtedly continue to be the most immediate source of support for the elderly in the future, but families will need help in caring for their elderly members. Assistance will be particularly important for families with low incomes, geographically distant elderly, and employed middle-aged women because these families will have special problems in meeting the needs of their elderly parents. Nutrition sites, senior centers, senior organizations, churches, and voluntary organizations will augment family support as they have in the past. However, programmatic efforts should not serve as substitutes for effective and instrumental support from families.

It is hoped that social policy will provide ways to alleviate the family burden of ill elderly members through services that offer respite to the family and independence to the elderly. The

148 resentment adult children often feel when they are caught between caring for their children and their elderly parents can be decreased by intervention strategies aimed at ameliorating the effects of the elderly person's poor health and the resulting poor relationships that often occur between elderly parents and their adult children.[11]

Preventive health care is a necessary societal goal that will affect the elderly person's health and the morale of the family. Preventive education needs to be directed toward maintenance of physical well-being and also toward improvement of family relations so that stresses precipitating disease will be decreased. Families also need assistance in how to effectively prevent secondary complications when the elderly already have a chronic disease.

Support of the elderly in the future will probably continue to come first from families, then from neighbors, and finally from bureaucracies. In order to be most effective in the care of the elderly, these groups must coordinate their efforts so that society is ready for the increasing numbers of elderly in the forthcoming years.

SUMMARY

The elderly in American society are not alienated from their families. However, there are inadequate data to judge the quality of family relations among the elderly and younger family members. Major psychosocial problems that threaten families include disengagement, enmeshment, infantilization, parentification, and scapegoating. Families with difficulties in these areas could benefit from professional assistance.

Changes in American society will require increased cooperation among families, social support groups, and bureaucracies. Elderly who do not have immediate family or who have family in distant places will be especially dependent on neighbors, other groups, and the government for help. The increasing number of employed women requires that new approaches be developed to care for the elderly because women will not be as readily available to assist their elderly parents as in the past. Assistance from a number of sources, however, may have a beneficial effect on family relations because the burdens of illness will not be placed on any one individual or group.

REFERENCES

1. US Department of Commerce, Bureau of the Census: *Demographic Aspects of Aging and the Older Population in the United States.* Current population reports, series PC-23, no 59. Washington, DC, US Government Printing Office, 1976.
2. Shanas E: Social myth as hypothesis: The case of the family relations of old people. *Gerontologist* 19:3–9, 1979.
3. Richmond JB: Health promotion and disease prevention in old age. *Aging,* May–June 1976, p 6.
4. Shanas E: The family as a social support system in old age. *Gerontologist* 19:173, 1979.
5. Minuchin S: *Families and Family Therapy.* Cambridge, Mass, Harvard University Press, 1974.
6. Walsh FW: Breaching of family generation boundaries by schizophrenics, disturbed, and normals. *Int J Fam Ther* 1:254–258, 1979.
7. L'Abate L, Weeks G, Weeks K: Of scapegoats, strawmen, and scarecrows. *Int J Fam Ther* 1:86–96, 1979.

8. Richmond J: Health promotion and disease prevention in old age. *Aging,* May–June 1979, p 15.
9. Pearlin LI, Shooler L: The structure of coping. *J Health Soc Behav* 19:2, 1978.
10. Treas J: Family support systems for the aged: Some social and demographic considerations. *Gerontologist* 17:486–491, 1977.
11. Johnson ES, Bursk BJ: Relationships between the elderly and their adult children. *Gerontologist* 17:90, 1979.

Health Care for Older Women: Toward a More Humanistic Approach

Pamela J. Heiple, R.N., M.S.
Instructor and Clinician
University of Rochester
School of Nursing
Rochester, New York

THE CONCEPTS OF HOLISTIC health, mind-body integration, and self-care, nourished by the "me" orientation of the 1970s, have become an integral part of health care delivery for many providers. The self-care orientation and consumer activism advocated by the women's health movement have raised the consciousness of many people concerning the deficiencies and needs of the present health care system. Some positive changes have been made. However, the main beneficiaries of self-care clinics, alternative healing, and "total person" health care have been essentially healthy young women. Most older women are still receiving traditional, medical-model, illness-oriented health care. It is time to investigate the factors influencing the quality of care received by older women and to explore means of providing more wellness-oriented, humanistic health care.

152 OLDER WOMEN AS HEALTH CARE CONSUMERS

Women use health care services more than men, and both sexes use health care services more with advancing age, probably because of the greater prevalence of chronic conditions among the elderly.[1] About 86% of noninstitutionalized elderly have one or more chronic conditions, but the majority suffer no interference with mobility and independence.[2] The elderly have more bed disability days, twice as many hospitalizations that last twice as long, and visit physicians 50% more often than young people. The elderly account for almost one third of the total health expenditures for the entire population.[2]

Sex differences are a factor in the nature of illness in older people. Older women (age 45 and over) are more likely to have a chronic condition than are men and are more likely to restrict their activity and to stay in bed longer.[1] Women live longer than men and have lower mortality for most causes of death, probably because of their constitutionally greater resistance to infection and degenerative disease.[3] Yet women continue to report more physical and mental illness than men. This is probably because of sex differences in socialization patterns and role expectations. Three possible explanations for this phenomenon have been suggested: (1) women report more illness than men because it is culturally more acceptable for women to be sick; (2) the sick role is relatively more compatible with women's other role responsibilities and incompatible with those of men; and (3) women's assigned social roles are more stressful than those of men, there-

fore they have more illness. There is theoretical support for all three explanations.[3]

As a result, older women evidently need a variety of health care services. The strong association among aging, chronic illness, and poverty is most likely the cause for this need and at the same time may be the basis for ageist attitudes and practices that prevent older women from receiving optimal health care.

AGEISM IN HEALTH CARE

Although ageism is an issue for all older women, its effects are particularly obvious in health care for the poor and minority groups.[4] Poverty has been characterized as being the root of ageism in health care because the lack of adequate finances and prevalence of chronic illnesses associated with the elderly make them prime candidates for the charity wards of hospitals.[5] Although it was hoped that Medicare would alleviate some of the financial strain of health care for the elderly, Medicare may also be contributing to ageist attitudes and practices.

Robert Butler, a physician who has repeatedly denounced the ageist attitudes inherent in the medical profession, reported that the quantity of paperwork, confusion, and delay in billing Medicare and Medicaid for older patients' care is a real problem for physicians. Some physicians are reluctant to see Medicare patients, and others have quotas. Butler gave other reasons for the ageist attitudes and practice of physicians: (1) treating the elderly is more time consuming because of the complexity of history and symptoms; (2) many elderly persons may want to talk at length; and (3) they do not respond to treatment as quickly as the young.[6] Many providers do not see the value of preventive care and treatment for older persons with a short life expectancy.

Ageist attitudes have also been found in medical students. A survey of freshman and senior medical students found the attitudes of these students toward the medical care of the elderly to be characterized by negativism, defeatism, and professional antipathy. The medical students perceived the elderly as more disagreeable, dull, socially undesirable, economically burdensome, and emotionally ill than youth or adults. Ageism was more prevalent than racism in this sample.[7]

SEXISM IN HEALTH CARE

Ageism is just one barrier preventing older women from receiving optimal health care. Another, perhaps more insidious barrier, is sexism. Sexism in the health care system has been described as having both individual and institutional aspects. Individual sexism is manifested by the attitudes of health care providers and how they relate to their clients; institutional sexism is evidenced by the lack of basic research funds appropriated for the study of chronic illnesses and problems of women.[8]

Sexist trends and practices in the present health care system have been well documented by the women's health literature.[9,10] Perhaps the most pervasive influence of sexism appears in the tendency for the medical profession to attribute women's illnesses and discomfort to psychological origins. The histori-

cal roots of this tendency and its influences on present practices have been described elsewhere.[11,12]

Paradoxically some providers complain that many women (especially older women) waste precious office time with social and emotional problems. However, this phenomenon may have an iatrogenic origin, as certain problems of women that have psychological causes and are treated by nonmedical interventions, such as loneliness and poor self-image, are often referred to the health care services.[13]

Recognizing the social and psychological needs of women is essential to provid-

In dealing with the elderly, attention must be given to the unique problems brought about by the emotional impact of illness and disability.

ing humanistic care. However, the practice too often has been to label the discomfort as psychosomatic in a derogatory way and declare that "nothing can be done." In dealing with the elderly, attention must be given to the unique problems brought about by the emotional impact of illness and disability. The older woman deserves sensitive treatment of her emotional needs without casual stereotyping.

THE WOMEN'S HEALTH MOVEMENT AND OLDER WOMEN

Are women's health activists forgetting their older cohorts? Is change occurring only in policies influencing health care for younger women? The overwhelming ma-

154 jority of literature published since the inception of the women's health movement in the early 1970s deals almost exclusively with reproductive issues such as birth control and abortion. *Our Bodies, Our Selves,* the "bible" of the women's health movement, is a well-researched, comprehensive health manual for women.[14] However, its content focuses mainly on health issues of the childbearing years, and the brief chapter on older women concentrates on the menopause. Health concerns of older women, such as breast cancer, estrogen replacement therapy, nutrition, and exercise, are mentioned in the literature; however, osteoporosis, urinary incontinence, and chronic gynecologic problems are barely mentioned.

Some women have looked to the ideology of radical feminism to improve health care. Radical feminists believe that sexism can be eliminated from health care by balancing the unequal power relationships that exist within the present system. Weaver has proposed that many of the problems women have with health care either stem from or are exacerbated by the relative power or lack of power that women possess in American society.[15] The older woman is especially viewed as powerless because of her age.

Radical feminist theory describes women's lack of power in health care as resulting from the patriarchal structure of the present health care system.[16] The physician (father, head of household) holds the power over the patient (child), while the nurse (mother, caregiver) acts as an intermediary between the two. Radical feminists propose that women should have more knowledge and understanding of their bodies in order to equalize the distribution of power and dispense with the patriarchy of the present system.

Radical feminist theory, with its advocacy of consumer rights, catalyzed women's self-help clinics. These health centers have a serious drawback because they deal primarily with the needs of the reproductive system and neglect women's other health needs. This fragmentation of services leads to inefficiency and increased cost of health care delivery to women and, moreover, does not meet the chronic health needs of most older women.

TOWARD MORE HUMANISTIC HEALTH CARE

What is humanistic health care, and how does it differ from traditional medical care, alternative therapies, or holistic health? Miles outlined five types of health care within the present system[17]:

1. "Allopathic" medicine (traditional), which is based on a reductionistic view of the life process, conceptualizes disease as the enemy, reduces the patient to a set of symptoms, and puts the majority of responsibility for improvement on the provider. Miles believes allopathic medicine is highly effective in situations involving infections and structural damage, and marginally effective in treating lifestyle problems and chronic degenerative disease.

2. Although practitioners of "alternative" medicine use less invasive methods of treatment (such as nutritional medicine or behavior modification), their

perceptions of illness and of clients' and providers' roles and responsibilities are similar to those of allopathic practitioners. Illness is viewed as the enemy and the provider has the responsibility to conquer it.

3. "Humanistic" medicine, on the other hand, views illness as a barrier to growth, emphasizes dealing with the feelings and anxieties of the client (and the provider), views the provider as a caring person, and places the responsibility of wellness on the client.

4. "Systemic-organic" medicine conceptualizes disease as an imbalance of energy systems, places providers in the role of "manipulator of energy flows," and gives them primary responsibility for the outcome of treatment.

5. "Holistic health," in Miles' framework, is different from the other four categories in that it "focuses on development of the joyful expression of good health, not on the achievement of normalcy or balance."[17] Disease is seen not as an enemy, but as a "feedback message to a choosing person." The provider facilitates the client's learning to recognize and act on life's stresses, and the client has sole responsibility for his or her wellness.

Most older women receive allopathic medical care in traditional hospital,

Many of the health care needs of the elderly center on adaptation to chronic illness or changes in lifestyle and are too complex to be reduced to a set of treatable symptoms.

clinic, or office settings. However, many of their health care needs center on adaptation to chronic illness or changes in lifestyle and are too complex to be reduced to a set of treatable symptoms. Chronic illness is the unwelcome companion, not the enemy, of many older women, and the efforts of health care professionals should be directed toward helping such women integrate their limitations into a realistic conception of wellness. Humanistic care, with its emphasis on psychological processes, can provide opportunities for such integration.

Howard and colleagues defined humanized health care as "care that enhances the dignity and autonomy of patients and health care professionals alike."[18] These are factors that can greatly influence the way older women feel about themselves and their health.

PROMOTING WELLNESS

Ardell described five dimensions of wellness: self-responsibility, nutritional awareness, physical fitness, stress management, and environmental sensitivity.[19] These concepts could be incorporated into health care for older women to help them reach and maintain their highest level of wellness.

Self-responsibility

Accepting responsibility for one's personal health encompasses some degree of self-care. There are many definitions of self-care. Some emphasize the individual aspects of the specific self-care act[20]; others maintain that self-care is a contin-

156 uous process, essential to an individual's sense of health and well-being.[21] Perhaps the most comprehensive definition was offered by Levin, who emphasized the cognitive dimensions of the self-care act as "a process whereby a layperson can function effectively on his or her behalf in health promotion and decision making, in disease prevention, detection and treatment at the level of the primary health resource in the health care system."[22]

This conception of self-care was used in the program for health activation for senior citizens instituted at Georgetown University. This program was based on the belief that by training the elderly to prevent, detect, and treat common illness and injury, less demand would be placed on primary care resources and more efficient and economical use of the primary care system would be facilitated.[23] This health activation program also has the promotion of high-level wellness as a goal.

Reduced demand on traditional primary care resources may also be a result of the psychological benefits of self-care. It has been reported that along with improving physical functioning, self-care also enhances components of well-being such as self-confidence, social competence, and coping ability.[24] Improvement in these areas would lead to an increased sense of mastery and, in turn, decrease the individual's dependence on outside resources.

There are many unresolved problems with self-care programs, one of which is the lack of a universal, operational definition of the self-care process. This lack of standardized measures of both input and outcome variables has been termed the major obstacle to advancing the scientific base of health education practice in self-care programs because it prevents the comparison of findings between studies and subsequently limits the generalizability of results.[25]

Problems with evaluation procedures should not limit the incorporation of self-care measures into the health care of older women. Self-care measures are essential for the monitoring of chronic illness and, paradoxically, also are suited for preventive care.

Self-care programs for older women would help challenge existing stereotypes.

By taking more responsibility for their health, older women would challenge the stereotype of themselves as being helpless and dependent, one of the manifestations of ageism and sexism.

Older women are frequently portrayed as hypochondriacs who are dependent on physicians and unwilling to assume responsibility for their health needs. However, a recent study indicated that older women have a much greater amount of perceived health care knowledge than younger women.[26] A self-care program could build on this preexisting knowledge and provide a structure for older women to put it to use. By taking more responsibility for their health, older women would challenge the stereotype of being helpless and dependent, one of the manifestations of ageism and sexism.

Nutritional awareness

Older women have some special nutritional needs, especially during menopause.[27] Some chronic problems of older women, such as osteoporosis and constipation, may be prevented or alleviated by good nutritional practices. What better place to promote nutritional awareness than at nutrition sites? Older women could share information about preparing soft foods, cooking with less salt, and how to choose sound nutritional foods when shopping on a limited budget. Although some older women may be reluctant to modify lifelong food habits, many older women may look to this period in life as a time of growth and change and may be willing to experiment with new foods and methods of preparation.

Physical fitness

The "me decade" taught individuals to know, respect, and enjoy their bodies. Thousands of people took to jogging tracks, racquetball courts, and yoga classes. Many older people realize the need for exercise; however, limiting factors must be considered and realistic goals identified. People with lower back problems should not be encouraged to jog on hard streets but to start a walking program instead. People whose idea of physical exertion is 18 holes of golf (using a cart) will probably not be able to tolerate a vigorous game of tennis. Yoga classes are now offered at some senior citizen centers, and many older people are reaping the psychological as well as the physical benefits of these gentle, muscle stretching exercises.

Activities involving some degree of physical exertion could be offered along with the traditional bingo games and crafts activities. Dancing is an excellent and enjoyable form of exercise and would be an acceptable activity to those women who were brought up believing that participation in sports or physical activity is unfeminine and undesirable. One note of caution: people who take the responsibility to encourage dancing must make sure that they are proficient in the latest dances because they will surely be asked to teach them.

Stress management

It is well accepted that old age can be a time of biological, psychological, and social stress. Dealing effectively with these stresses is essential to maintaining a high level of wellness. In some instances helping the older woman with an instrumental task, such as filling out social security forms or arranging transportation, may alleviate the stress. However, maintaining wellness in the presence of such ongoing stresses as adaptation to chronic illness or frequent losses requires considerable skill. Many older women deal effectively with stress by adopting a "you take what comes to you, there's no use crying about it" attitude; others use alcohol or drugs, or become depressed or physically ill.

The mind-body relationship often is not news to older women; many of those with arthritis can identify a relationship between their mood and degree of physical discomfort and disability. Techniques available to younger people, such as tran-

158

scendental meditation, biofeedback, or relaxation exercises, may be beneficial to older women. Many older women find that spiritual measures such as praying are extremely helpful in times of stress. Support groups encouraging expression of feelings, sharing of common experiences, and mutual problem solving are other means by which older women may decrease stress.

Environmental sensitivity

The older woman has a unique, interdependent relationship with her environment. Environmental cues and orienting devices may help compensate for a memory impairment, and modifications in the physical environment (handrails in bathrooms, cabinets within reaching distance) may help older women maintain their highest level of functioning. Architectural design for the elderly has become a subspecialty,[28] and many housing projects, senior citizen centers, and long-term care facilities incorporate these concepts. Transportation, heating, and safety from crime are priority environmental issues for the elderly. Education regarding environmental hazards and ways to deal with them could be incorporated into preexisting programs for the elderly. Older women could be encouraged to form activist groups to lobby for issues such as better programs for energy conservation and transportation.

ADVOCACY FOR BETTER HEALTH CARE

Maggie Kuhn, national leader of the Gray Panthers, described the present health care system as one of the two massive systems that oppresses rather than serves older people.[29] It is time for older women to become aware of their rights as consumers and demand some changes in the present system of health care delivery. In a recent speech to the American Gerontological Society, Butler called for an alliance of advocacy with science.[30] During the past decade scientific advances have been made in the areas of cause and treatment of disease, identification of environmental hazards to health, and ways to prolong life.

Advances have been made in knowledge of nutrition, exercise, and psychological factors influencing health. Older women, younger women, and health care providers must unite to advocate changes in the health care system based on scientific advances in the health care system. The 1980s could be the decade when truly humanistic, nonageist, nonsexist, wellness-oriented health care is made available to all older women.

REFERENCES

1. Shanas E, Maddox G: Aging health and the organization of health resources, in Binstock R, Shanas E (eds): *Handbook of Aging and Social Science*. New York, Van Nostrand Reinhold, 1976, pp 592–618.
2. Brotman H: Every tenth American: The 'problem' of aging in Lawton MP, Newcomer RJ, Byerts TO (eds): *Community Planning for an Aging Society*. Stroudsburg, Pa, Dowden, Hutchinson and Ross, 1976, pp 5–18.
3. Nathansen C: Illness and the feminine role: A theoretical review. *Soc Sci Med* 9(2):57–62, 1975.
4. Jackson J: The plight of older black women in the United States. *Black Scholar* 7(7):47–55, 1976.
5. Roseman I, Burnside I: The United States of Ameri-

ca, in Brocklehurst JC (ed): *Geriatric Care in Advanced Societies.* Lancaster, England, MTP Press Ltd, 1975, pp 85–111.

6. Butler RN: *Why Survive? Being Old in America.* New York, Harper & Row, 1975.

7. Spence D, Fugenbaum E, Fitzgerald F, Roth J: Medical student attitudes towards geriatric patients. *J Am Geriatr Soc* 16:976–983, 1968.

8. Krause E: *Power and Illness: The Political Sociology of Health and Medical Care.* New York, Elsevier, 1977.

9. Frankfort E: *Vaginal Politics.* New York, Bantam Books, 1972.

10. Corea G: *Women's Health Care: The Hidden Malpractice.* New York, William Morrow & Co 1977.

11. Ehrenrich E, English D: *Complaints and Disorders: The Sexual Politics of Sickness.* Old Westbury, Feminist Press, 1974.

12. Lennane K, Lennane R: Alleged psychogenic disorders in women—A possible manifestation of sexual prejudice. *New Engl J Med* 288:288–292, 1973.

13. Muller C: Methodological issues in health economics relevant to women. *Soc Sci Med* 11:819–925, 1977.

14. Boston Women's Health Collective: *Our Bodies, Our Selves.* New York, Simon & Schuster, 1977.

15. Weaver J: *National Health Policy and the Underserved.* St Louis, The CV Mosby Co, 1976.

16. Fee C: Women and health care: A comparison of theories. *Intl J Health Serv* 5:279–288, 1975.

17. Miles R: Humanistic medicine and holistic health care, in Bauman E, Brent A, Pyser L, Wright P, (eds): *The Holistic Health Handbook.* Berkeley, Calif, And/Or Press, 1978.

18. Howard J, Davis F, Pope C, Ruzek S: Humanizing health care: The implications of technology, centralization, and self-care." *Medical Care* 15:5 (Supplement, May 1977) pp 11-26.

19. Ardell D: *High Level Wellness.* New York, Bantam Books, 1979.

20. Butler R, Gertman J, Oberlander D, Schindler L: Self-care, self-help and the elderly. *Intl J Aging Hum Dev* 10:95–117, 1979–1980.

21. Orem D: *Nursing: Concepts of Practice.* New York, McGraw-Hill, 1971.

22. Levin L: Forces and issues in the revival of interest in self-care: Impetus for redirection in health. *Health Educ Monogr* 5:115–120, 1977.

23. Nocerine J, Pringle W, Schnert K: *Health Activation for Senior Citizens.* Virginia, Health Activation Network, 1977.

24. Levin L, Katy A, Holst E: *Self Care: Lay Initiatives in Health.* New York, Prodist, 1979.

25. Green L, Werlin S, Shaeffer H, Avery C: Research and demonstration issues in self care: Measuring the decline of medicocentrism. *Health Educ Monogr* 5:161–187, 1977.

26. Kerschner P, Tiberi D: Health and older women. *Gerontolog Nurs* 4(4):11–15, 1978.

27. Seaman B, Seaman G: *Women and the Crisis in Sex Hormones.* New York, Rawson Associates, 1977.

28. Jordan J: *Senior Center Design.* Washington DC, National Council on Aging, 1978.

29. Kuhn M: What older people want for themselves and others in society, in Kershner P (ed): *Advocacy and Age.* Los Angeles, Ethel Percy Andrus Center, University of Southern California, 1976.

30. Butler RN: *Alliance of Science with Advocacy.* Paper presented at the Gerontological Society annual meeting, Washington, DC, November 1979.

Inadequate Nutrition in the Elderly: A Stumbling Block to Good Health

Pearl Skaien, P.Dt.
Therapeutic Dietitian
Regina Community Home Care
  Program
Regina, Saskatchewan
Canada

ADEQUATE NUTRIENT INTAKE throughout life is vital to good health. Food and drink should be a daily source of enjoyment, as well as provide adequate nutrition. Many fond memories have been created by the sharing of food and drink with family and friends.

In the latter part of life the elderly person's family has probably left home and friends are fewer. The subsequent loss of a spouse may leave an individual largely on his or her own. What is this person to do now? How can each day be filled? Where is the motivation to prepare a full meal for those who have been accustomed to having meals prepared for them or who have been used to preparing food for a family unit? Who cares?

There are many solutions offered for the nutritional problems of the elderly. However, not all of them are based on scientific facts. Nutritional requirements of the elderly are not significantly different from those of younger adults. However, economic status, disease, life-

162 style, and psychological change modify the food pattern.[1]

Because of decreasing physical activity the elder citizen's energy requirement is less. Caloric intake should decline by approximately 7% between the ages of 20 and 35, and by 2 to 3% per decade for the next 20 years. After the age of 55, energy requirements vary according to health and degree of mobility.[2] When a lower caloric intake is indicated, it is wise to restrict concentrated sweets, high-fat foods, and an overabundance of starchy foods, so that an adequate daily nutrient intake can be attained.

OBSTACLES TO ADEQUATE NUTRIENT INTAKE

Physical barriers

The individual's ability to chew and swallow may affect what can be eaten.[3] No teeth, not enough teeth, or loose-fitting dentures could prevent the proper chewing of most raw fruits and raw vegetables and certain cuts of meat. As a result of disease the elderly may have difficulty moving food from the front of the mouth to the back of the mouth. The swallowing reflexes may also be affected. Digestion may be impaired as well because of improper functioning of the stomach, the bowels, or both.[3]

A diminished sense of smell or taste may deprive the individual of the stimulus to eat. This could interfere with the optimum secretion of saliva and gastric digestive juices, creating distress during digestion. Certain drugs can interfere with the proper functioning of the taste buds. This distortion could result in foods tasting too sweet, too salty, or too bland.

As a consequence normally sweetened foods, normally salted foods, or normally spiced foods cannot be tolerated.

Obesity can impede mobility and increase the risk of cardiovascular disease, diabetes, and renal disorders. Fad diets, sometimes associated with weight loss, can be lacking in various nutrients and can lead to malnutrition.

Irregular bowel movements can interfere with adequate nutrient intake. Mineral oil given regularly as a laxative can deplete the body's stores of fat-soluble vitamins.[3(p28)] Inadequate fluid intake (dehydration) can upset the electrolyte balance of the individual. This dehydration can cause confusion and weakness as well.[3(p49)]

Problems obtaining food

The cost of food may affect food intake, particularly if individuals are on a fixed income. Limited cooking facilities can also be detrimental to adequate food intake. Individuals with only a hot plate are limited in the kind and variety of food they can prepare.

Immobility and the resulting lack of exercise can affect the appetite. If the physical effort of preparing a nutritious meal is too great, individuals may settle for toast and tea.

The degree of immobility can affect the actual purchasing of food. If the elderly can only arrange to purchase foods once a month, nonperishable foods will probably comprise the largest part of grocery purchases. The diet then could be sparse in fresh fruits, fresh vegetables, and possibly meat.

A lifetime of accumulated eating habits, good and bad, greatly influences the choice of food. The elderly must be given an "attentive ear" to learn why certain foods may not be acceptable to them. For example, skim milk in any form may be rejected because it could be associated with times of economic depression, or recalled as a product to be fed to the pigs.

Misconceptions abound regarding "proper" nutrition. Elderly individuals are particularly open to suggestions that good health can only be attained by eating "natural" or "unprocessed" foods.[3] The high cost of these foods can cut into minimal budgets, leaving inadequate funds to buy foods from the four food groups.

There is a common fallacy that milk is required only for pregnant women and growing children when, in fact, people never outgrow their need for milk. Cheese and milk have been maligned because of their supposed constipating effects. There is no basis for this assumption.

Emotional barriers

The realized need for a therapeutic diet can be a traumatic experience. It could mean that eating habits formed over many years must be altered. Loneliness can have an adverse effect on food intake. A nourishing meal may be replaced by coffee and a doughnut, because there is no incentive to prepare an adequate meal if it will be eaten alone.

HOW CAN THESE OBSTACLES BE OVERCOME?

Nutritional problems of elderly individuals may be alleviated to some degree by providing them with nutrition educa-

tion, either through group counseling or on a one-to-one basis.

163

Nutritional evaluation

All health care professionals should have a good basic knowledge of nutrition to support the dietitian in the nutritional education of the elderly. The nutritional status of each individual should be evaluated.[1] This should include a diet and social history, as well as appropriate laboratory tests, to identify any deficiency states that may exist.[1]

The diet and social history will indicate the individual's eating habits, mobility, food resources, attitudes, and living conditions.[1] If a deficiency state exists, then suitable measures should be taken to rectify the situation. Medical disorders that might affect metabolism and necessitate a change in dietary management should be identified[1]; examples are allergies, diabetes, hyperlipidemia, cardiovascular disease, renal disease, and cancer.

All elderly individuals should have their height and weight recorded regularly. Height and weight are two of the indicators used to assess nutritional status. A significant weight gain or weight loss without known cause should be investigated. When obese people are encouraged to lose weight, it is essential that they follow only nutritionally adequate weight loss programs and avoid fad diets, which are often nutritionally deficient.

Health care professionals should be

The nutritional status of each elderly individual should be evaluated.

164 aware of all drugs and medications prescribed for a geriatric person and the possible interactions of these drugs with specific nutrients.[4]

Specific measures

Cancer

A nutritional evaluation is a necessity when cancer therapy is required.[5] The cancer patient should be optimally nourished before therapy has begun.[5] This state of nourishment should be maintained throughout the course of the therapy.[5] Response to the cancer therapy is increased if the patient's nutritional status is preserved.[5] A weight loss of 4 to 5 kg should require a reevaluation of that person's nutritional status,[5] and effective measures should be taken to prevent further weight loss.

Urinary infections

Elderly individuals who are immobilized for long periods of time may develop urinary calculi and urinary infections. Skin breakdown may also become apparent. A nutritionally adequate diet then becomes essential, along with an increased fluid[3] and ascorbic acid (vitamin C) intake.[4] Confusion and weakness in the elderly may be attributed to "old age" when an increase in the fluid intake (1.5 to 2 liters per day) could help eliminate these symptoms.

A substantial increase in ascorbic acid in the diet can change the acidity of the urine and help in the prevention and treatment of urinary calculi and urinary infection.[4] If foods alone cannot increase the ascorbic acid intake sufficiently, then ascorbic acid tablets could be prescribed.

Because ascorbic acid is a water-soluble vitamin, the total amount should be divided and given three to four times daily for maximum benefit.

Cranberry juice has been used in an attempt to acidify the urine. It has been found that 1.5 to 4 liters of cranberry juice is required daily to have even the slightest effect on the acidity of the urine.[4] The caloric intake is high, and the tolerance for that amount of cranberry juice is poor.[4]

Eating

When an individual has problems swallowing, external stimulation of the throat with the hand or rubbing an ice cube on the throat may help induce swallowing. For those individuals who must take soft or blended food, a multiple vitamin supplement may be an asset. Caution must be exercised when using fat-soluble vitamin preparations. Fat-soluble vitamins are stored in the body, and an overdose of these vitamins could produce toxic effects. Multiple vitamins are not recommended for those who can and do eat the necessary foods daily from the four food groups.

Presenting small portions of food attractively can be an incentive to people when their senses of taste and smell are diminished and their appetite is poor. Small amounts of food, taken often, are generally more acceptable to those who may have difficulty digesting food.

Careful attention should be given to purchasing the more economical foods when the elderly are living on a limited income. Foods that are high in calories, low in nutrients, and often expensive should be eliminated from the grocery list. Common examples are potato chips, carbonated beverages, sugar-coated cereals, and chocolate bars.

An increase of dietary fiber in the diet can promote regular bowel movements and soften the stool for easier evacuation.[3(p359)] Cereal fiber added to the diet can reduce the symptoms of diverticulosis.[3(p358)] There is fiber in all fruits and vegetables. However, cooking breaks down the fiber somewhat. Therefore, raw fruits and vegetables are recommended when a fiber increase is required. Whole grains, bran (the skin or husk of cereal grain), and products containing these are excellent sources of cereal fiber.

COMMUNITY SERVICES

Many communities are supplying "Meals on Wheels" to individuals who are not able to prepare an adequate meal for themselves. Each meal should supply at least one third of the daily required nutrients. A more recent addition to the services offered by some communities is "Wheels to Meals." Meals are provided in a central area, and the older person is transported to that point. In this way meals can be enjoyed in the company of others.

Volunteer visitors can greatly increase the enjoyment of the day and allay loneliness. When an elderly individual finds it difficult to get to existing facilities, home visits by health care professionals can provide needed services. A physician, nurse, dietitian, physical therapist, occupational therapist, and social worker, working as a unit, can aid older citizens in their quest to be independent. Patience and concern by the health care practitioner for the elderly individual are of prime importance when offering services in the home.

A venture by a local supermarket to provide a bus to transport senior citizens to and from the shopping center could be of mutual benefit. Assistance would be required to load and unload their purchases. This service should be offered during slack periods at the shopping center.

CONCLUSION

The story is told that John Jones, a 104-year-old gentleman, went to his physician. "Doc" he confided, "I want you to look at my right knee, it is swollen and sore. I'm having a hard time walking."

The physician examined the knee and replied, "Well, John, that knee is 104 years old and you must expect problems at this stage of the game." John Jones scratched his head and countered softly, "That's a strange thing, Doc, because my other knee is 104 years old too, and it doesn't bother me a bit!"

Do not mask conditions as simply a result of old age. When dealing with the elderly, it is important to consider the specifics of the condition and to handle the condition with the same intensity that it would be handled with a younger person. This includes a nutritional assessment. Altering food intake to include the required daily nutrients can produce a significant response in the mental and physical well-being of the elderly individual. This response can be gratifying to the individual and to the health care professional involved.

166   Nutrition education provided to the elderly can enhance their quality of life. Who cares? It is the responsibility of people working with senior citizens to let them know that they care.

REFERENCES

1. Todhunter EN, Darby WJ: Guidelines for maintaining adequate nutrition in old age. *Geriatrics* 33:49–56, June 1978.
2. Bray GA: Energy requirements of the aged. In *Nutrition of the Aged,* Proceedings of a symposium presented by the Nutrition Society of Canada, June 20, 1977, University of Calgary, Calgary, Alberta, Canada, pp 45–52.
3. Mitchell H, Rynbergen H, Anderson L, Dibble M: *Nutrition in Health and Disease,* ed 16. Philadelphia, JB Lippincott Co, 1976.
4. Brin M: Drug-vitamin interrelationships. *Nutr MD* 3:1, November 1976.
5. Pelham M, Woolard J: Nutritional support of cancer patients. *Dietetic Curr* 5:12, May–June 1978.

Preventive Group Interventions for Elderly Clients: Are They Effective?

Sue Nickoley-Colquitt, R.N., M.S.
Instructor/Clinician II
Interim Program Director
Gerontological Nursing
University of Rochester School of
*   Nursing*
Rochester, New York

ARE GROUP INTERVENTIONS an effective strategy in promoting the health of elderly clients? Despite the recent proliferation of group approaches designed to promote health, an analysis of reported literature on preventive group interventions reveals several critical issues that need to be examined before an answer to this complex question can be determined. What needs of the elderly population are being addressed through group methods? What factors have been identified as health promoting? Are there factors common to all groups? What process occurs during a group that leads to desired health outcomes? What evaluatory processes are needed to link group interventions to the desired outcome? What further steps are needed to address these issues?

SHIFTING EMPHASIS

Reports of group interventions with elderly clients began to emerge in the

168 early 1950s and have grown rapidly. Early work focused on the ill, hospitalized, or institutionalized elderly with group approaches serving as part of a treatment program for a recognized physical or mental pathology. Successful outcomes were claimed using such group techniques as reality orientation, remotivation, and reminiscing. These reports were primarily descriptive anecdotal accounts of observed patient improvement. Further, experimental studies employing control groups were seldom reported.

During the past decade group approaches emphasizing health promotion emerged. This shifting emphasis parallels the preventive trend in the health care system that aims to reduce the incidence of health deviance by managing harmful conditions in the environment and strengthening the ability of people to endure stress and change.[1] Preventive interventions examine patterns of adaptation to developmental and situational life circumstances and seek to improve handling of change to facilitate healthy adaptation. This approach advocates intervening before the onset of disease or dysfunction and focuses on the whole person rather than limiting attention to an identified pathology.

Changing conceptualizations have emerged defining health as more than the absence of disease. Health has been described in terms of achieving high-level wellness: "an integrated method of functioning which is oriented toward maximizing the potential of which the individual is capable within the environment where he is functioning."[2(p208)] This definition supports the need for interventions designed to promote the highest level of functioning possible and supports the belief that continued learning and development can take place during all stages of life.

Health-promoting strategies imply the need for a policy of minimal intervention, that is, interventions that are least disruptive of usual functioning in the usual setting. Decentralization and demedicalization of services that foster client control and responsibility versus passivity toward health maintenance are also desirable.[3]

With the changing emphasis toward health and with the expansion of services from institutional to community settings, there is an increase in reports of group interventions conducted with healthy elderly individuals.

REVIEW OF PREVENTIVE GROUPS

A review of 18 group interventions involving an elderly population or their family members was made (Table 1). Leaders conducting these groups represent a variety of health care workers, including peer counselors, social workers, psychiatrists, psychologists, and nurses. A diversity of client and group characteristics can be observed. Some groups were conducted with "young" old or "old" old clients, while others included clients of all ages. Family members with aging relatives were the focus of still others. Groups included persons from short-term interventions of several sessions over a time span of weeks to those ongoing over a period of years.

However, despite the individuality and variability observed, all had a common

Table 1. Literature review of preventive group interventions

Year	Author	Type of group	Client characteristics	Group characteristics	Goals	Evaluation	Reported outcomes
1972	Altholz[1]	Socialization; problem solving	Male, female; age range 57–84; prior individual treatment; depressed	Setting: outpatient clinic; one group, 15 members (average 5); weekly sessions for 1 hour; long-term, open membership	Resolve problems in adapting to growing older; improvement of reality testing; social interaction	Observation by group leaders	Descriptive examples of client progress
1976	Maney and Edinberg[2]	Social competency	Male, female; mean age 71	Senior citizens center setting; one group; 6 members, 8 sessions; short-term	Assist with problems of self-maintenance; use of each other as resources in problem solving; develop meaningful relationships with others; provide support, test new behaviors, source of feedback	Observation by group leaders	Descriptive examples of client behaviors

Table 1. (continued)

Year	Author	Type of group	Client characteristics	Group characteristics	Goals	Evaluation	Reported outcomes
1976	Petty, Moeller, and Campbell[3]	Support	Male, female; age range 62–85	Community health setting; 4 groups, N = 30, 6–9 members; 10 two-hour sessions; short-term	Present information on normal aging changes; develop interpersonal skills to cope with change	Observation by group leaders; pretests: attitudes toward old age, satisfaction with daily activities, physical and psychological concerns, beliefs about similarity of own concerns and those of other older persons; posttests: changes in attitudes and behaviors; satisfaction with group	Increase development of new friendships; increase use of community resources; increase development of problem-solving skills; engagement in new coping behaviors; attitude changes about the uniqueness of problems of old age
1977	Butler and Lewis[4]	Age-integrated; life crisis	Male, female; age range 15–80+; absence of active psychosis; presence of life crisis	4 groups, 8–10 members; weekly 1½ hour sessions; long-term (2 years)	Decrease suffering; overcome disability; opportunities for new experiences of intimacy and self-fulfillment; verbalization of emotions	Not reported	Not reported

1977	Toseland[5]	Problem solving concerning interpersonal social situations	Male, female; ages 55+; volunteers; identified as lacking problem-solving skills	Senior citizens center setting; one group, 6 members; 6 weekly 1½-hour sessions; and a pregroup and postgroup assessment session; short-term	Describe and practice using a problem-solving technique	Anxiety measure (assertion inventory); behavioral role playing testing problem-solving technique	Increase social skills
1977	Waters and White[6]	Group counseling using peer counselors	Male, female	Community center settings; large group sessions (12–30 members) followed by small group sessions (5–6 members); 7 two-hour sessions; short-term	Encourage self-exploration; increase involvement with others; encourage making choices; recognize need and ask for help; increase responsiveness to others	Verbal and written report of leaders and members of observable and reported behavioral changes	Increase self-confidence, feelings of warmth and closeness to others; increase interaction with and interest in others; increase responding in a helpful manner; increase willingness to try new behaviors
1978	Ingersoll and Silverman[7]	Well-being; "Here and Now" and "There and Then"	Male, female; mean ages 69.5–69.8; all experiencing anxiety or depression resulting from age-related losses	2 groups, 8–9 members; 8 two-hour sessions	"Here and Now" group: increase coping with anxiety; develop awareness of body tension; progressive relaxation training; "There and Then" group; reminiscing life review; enrich sense of identity	Pretest and posttest measures: self-esteem, anxiety, and somatic behavior; progress notes (group content, participants' verbal and nonverbal behavior); debriefing interview to determine reactions to group experience	Improvement in somatic behavior—"There and Then" group; descriptive report of selected comments showed awareness that others had similar problems was helpful

Table 1. *(continued)*

Year	Author	Type of group	Client characteristics	Group characteristics	Goals	Evaluation	Reported outcomes
1978	Nickoley[8] and Leavitt[9]	Support	Females; age range 65–83; intact mental functioning; experiencing some life change events in recent past	Senior citizen high-rise apartment complex setting; one group, 11 members; 12 one-hour sessions twice weekly, each followed by one-half hour socialization/refreshment period	Provide information: normal age changes, availability and use of community resources; promote: perception of greater control over self and environment, increased functional level of health, increased interaction and participation in environment, use of group as a support system during and following group experience; strengthen problem-solving skills and interpersonal effectiveness; improve life satisfaction and ego identity; increase ability to cope effectively with changes specific to the aging process	Pretest and posttest measures perception of control; functional level of health; life satisfaction; ego identity; social support, interaction, and participation	Descriptive, observable but not measurable outcomes

1978	Rosenfeld[10]	Senior actualization and growth exploration (Sage)	Male, female; ages 60–84; good health	Community setting; eight groups, 12–15 members; 6-month, 2-hour weekly individual session and weekly group session followed by group sessions only; commitment of at least 9 months participation	Progression of techniques teaching relaxation, enjoyment of body, free movement; stimulate sensory awareness; share feelings more openly; develop better self-image	Questionnaires	Increase coping; increase memory
1978	Rosenfeld[10]	Interpersonal skill training	Age 55 and older; community volunteers	15 small groups, 3–5 members; 6 90-minute sessions; 3 months training	3 training approaches: behavioral role play, social, problem solving; behavioral approach emphasized demonstrating and acting out ways to handle problem situations rather than simply talking about them; active rehearsal of appropriate responses with feedback	Role-playing test	Ability to handle difficult social situations was greatest in behavioral role training, significantly better than social group, and better (not statistically significant) than problem-solving group; 3 months after training, no significant differences although social group showed less improvement

Table 1. (continued)

Year	Author	Type of group	Client characteristics	Group characteristics	Goals	Evaluation	Reported outcomes
1979	Baum-Baicker and Kessler[11]	Personal growth (support)	Male, female; mean age 85; alert residents	Nursing home setting; one group, 10 members; 10 meetings for 10 weeks	Increase communication; increase feelings of self-worth; increase feelings of independence; increase knowledge of aging changes; increase effectiveness of interpersonal skills	Observation by group leaders	Goals achieved by most members
1979	Berland and Poggi[12]	Expressive psychotherapy	Male, female; age range 72–99; no disease interfering with group participation; no severe organic central nervous system disease interfering with memory or ability to communicate	Private retirement home setting; one group, 9 members; weekly 1-hour sessions	Teach therapists what it is like to grow old; therapists share what they thought about members; members learn more about self (psychoanalytical growth and problem solving)	Observation by group leaders	Allowed expression of themes of death and loss; development of transference relationship; experiencing and talking about members; allowed members to help and support each other; increase member interaction outside of group; increase protest for better service in home; increase activity in affairs of home; increase in-

1979	Borus and Anastasi[13]	Support	Female; ages 55–70; Italian American; interpersonally isolated; mainly widowed; lonely; at times depressed	Community health center setting; one group, 18 members, growing to 50 members; ongoing–6 years meeting weekly; leadership change to elected officers in fourth year	Provide meaningful community roles; productive socialization; peer support network; sharing of aging experiences; health education	Observations by group leaders	volvement with others; redirection of cathexes to external objects Increased activity in neighborhood and city affairs
1979	Borus and Anastasi[13]	Preventive support	Female; age range 75–90+; European born, Italian speaking; socially isolated widows	Community health center setting; one group, 40 members increasing to over 200; began with monthly Italian movie; changed to 2 weekly discussions; social hour before and after	Reminisce about past; mourn personal losses and traditions; talk about daily lives	Observation by group leaders	Facilitated development of social network; increased member interaction outside of group; members began receiving regular health care, participated in nutrition program, and some moved from isolated apartments to housing center for elderly

Table 1. (continued)

Year	Author	Type of group	Client characteristics	Group characteristics	Goals	Evaluation	Reported outcomes
1979	Hausman[14]	Support	Male, female; mean age 52 (range 26–70); family members of elderly people	Five groups, 6–15 members each; weekly 1 1/2 hour sessions; short-term (8 weeks)	Find balance between responsibility to self, nuclear family, and parents; make decisions about extent and limits of duties and obligations; learn to deal with parents in mature way, leaving behind conflicts of earlier years	Evaluation questionnaire about initial expectations of group, whether expectations were met, and benefits of group; observations by group leader	
1979	Lieberman and Gourash[15]	Actualization and growth encounter	Male, female; age 60–80+; volunteers; highly educated; healthy	4 groups (N = 60), 15 members; weekly 3–4 hour sessions over 9 months	Dispel myths of aging; provide novel experiences; teach new skills	Pretests and posttests; psychiatric symptoms; self-esteem; anxiety; depression; measures of coping strategies; physical health and health behaviors; social functioning; social resources; life satisfaction; anomie; interpersonal reaction patterns; developmental themes.	Control group; increase depression; increase anxiety; increase anomie; increase parental strain; decrease life satisfaction; experimental group; better accomplishment of goals; more engaged in desired activities; decrease psychiatric symptoms; increase in self-esteem;

| 1979 | Silverman[16] | Support | Adults with aging parents | Several groups (N = 125); 6 2-hour sessions; short-term | Increase knowledge about aging process; increase understanding of emotional reactions of older people; increase problem solving; increase access to community supports; development of support system; develop greater awareness of responses of parents and own aging | change in perceptions of degree to which health problems affected lives; decrease health anxiety; increase coping with marital strain; increase emphasis on current interactions as source of feedback in maintaining self-esteem
Increase communication with elderly relatives; increase coping; increase knowledge of aging; increase utilization of community resources; increase recognition of own needs, responsibility to self, and setting realistic limits |

Table 1. (continued)

Year	Author	Type of group	Client characteristics	Group characteristics	Goals	Evaluation	Reported outcomes
1979	Weiner and Weinstock[17]	Resocialization; problem solving versus talk group	Male, female; mean age range 71.5–74.4	Large metropolitan general hospital setting; 3 conditions: 2 resocialization/problem solving with active leader (N = 27), 2 talk groups with passive leader (N = 20), control group (N = 20); weekly meetings for 12 weeks	Resocialization group: acquire alternate ways of functioning in response to expressed needs; use of self and others as resources; increase problem solving; modeling after peers who cope and function well; Talk group: passive leader intervention limited to acceptance that problems exist	Tape analysis of group tempo measuring member-to-member interaction; pretests and posttests: cognitive functioning, medical index; group evaluation questionnaire	Problem-solving group showed faster group tempo and more satisfaction with group; control group showed negative changes on cognitive functioning and medical index measures

1. Altholz J: Group psychotherapy with the elderly, in Burnside I (ed): *Working with the Elderly: Group Processes and Techniques*. North Scituate, Mass, Duxbury Press, 1978, pp 354–370.

2. Maney J, Edinberg M: Social competency groups: A training and treatment modality for the gerontological nurse practitioner. *J Gerontol Nurs* 2(6):31–33, November–December 1976.

3. Petty B, Moeller T, Campbell R: Support groups for elderly persons in the community. *Gerontologist* 15(6):522–528, December 1976.

4. Butler R, Lewis M: *Aging and Mental Health: Positive Psychosocial Approaches*. St Louis, The CV Mosby Co, 1977, pp 271–272.

5. Toseland R: A problem-solving group workshop for older persons. *Soc Work* 22(4):325–326, July 1977.

6. Waters E, White B: Helping each other, in Troll L, Israel J, Israel K (eds): *A Woman's Guide to the Problems and Joys of Growing Older*. Englewood Cliffs, NJ, Prentice-Hall, 1977, pp 184–193.

7. Ingersoll B, Silverman A: Comparative group psychotherapy for the aged. *Gerontologist* 18(2):201–206, February 1978.

8. Nickoley S: *Promoting Functional Level of Health and Perception of Control in Elderly Women in the Community through Supportive Group Intervention*. Master's thesis, University of Rochester, 1978.

9. Leavitt D: *The Effects of a Support Group on Adjustment to the Changes of Aging in Elderly Women Living in the Community*. Master's thesis, University of Rochester, 1978.

10. Rosenfeld, in US Dept of Health, Education, and Welfare: *New Views on Older Lives*, DHEW Pub no (Adm)78-687, 1978, pp 66–75.

11. Baum-Baicker C, Kessler J: *A Personal Growth Group within the Nursing Home Setting*. Paper presented at the 32nd Annual Meeting of the Gerontological Society, Washington, DC, November 1979, pp 1–7.

12. Berland D, Poggi R: Expressive group psychotherapy with the aging. *Int J Group Psychother* 29(1):87–108, January 1979.

13. Borus J, Anastasi M: Mental health prevention groups in primary-care settings. *Int J Mental Health* 8(2):58–73, 1979.

14. Hausman C: Short-term counseling groups for people with elderly parents. *The Gerontologist* 19(1):102–107, 1979.

15. Lieberman M, Gourash N: Evaluating the effects of change groups on the elderly. *Int J Group Psychother* 29(3):283–304, July 1979.

16. Silverman A: As Parents Grow Older: A Community-Based Intervention Strategy. Paper presented at the 32nd Annual Meeting of the Gerontological Society, Washington, DC, November 1979, pp 1–15.

17. Weiner M, Weinstock C: Group progress of community elderly as measured by tape recordings, group tempo and group evaluation. *Int J Aging Hum Devel* 10(2):177–185, 1979–1980.

180 focus—providing group interventions for clients or their family members who were experiencing common developmental and situational changes or stresses. Each group fit within a health-promoting framework that emphasized the understanding and management of change or the effects of such change.

NEEDS ADDRESSED BY GROUP INTERVENTIONS

The importance of identifying needs when selecting clients and intervening with a group experience cannot be overlooked. Unmet needs serve as a basis for group formation. In the literature a number of perceived elderly client needs were identified and commonly addressed through health-promoting group interventions (see boxed material).

Implementation of preventive approaches requires an understanding of what supports or interferes with health. Two major items identified are stressor factors (such as psychosocial stress, loss of social supports, and physical illness[4]), which enhance susceptibility to altera-

---

Change, with its resultant stress, makes the individual susceptible to physical and psychological illness.

---

tions in health, and protective factors, which minimize the negative or harmful conditions experienced.[5]

Stressor factors

An examination of the frequent developmental or situational changes associated with aging reveals why these identified needs are frequently unmet. The many changes commonly experienced may produce stress. Further, with increasing age, many physical and psychological adaptive systems are operating near the edge of reserve capacity. Change, with its resultant stress, makes the individual susceptible to physical and psychological illness.

It is hypothesized that illness onset is influenced by an individual's perception of events as stressful and the lack of ability to adapt to the stressful conditions. Speed of change, length of exposure, novelty, and unpredictability, as well as lack of preparedness or previous experience, increase the association of stressful events and the development of illness.[6,7]

This period of change may be experienced in a nonsupportive social environment. In times of change, guidelines for behavior may no longer be the same, and the resulting uncertainty may not be adaptive to new conditions. Role loss may occur that excludes the elderly person from familiar social participation and meaningful use of time. Norms for behav-

---

Needs Addressed Through Preventive Group Intervention
- Knowledge about aging process, changes, and use of supportive resources
- Management of change
- Development and use of effective coping strategies
- Control and mastery
- Self-esteem
- Continued growth and use of potential
- Communication, feedback, effective interpersonal skills, expression of feelings
- Affiliation, social interaction
- Meaningful roles

ior may be nebulous or inappropriate, thus placing the elderly in marginal or alienated positions within the larger society.[8] Individuals lack socialization to the aging process; therefore expected behaviors may be unclear. Further, cogent reference groups with whom to associate may be lacking.

These social conditions limit the feedback available and may lead to vulnerability and dependence on others. Moreover, the societal view of the aging process is often negative, which may result in negative self-labeling by the elderly person.

Thus, for some, aging may be viewed as a developmental crisis resulting in unmet needs. Usual patterns of managing and coping may have been disrupted, leaving individuals confronted by changes for which they may have no available solution.[9]

Protective factors

Preventive groups, which may serve as a protective mechanism supporting the maintenance of health, help individuals understand and manage change. The use of groups has been considered economically efficient because they provide an intervention that allows the involvement of more than one individual at a time. Further, with the limited number of health care professionals available, it represents an efficient use of personnel.

Additional reasons exist for the use of group interventions. A variety of frameworks were used in the preventive group literature which were believed to assist individuals to cope with and manage change: socialization, problem solving, support, reminiscing, actualization and growth experiences, here and now focus, and social competency. As a beginning step in answering the question of group effectiveness, the group process used requires further clarification to identify what actions carried out during the group produce the desired outcomes.

Careful examination of the reported interventions reveals two common themes that may be useful in guiding the design of health-promoting group interventions. Support and control may serve as unifying elements for a preventive group framework.

Support elements

Support, as defined by Caplan from his work in preventive psychiatry, consists of three elements:

1. Helping to mobilize psychological resources and master emotional burdens;
2. Sharing of tasks; and
3. Providing tools, skills, and cognitive guidance to improve handling of the situation.[1]

Education was an integral part of many reported groups. Content often focused on normal aging changes and the availability and use of community resources. One series of group sessions entitled "As Your Parents Grow Older" sought to teach family members more about the aging process not only to develop a greater understanding of relatives' but also their own aging.[10] This educational component fits within the framework of support as providing cognitive guidance.

The reminiscing, relaxation, and problem-solving techniques taught and prac-

182 ticed during group experiences serve as examples of tools and skills to improve handling of current and future situations. Reminiscing as a technique also fits into the element of helping to mobilize psychological resources and master emotional burdens. This may be helpful in meeting the need for a positive self-esteem and might be used in assisting individuals to identify previously used coping skills.

Sharing of tasks may be accomplished through group process as "groups allow for the development of mastery through specialization of function, pooling resources and information, and developing reciprocal help-giving relationships."[11(p35)] Participation in a group experience may assist the elderly person in developing new roles, provide norms, for effective behavior, and provide a reference group that assists in socialization to growing older.[12]

Control elements

The second factor identified as common to the preventive groups is control. Use of group interventions supports the belief that an individual's active participation in maintaining health is essential. The element of control may be a critical factor that influences an individual's management of change and results in healthy adaptation.

The relationship between demands confronting individuals and their resources to manage these demands must be considered. Control involves a belief that an individual's actions produce an effect on the environment that minimizes anxiety, satisfies needs, and promotes self-esteem.[13] Individuals who do not

Personal responsibility and a sense of control over life were fostered during the group experiences.

perceive this relationship are less likely to initiate adaptive behaviors. But the positively experienced outcomes of behavior lead to a sense of mastery that may motivate further adaptive behavior.[14,15]

It is evident from the literature that personal responsibility and a sense of control over life were fostered during the group experiences. Sessions often encouraged this by providing knowledge, opportunities for learning and practicing effective coping and problem-solving techniques, and encouraging decision making that led to successful management of change. Thus group members could learn that their actions often produced desired outcomes.

GROUP CHANGE MECHANISMS

Common elements

Eleven factors that are felt to be important conditions necessary for or serving as mechanisms of change[1] have been identified as occurring during the group process.[6] Ten of these appear to relate directly to fulfilling unmet needs of elderly clients through the preventive group approach: instillation of hope, universality, imparting of information, altruism, catharsis, development of socializing techniques, imitative behavior, interpersonal learning, group cohesiveness, and existential factors (including the belief that individuals must take ultimate responsibility for their lives despite the guidance and support received from others). Examination of these change factors in light of the elements of support and control reveals similarities in content (Table 2).

Various examples of change factors were noted in the group literature. The importance of the universality of the problems experienced by group members was reflected in client comments such as, "It helps to know others have similar problems" and "My situation is not unique." Groups used imparting of information. This was helpful because there were many areas of content with which the elderly individuals and their families had little familiarity. Offered an opportunity for catharsis, group members were encouraged to express feelings, and they received feedback from multiple sources

through the group experience. Interaction fostered the development of socialization techniques and often led to the establishment of a supportive network of relationships that continued outside the sessions and beyond termination of the formal group experience.

Thus the group frameworks that were reviewed shared the elements of providing support, promoting control, and fostering the development of the change factors identified. However, further identification and documentation of the process and mechanisms of change that occur during a group are required to answer the question of effectiveness.

Most assessments of group process have not been thorough enough to develop a definitive synthesis of health-promoting factors. While the reported group experi-

Table 2. Similarities among support, control, and change factors

	Group framework		
Needs	**Support**		**Change factors**
Positive self-esteem	Helping to mobilize psychological resources and master emotional burdens		Instillation of hope
Development and utilization of effective coping strategies			Catharsis
Expression of feelings			
Affiliation, social interaction	Sharing tasks		Universality
Communication, feedback, effective interpersonal skills			Altruism
			Imitative behavior
Increased knowledge about changes, aging process, and availability and use of supportive resources	Providing tools, skills, and cognitive guidance to improve handling of situation		Interpersonal learning
			Group cohesiveness
Successful management of change			Imparting of information
Sense of mastery and control			Development of socializing techniques
Continued growth and use of potential	**Control**		Existential factors (personal responsibility for life)
Meaningful roles	Promoting attitude of personal responsibility and control		
	Developing belief that actions can produce an effect in managing change		

184 ences appear to share common elements, further analysis through research testing is required. Incorporating similar elements in a group framework would allow consistency in approach while providing enough latitude to vary the specific intervention techniques to meet group member needs and leader method preference.

Critical questions

An additional critical question must be addressed in preventive group designs: are desired outcomes achieved? Practitioners must not accept good intentions as sufficient, but rather seek to evaluate outcomes to determine what was accomplished through their actions. Many leaders rely on anecdotal, descriptive accounts of client benefit. A systematic investigation of group interventions is needed that uses evaluation techniques that produce reliable and valid outcomes. Various evaluative approaches have been reported; some focused on group outcomes, while others examined individual outcomes. These ranged from observation of behavior change to a client's subjective response to interview questions or questionnaires.

The use of control groups, a critical requirement of experimental studies, is often lacking. Recently attempts to replicate a particular group framework have been made.[10] Such studies are greatly needed. The combined efforts of practitioners and researchers may be necessary for better design and evaluation of group experiences.

Consideration must be given as well to commonly identified problems interfering with the implementation of preventive groups. Hesitancy to conduct group experiences with the well elderly and their families may occur due to limited experience with interventions geared toward healthy individuals. Better articulation of the preventive group framework and guidelines for leader behaviors may prove to be useful.

The population addressed by this type of intervention often is unfamiliar with health promotion and may not see a need for any assistance. The present-day cohort of elderly clients associates the provision of care with the treatment of a specific problem or illness. Not seeing themselves as ill, they may lack reasons for joining a preventive group. Further, formal group experience is often lacking, and a tendency exists to equate any group intervention with the more familiar use of groups to treat psychiatric illness. Therefore leaders are encouraged to identify a relevant subject or activity to interest potential clients and motivate participation.[17(p62)] This approach, coupled with a clear description of what the experience might offer, will avoid problems often experienced in obtaining and retaining a sufficient number of participants. Accessibility of the group meeting site must also be considered to avert attendance problems. Familiar, convenient settings that are frequented by potential group members are recommended.

The issue of lack of funding or reimbursement for group interventions has yet to be addressed. While legislative support exists for a preventive focus, actual payment for services of this nature is often missing.[17(p72)] The determination that groups are an effective strategy in promoting health would greatly assist resolution of the payment issue.

EVALUATION

A review of preventive group strategies with an elderly population reveals what steps have already been taken to answer the question of group effectiveness. Theoretical and methodological issues remain. Unmet client needs are often not clearly delineated, yet these needs must serve as a basis for the development of appropriate group goals. Further identification and clarification of the preventive group approach are required to determine what leads to desired health outcomes. Finally, the outcomes must be evaluated. Each element of the group design can influence the final results. These issues must be addressed before the answer to the question of group effectiveness will be found.

REFERENCES

1. Caplan G: *Support Systems and Community Mental Health*. New York, Behavioral Publications, 1974.
2. Greifinger R, Grossman R: Toward a language of health. *Health Values: Achieving High-Level Wellness*. 1:207–209, September-October 1977.
3. Kahn R: The mental health system and the future aged. *Gerontologist* 15:24–31, February 1975.
4. Blazer D: The epidemiology of mental illness in late life, in Busse E, Blazer D (eds): *Handbook of Geriatric Psychiatry*. New York, Van Nostrand Reinhold Co, 1980, pp 249–271.
5. Kaplan, B, Cassel J, Gore S: Social support and health. *Med Care* 15:47–58, May 1977.
6. Eisdorfer C, Wilkie F: Stress, disease, aging and behavior, in Birren J, Schaie W (eds): *Handbook of the Psychology of Aging*. New York, Van Nostrand Reinhold Co, 1977, pp 251–275.
7. Rabkin J, Struening E: Life events, stress, and illness. *Science* 194:1013–1020, December 3, 1976.
8. Rosow I: The social context of the aging self. *Gerontologist* 13:82–87, Spring 1973.
9. Weiss R: Transition states and other stressful situations: Their nature and programs for their management, in Caplan G, Killilea M (eds): *Support Systems and Mutual Help: Multidisciplinary Explorations*. New York, Grune & Stratton, 1976, pp 213–226.
10. Silverman A: As parents grow older: A community-based intervention strategy. Paper presented at the 32nd annual meeting of the Gerontological Society, Washington, DC, November 1979, pp 1–15.
11. Mechanic D: Social structure and personal adaptation: Some neglected dimensions, in Coelho G, Hambury D, Adams J (eds): *Coping and Adaptation*. New York, Basic Books, 1974, pp 32–55.
12. Rosow I: *Socialization to Old Age*. Los Angeles, University of California Press, 1974.
13. White R: *Lives in Progress*. New York, Holt, Rinehart & Winston, 1975.
14. Kuypers J: Internal-external locus of control, ego functioning, and personality characteristics in old age. *Gerontologist* 12:168–173, 1972.
15. Bengston V: Self-determination: A social-psychologic perspective on helping the aged. *Geriatrics* 28:118–124, December 1973.
16. Yalom I: *The Theory and Practice of Group Psychotherapy*. New York, Basic Books, 1975.
17. Borus J, Anastasi M: Mental health prevention groups in primary care settings. *Int J Ment Health* 8(2):58–73, 1979.

Lifestyle Change in Elderly Hypertensive Persons: A Multifaceted Treatment Program

Gwen C. Uman, R.N., M.N.
Gerontological Nurse Practitioner
Senior Health and Peer Counseling
Center
Santa Monica, California
Doctoral Student
School of Education
University of Southern California
Los Angeles, California

Madeline A. Hazard, M.P.H.
Director of Health Screening and
Education
Senior Health and Peer Counseling
Center
Santa Monica, California

HYPERTENSION IS PREVALENT and difficult to treat in elderly individuals. Widespread public awareness of the serious complications of hypertension has aroused a high demand for blood pressure measurement. Unfortunately the checking rarely leads to any rational plan aimed at better blood pressure control. Worried elderly persons often waste their scarce resources and overtax the medical care system by visiting their physicians too often for blood pressure monitoring. In contrast, there are still some undiagnosed or inadequately treated elderly hypertensive persons who do not have physicians or do not avail themselves of their physicians' care for a variety of reasons.

The program described in this article is

The authors thank Estelle Tuvman, Nora Freed, and Davida Coady for help in program design and implementation. The authors also thank Edison Goldsmith, Stanley S. Franklin, Nancy L.R. Anderson, and Margo Kipps for their help.

188 designed to provide elderly persons with the knowledge, skills, and support needed to make significant changes in their lives that are likely to lower their blood pressures.

EVOLUTION OF THE PROGRAM

Rationale

The Senior Health and Peer Counseling Center, a free clinic founded by concerned senior citizens, serves a community whose elderly residents make up 22% of the city's 100,000 population. Citizens from surrounding areas also use the center's services. Persons using the center range in age from 60 to 97 years. Formerly of the middle economic class, most members of this group now experience fixed and dwindling incomes as they struggle to maintain established styles of living.

A small percentage of the clients suffer more extreme poverty. Still another group has no financial needs, but attends the center for reasons such as distrust of the medical system or death of a long-time personal physician. Center consumers are well informed about the prevalence and risks of hypertension.

Total program cost is estimated at $20,000 per year with an estimated cost per visit of $8). Half of this cost is actually in-kind donation of services by health care professionals and senior volunteers.

In 1977 the center responded to a heavy demand for blood pressure screening by scheduling volunteer registered nurses (RNs) to take blood pressures two mornings per month. This service was overattended and clinically unsatisfactory. In most cases health advice was given inconsistently by the nurses, not enough baseline health data were obtained, and compliance was deemed unsatisfactory. Many participants seemed to feel that by having their blood pressures measured, they were engaged in a preventive act; that is, measurement would protect them from the complications of hypertension.

Some participants used the blood pressure reading as a guide for self-medication, rather than remaining on a consistent medication regimen as prescribed by their personal physician. It is not surprising that these health behaviors were exhibited even by relatively sophisticated participants. The difficulty of achieving compliance in the treatment of an asymptomatic chronic disease is well documented.

Antihypertensive medications often have perceptible or well-publicized side effects that further decrease motivation to adhere to dosage schedules. Elderly persons' drug compliance has been shown to be poor because of inadequate vision, lack of understanding, memory problems, and multiple-drug regimens.[1] To further compound the problem, the low income of participants discourages them from purchasing medicine or visiting a physician to renew prescriptions.

The inadequacy of simple screening and the health care behaviors of the parti-

The difficulty of achieving compliance in the treatment of an asymptomatic chronic disease is well documented.

cipants led to a new program design for hypertension screening and counseling. The staff wanted to create a positive, healthful approach that would counteract the nihilism elderly people frequently face in the traditional health care system and that would also provide an alternative to the occasional overtreatment of hypertension in elderly people. There was a desire to provide worried participants with some tools for self-care and hence greater control over their lives.

The staff further hoped that by decreasing the frequency of physician visits and hospitalizations, the program might conserve participant financial resources without sacrificing high-quality health care supervision. Incidentally some physicians might be relieved of inappropriate patient demands on their time. The underlying assumption of the new program design was that elderly ambulatory hypertensive persons could be helped to change specific health care behaviors, which would have a positive effect on their blood pressure.

Goal and objectives

The overall goal of the program is to prevent the complications of hypertension by lowering or maintaining blood pressure within a safe range.[2] Specific objectives of the program have been defined by the staff as follows:
- To screen 2,000 elderly persons for hypertension annually;
- To classify blood pressure as normal, borderline, elevated, or dangerous;
- To evaluate health status and current blood pressure regimen and recommend changes in treatment plan to

participant and his or her personal physician;
- To encourage compliance with the physician's treatment plan;
- To inform participants about health behaviors that are correlated with the lowering of blood pressure;
- To teach methods of integrating these positive health behaviors into participant's daily life; and
- To encourage ongoing compliance with the aforementioned behaviors over time.

DESCRIPTION OF THE PROGRAM

Participants may enter by way of self-referral, private physician referral, or referral from another center or community program. Once having been channeled into the program, participants may be involved in three phases—initial intake, screening, and counseling.

Initial intake includes collection of demographic information and determination of hypertension status. This phase of the program is the responsibility of a senior citizen volunteer who asks the participant whether he or she has ever been diagnosed as hypertensive, has ever taken antihypertensive medications, or is currently taking such medication.

Screening

The screening process is based on the accumulation of three blood pressure measurements, each taken 1 week apart by retired volunteer RNs or nursing students. The average blood pressure is then used to classify the participant

190 according to the following categories (Fig 1):

Normal (or controlled): Systolic ≤ 140; Diastolic ≤ 90
Borderline: Systolic = 141 to 160; Diastolic = 91 to 95
Elevated: Systolic = 161 to 229; Diastolic = 96 to 119
Dangerous: Systolic ≥ 230; Diastolic ≥ 120

The screening process is based on recommendations of the Joint National Committee on Detection, Evaluation, and Treatment of High Blood Pressure.[3] Blood pressure is measured with the participant seated. Systolic and diastolic pressures are recorded using a mercury sphygmomanometer; a written report and verbal explanation are given to each participant. According to the committee, participants over age 50 with blood pressures between 140/90 and 160/95 should be reevaluated within 6 to 9 months.

Because the center's major function is preventive, more attention is given to this "borderline" group than is recommended. While the committee emphasizes only the diastolic blood pressure, Ram et al point out that although some rise in systolic pressure accompanies aging, increased morbidity and mortality correspond to this rise.[4] They conclude that it is erroneous to consider systolic hypertension normal in elderly people, citing a systolic pressure of above 160 mm Hg as treatable. In concurrence Colandrea et al found an increase in morbidity from coronary artery disease, stroke, and intermittent claudication, and an increase in overall mortality among elderly people with systolic hypertension as compared with those with normal blood pressure.[5] An analysis of data from the Framingham study showed that stroke, coronary artery disease, and congestive heart failure were associated with increased systolic, diastolic, and mean blood pressures.[6] The Veterans Administration Cooperative Study Group conclude that treatment of hypertension is effective in reducing the frequency of complications in elderly patients when the systolic blood pressure is higher than 164 or the diastolic pressure is above 104 mm Hg.[7] The blood pressure classification scheme of

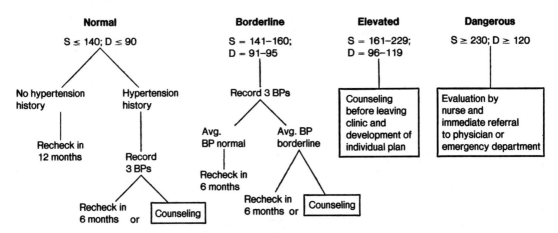

Fig 1. Blood pressure (BP) classification flow chart. S, systolic pressure; D, diastolic pressure.

this program thus considers systolic and diastolic blood pressures as two separate and important issues.

Fig 2 shows how participants proceed from the screening phase into the counseling phase of the program. Normal blood pressure participants with a history of hypertension or those having borderline and higher readings regardless of hypertension history are encouraged to participate in the counseling phase. The majority of participants who fall into the normal blood pressure category are actually hypertensive persons who are controlled on medication. Only a small number are without hypertension and attend only for periodic reassurance. The screening process is designed so that (1) many individuals can be introduced into the program; (2) those determined to be at risk are encouraged to enter the counseling phase; and (3) those not at risk would be involved to a minimal degree, allowing for a focus on those most in need of supervision. Some people with controlled hypertension elect to obtain counseling in hopes of lowering their blood pressures by mechanisms other than medication.

COUNSELING

The counseling phase consists of three components: (1) individual care by the nurse practitioner or hypertension nurse (referred to throughout this article as

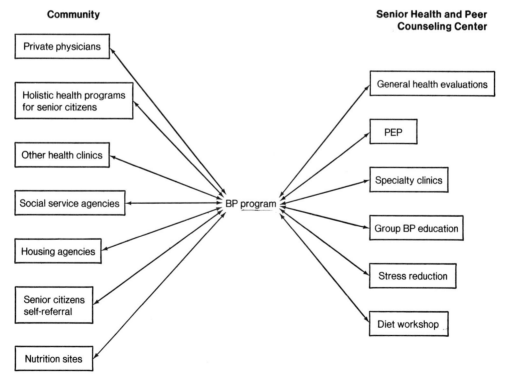

Fig 2. Referrals to and from the blood pressure (BP) program.

"counselor")[8,9]; (2) support for ongoing contact with private physician; and (3) participation in appropriate group experiences.

Individual counseling

Pertinent information

The counselor collects a data base on each participant consistent with recommendations from the Joint National Committee.[3] A brief history of hypertension and its treatment is recorded, followed by a complete drug list that includes all prescription and over-the-counter medicines and doses. Past medical history and family history of cardiovascular and renal disease, diabetes, and hyperlipidemia are determined. Finally health care behaviors felt to be contributory to increased risk of hypertensive complications are determined. These include obesity, history of smoking, alcohol intake,[10] sodium intake, exercise, and self-perception of life stress.[11]

Physical evaluation includes height, weight, two blood pressures (which are averaged), pulse, ophthalmoscopy, thyroid palpation, carotid and jugular evaluation, heart and lungs, abdomen examination for bruits, kidney tenderness or enlargement, and examination of the extremities for edema, pulses, and neurologic abnormalities. Student nurses are assigned to take home blood pressures on those with labile hypertension to determine the predominant blood pressure range. Laboratory reports are obtained from the participant's physician. Referral is made for more extensive workup if secondary hypertension is suspected, based on the data gathered.

Health care goals

Having collected the most pertinent information, the counselor then shares his or her knowledge and values about hypertension with the participant and elicits information on the participant's knowledge and values regarding this health care problem.[12] It is the role of the counselor to encourage and help the participant to set up realistic health care goals. The counselor and participant contract to work toward such goals as achieving a blood pressure below 160/95, losing weight to within 10% of ideal body weight, decreasing sodium intake, increasing aerobic exercise, or complying with the medication regimen. The counselor helps the participant understand that hypertension is a polygenic, multifactorial disease and teaches various appropriate means by which health care goals can be met.

Follow-up counseling

Ongoing follow-up counseling involves reassessment of symptoms, medication compliance, diet, exercise, stress and activities to counteract it, review of new and ongoing health care problems, two blood pressures, weight, other examination as necessary, and identification of new short-range goals and plans.

The counselor takes responsibility for drug education and exercise prescription and provides some general nutrition information. Participants are taught the mechanism of action and important side effects and interactions of their drugs.

The exercise prescription designates how long and how often the participant should walk and the pulse rate that should be achieved during walking.[13] Because walking becomes an aerobic exercise for most people over age 65 years, it is an adequate cardiovascular fitness exercise that represents little risk. Most participants have never had an exercise stress test (treadmill), so prescriptions are based on general guidelines for safe pulse level for age.[14] The counselor teaches the participant how to take the pulse and provides a form for recording preexercise and postexercise pulse rates. Contraindications to the exercise program are recent myocardial infarction, angina pectoris, cardiac arrhythmia, and painful arthritis of weight-bearing joints.[15]

Counselor-participant relationship

The final important aspect of individual counseling is the consistent counselor-participant relationship. This ongoing relationship allows for feedback and evaluation, which ideally leads to motivation to continue with the plan of action. There is little doubt that for some people the counseling sessions are more than a series of planning and clinical evaluation sessions. Rather they are intrinsically therapeutic, providing the participant with a caring relationship and a person to whom concerns can be ventilated. In addition, the participant becomes active

---

For some people the counseling sessions are more than a series of planning and clinical evaluation sessions. Rather they are intrinsically therapeutic.

---

in the health promotion process and is motivated to make return visits.

Contact with private physician

Communication among the counselor, the participant, and the private physician is essential for effective hypertension management. Participants are encouraged to maintain regular contact with their physicians and are also advised to seek a physician's care when their clinical status changes (eg, symptoms of hypokalemia). Responsibility for prescribing medication and laboratory work resides with each participant's physician. The counselor communicates changes in clinical status to the physician by phone or in writing.

Participation in group experiences

Resources within the center and in the surrounding community are used to further assist participants in meeting their health care goals. The two-way arrows in Fig 2 demonstrate this relationship. For example, a cost-effective group method of providing basic hypertension education has been designed and successfully piloted. The diet workshop, taught by a nutritionist, meets twice per month. Topics of discussion include obesity; carbohydrates, protein, and fat; exercise; spices other than salt; food and drug interactions; vitamins and minerals; and recipe modification. The course is undergoing revision so that it will focus mainly on weight loss techniques and ongoing support, supplemented by information on sodium restriction.

A stress reduction course is taught by a

194 volunteer psychologist. At the present time three groups (beginning, intermediate, and advanced) are meeting concurrently once per week. The basic course outline includes relaxation response, deep breathing techniques, progressive relaxation, guided imagery, autoregulation techniques, and stress management techniques.

For participants who suffer from anxiety or depression, the Peer Counseling for Elderly Persons (PEP) program is available as a component of the center. PEP is a 3-year project funded by the California State Department of Mental Health 314d funds in which 25 specially trained and supervised elderly persons provide individual and group counseling for their peers. Hypertension program participants who have emotional problems related to the aging process but who are not interested in the stress reduction class are often referred to PEP for further help.

A group of elderly persons have been trained by Center professional staff to serve as "Peer Health Advocates" to further assist individuals and groups achieve lifestyle changes. They are prepared to assist participants in weight loss, learning of circumscribed stress reduction techniques, stretching and aerobic exercises, and use of community resources. The staff believes it is possible that these peers will be more effective in assisting participants actually change their behaviors than the Center has previously been. The Peer Health Advocates are just beginning to work with clients, supervised by a Nurse Practitioner.

As participants continue in the counseling phase, with its individual and

---

PARTICIPANT INVOLVEMENT

Phase 1: Intake—Minimal involvement of communicating medical information

Phase 2: Screening—Increased involvement of keeping personal record of blood pressure and returning for weekly blood pressure readings

Phase 3: Counseling—Additional involvement of evaluating lifestyle, signs and symptoms, learning drug information, and setting goals

---

group activities, their level of active involvement with their own health care increases (see boxed material).

EVALUATION AND RECOMMENDATIONS

The blood pressure program was begun as a community service project rather than for purposes of research. However, the staff recognized the need to evaluate program effectiveness, and such an evaluation was attempted 1 year after the program was first implemented. Charts of the first 100 participants were studied because these participants began the program about the same time. The evaluation attempted to consider the following information:

- Demographic data (age, sex, marital status);
- Use of the program;
- Effects of the program, including changes in physical indicators (blood pressure, weight), lifestyle changes, and changes in obtaining medical care.

The source of information was participant records. From the outset it was apparent that the records were often inadequate in supplying information for evaluation. This was partly because of the lack of specific objectives before the medical record forms were designed and partly because of inconsistencies in recordkeeping. Also, baseline health status data were not collected on participants unless they entered the counseling phase, thus creating a data void that prevented the comparison of participants with normal blood pressure or controlled hypertension with those whose blood pressures were borderline or elevated. Clear criteria for measurement of lifestyle change had not been established at the program outset, so conclusions about these data are tentative.

Demographic data

The mean age of the sample (N = 100) was 73.06 years (Table 1), and participants were predominantly white. Three fourths of the sample were women; 40% were married, 40% were widowed, and the remainder were divorced or single.

Use

The program was successful in having participants revisit the program. Of those persons with an elevated pressure at the

time of initial intake, 73% made at least one revisit; the average was 5.2 visits. Hypertensive persons used the counseling phase more than did persons with normal blood pressure. Those who changed blood pressure class from normal to hypertensive during the year were successfully transferred into counseling. However, those who changed class from normal to borderline remained in the screening phase; one third of these eventually developed elevated blood pressures. Participants with normal blood pressure have been unwilling to comply with program guidelines of rescreening at 6- to 12-month intervals and, for various reasons, have requested monthly screenings. The effect of providing this reassurance and service in terms of excess strain on the program remains to be evaluated.

Physical indicators

Changes in blood pressure were evaluated in two ways. First, changes in blood pressure classification were examined. Second, changes in systolic and diastolic pressures were scrutinized. At the beginning of the program 34% of the sample had elevated blood pressures, 38% were in the borderline category, and 28% were in the normal range (Table 2). For purposes of evaluation data on persons with normal and borderline blood pressure are com-

Table 1. Age distribution

Statistic	Men (n = 25)	Women (n = 75)	Total
Mean	70.04	73.95	73.06
Median	78	74	75
Range	62–90 (28)	61–97 (36)	61–97 (36)

Table 2. Blood pressure class at first visit

Blood pressure	Men (%)	Women (%)	Total (%)
Elevated			
Systolic 161–229			
and/or	35	34	34
Diastolic 96–119			
Borderline			
Systolic 140–160			
and/or	35	38	38
Diastolic 90–95			
Normal			
Systolic 140			
and	30	28	28
Diastolic 90			

bined and considered "acceptable" because there is no documented increased risk or evidence of treatment benefit when blood pressure is at or below 160/95 in elderly persons.

Table 3 shows that two thirds of the total sample began the program with acceptable blood pressures; one third of the sample began with elevated (>160/95 mm Hg) blood pressures. Of those whose blood pressures were initially in the acceptable range, two thirds remained in this category, but one third (n = 22) developed elevated blood pressures. These participants were 7.5 years older than their counterparts whose blood pressure remained acceptable, and they made more total visits and counseling visits than did participants with acceptable blood pressures.

Table 3. Changes in blood pressure (BP) class

BP class at program start	Total sample (%)	BP class at time of evaluation	Mean age	Sex	Married (%)	Mean no. of visits (Total/ Counseling)	
Acceptable*	67	Acceptable (66%)	73.45	Men (32%) Women (68%)	29	3.8	1.0
		Elevated (34%)	80.9	Men (25%) Women (75%)	29	5.7	2.9
Elevated†	33	Acceptable (51%)	73.9	Men (18%) Women (82%)	78	6	3.4
		Elevated (49%)	75.6	Men (8%) Women (92%)	10	7.5	4

*BP ≤ 160/95 mm Hg.
†BP > 160/95 mm Hg.

Of the one third (n = 33) participants who began the program with elevated blood pressure, one half progressed into the acceptable blood pressure range and one half had persistent blood pressure elevations. Those whose blood pressure remained elevated were older by 2 years, and a greater proportion were female and unmarried, when compared with those whose blood pressure improved. Those whose blood pressure remained elevated made slightly more counseling visits and visits overall.

Mean change in blood pressure tended to be obscured when considering the entire sample. There was a mean systolic change of -5.60 mm Hg (range $+48$ to -52), and a mean diastolic change of -0.45 mm Hg (range $+16$ to -26). Singling out the group of 17 participants whose blood pressure changed from the elevated to acceptable categories, there was a mean systolic change of -30.5 mm Hg and a mean diastolic change of -7.6 mm Hg.

Height and weight information was available from 37% of the participants. Of these patients, 22% were obese at the start of the program. All of those classified as obese had blood pressures above normal (75% borderline and 25% elevated). An average of 7 pounds was lost among those who were obese.

Lifestyle change

Areas of potential change were diet, exercise, stress reduction, medications, and visits to personal physician. It was expected that acceptance of new behaviors would correlate with blood pressure declines, but the data available showed

It was expected that acceptance of new behaviors would correlate with blood pressure declines, but the data available showed equivocal results.

equivocal results. Participants in all blood pressure categories reported high levels of compliance with recommended dietary changes, irrespective of success in normalizing blood pressure.

Aerobic exercise was reportedly complied with almost as well as diet changes, although lower rates of exercise were found among those whose blood pressure remained or became elevated. Medication compliance and physician visits were next in frequency of adherence and show no relationship to objective change in blood pressure. Stress reduction methods were least often acceptable as lifestyle changes, perhaps because of their nontraditional nature. Once again there was no consistent pattern related to blood pressure change.

SUMMARY

The hypertension program was largely attended by persons whose blood pressures were controlled within acceptable ranges. However, a total of 52 persons in the sample of 100 studied had elevated blood pressure at some time during the year and were assisted to obtain or maintain medical treatment for this condition. Approximately 5% of the sample were persons with newly discovered hypertension and were referred to physicians for initiation of treatment. There were no known hospitalizations or deaths related

198 to hypertension in the sample. The participants were approaching the old old-age group (75 years and older), which is a recognized high-risk group sometimes referred to as "frail elderly." Minority groups in the community served were distinctly underrepresented.

The 39 participants who developed or persisted in elevated blood pressure were older, lacked a significant other (spouse) more often, and were more predominantly women. Whether they represent a resistant group who will not improve because of advanced age and overall health status, an undertreated group, or a noncompliant group, or were affected by other exogenous factors (eg, the concurrent housing cost crisis) cannot be determined by this evaluation. They received more attention in this program than any other category of participants, so it is possible that factors not directly addressed by the program may play a major role in blood pressure elevations.

Revisions

The program evaluation points toward several important revisions:

1. Critical analysis of the characteristics of those who maintain or develop elevated blood pressure;
2. Development of detailed program objectives with corresponding evaluation criteria for better measurement of program outcomes;
3. Improvement of orientation and in-service education of all program staff in the three phases of the program;
4. Recruitment and training of additional volunteers to take complete hypertension histories on all participants;
5. Revision of medical records and the data collection system;
6. Revision of medical protocol to focus more resources on participants in the borderline classification;
7. Increase in participants' active role in their progress evaluation by keeping personal notebooks of physical findings and plans[16];
8. Change in focus of diet workshop to weight loss education and support with ancillary assistance in sodium restriction; and
9. Institutionalization of the blood pressure orientation class for all participants.

Although the program began as an experiment outside the center budget, the center's board of directors and administration are committed to this cost-effective method of identifying and referring elderly hypertensive persons and supporting them as they make lifestyle changes to control their blood pressures. Steps are being taken to further institutionalize and overcome deficiencies of the program.

REFERENCES

1. Lofholm P: Self medication by the elderly, in Davis RH (ed): *Drugs and the Elderly*. Los Angeles, University of Southern California Press, 1974, pp 7–24.
2. US Department of Health, Education, and Welfare, National Institutes of Health: *National High Blood Pressure Education Program*. Pub no (NIH) 78–1086. Washington, DC, US Government Printing Office, 1978.
3. Joint National Committee on Detection, Evaluation,

and Treatment of High Blood Pressure: Report of the Joint National Committee on Detection, Evaluation, and Treatment of High Blood Pressure—A cooperative study. *JAMA* 237:255–262, January 17, 1977.

4. Ram C, Venkata S, Kaplan NM: Systolic hypertension. *Practical Cardiol* 3:17, October 1977.

5. Colandrea MA, Friedman GD, Nichaman MZ, Lynd CN: Systolic hypertension in the elderly—An epidemiologic assessment. *Circulation* 41:239, 1970.

6. US Department of Health, Education, and Welfare, National Institutes of Health: *Some Characteristics Related to the Incidence of Cardiovascular Disease and Death: Framingham Study, 18-year Follow-Up.* Pub. no. (NIH) 74–599. Washington DC, US Government Printing Office, 1974.

7. Veterans Administration Cooperative Study Group on Anti-Hypertensive Agents: Effects of treatment on morbidity in hypertension. II. *JAMA* 213:1143–1152, August 17, 1970.

8. Clark AB, Dunn M: A nurse clinician's role in the management of hypertension. *Arch Intern Med* 136:903–904, August 1976.

9. Ward GW, Bandy P, Fink JW: Treating and counseling the hypertensive patient. *Am J Nurs* 68:824–828, May 1978.

10. Klatsky AL, Friedman GD, Stegelaub AB, Gerard MJ: Alcohol consumption and blood pressure. *N Engl J Med* 296:1194–1199, May 26, 1977.

11. Sokolow M, Werdeger D, Perloff DB, et al: Preliminary studies relating portably recorded blood pressures to daily life events in patients with essential hypertension. *Bibl Psychiatr* 144:164–189, 1970.

12. Kuhn A: *The Logic of Social Systems.* San Francisco, Jossey-Bass Publishing Co, 1974.

13. Wilmore, J: Individual exercise prescription. *Am J Cardiol* 33:757–759, May 20, 1974.

14. Zohman LR: *Beyond Diet . . . Exercise Your Way to Fitness and Heart Health.* Englewood Cliffs, NJ, CPC International, 1974.

15. Wear RE: Conditioning exercise programs for normal older persons, in Harris R, Frankel LJ (eds): *Guide to Fitness After Fifty.* New York, Plenum Press, 1977, pp 253–270.

16. Katz AH, Levin L: *Self-Care: Lay Initiatives in Health.* New York, Prodist, 1976.

Meeting Human Needs of Elderly Patients

Doris Schwartz
Senior Fellow, Geriatric Nursing
University of Pennsylvania School of
  Nursing
Formerly Associate Professor
School of Nursing
Cornell University
New York Hospital
New York, New York

TO PRACTICE HEALTH CARE with the elderly, people need, in addition to the required clinical knowledge, compassion, patience, a sense of proportion, humor, and adequate awareness of the dynamics of human behavior. They need to have genuine respect for people. This cannot be counterfeited; patients know.

TIME FOR TRUST

When initial assessments are being done (ie, physical, social, psychological, or environmental), health care practitioners should treat patients with courtesy and friendliness and ask permission before seeking information or performing required tests and procedures (eg, "I'd like to ask you some questions. May I?" or "I'd like to test your vision. May I?"). This has two advantages. Practitioners let patients exert control, informing them in advance of what is planned. In doing so,

202 the practitioners imply that patients are partners, with the right to refuse permission or to question the reason for whatever is to be done without creating chaos. Also through this method, any reluctance by patients becomes apparent almost immediately.

This habit of asking permission along the way can be adopted as a technique, but in the hands of a courteous and thoughtful health care worker, a technique cannot be distinguished from the person. Perhaps this synthesis of person and technique is one criterion of the ability to work well with the elderly.

During initial interviews when personal information is first volunteered, interviewers should pause for several intervals before continuing with questioning. At first these pauses may seem overlong. Elderly patients may not yet trust enough to volunteer more information or perhaps they have no more to volunteer. Such pauses might be awkward because neither patients nor professionals fill the gap. However, they give the elderly an understanding that although they may not want to use it now, there will be "listening time" and a "listening attitude" later if needed. However empty these first pauses, they teach the elderly something. Among other things they teach the elderly that they are working with health care workers with whom it is comfortable to be alone and to think.

Sometime during initial interviews and assessments something happens that amuses both practitioners and elderly patients. Laughter, shared spontaneously, draws them together quickly. Planned humor can never substitute for this experience, for in spontaneous laughter comes a feeling of comradeship. By the end of the first session the practitioners may or may not be able to give the patients a reasonable amount of information about their health. This may have to wait for further investigation. What practitioners can and should be able to give is intangible, not necessarily requiring words: a knowledge that whatever the problem, from this moment, they are going to seek a solution to it together. This is advocacy.

However faulty patients' health habits, the first visit is not the time for "beating" new ones into them. If they are ill, weak, or deeply troubled, they will usually not be ready to change, or even to remember much advice, and readiness is fundamental to all learning. Patients are already likely to be aware if habits have been poor and are basically the cause of health problem(s). That awareness often makes the elderly resistant because of guilt feelings. They have had a lifetime in which to change their habits. If they are rebels, pressure at this point may lose them entirely to follow-up. Also the elderly may line up on the opposite side of the fence so effectively that conflict rather than cooperation becomes the dominant note in the health care worker-patient relationship on future visits.

CIRCLE OF SAFETY

From anthropology one learns about a ceremony during which certain primitive tribal members approach the council fire. Rare, colored sand is sprinkled in a great circle outside the fire area. Inside that circle there is peace and safety; quarreling, grudges, and the day-to-day problems of tribal life are abandoned, once the circle has been crossed. Within the circle, at the fire, is found a kind of fellowship that enables the participants to take up the problems of daily life again once they have finished with their session and left the council fire area.

This provides a model for health care workers and elderly patients. When a professional worker whom an elderly person trusts facilitates a similar interaction, the patient gets a feeling of safety like that which those tribespeople found at the council fire. The setting may be varied: the patient's home, a public clinic, or a geriatric center. Often there is nothing profound in the conversations that take place, but it is easy to talk. Often no special answers are found to problems, although sometimes these occur unexpectedly in the conversation. Mostly the troubled older patient figures out answers later. But talking about the problems with somebody who is really concerned makes it easier to think straight.

The health care practitioner's conscious goal may be to abstain from praise and blame. Even if that is tried, a value system may show through, making some of the practitioner's beliefs apparent. This is not necessarily a disadvantage. It is as though the practitioner has a dual role: that of counselor (no praise or blame for what the elderly person says or does) and that of friend (a warmth for shared goals and ideas). This again is the synthesis of technique and humanness that is inseparable but that makes patients know that

---

The practitioner has a dual role: that of counselor . . . and that of friend.

---

they have chosen nurses or physicians wisely (or had the good luck to be well directed).

SUPPORT FROM FRIENDS

One of the things the elderly person finds with such support is that it is progressively easier to think clearly and more honestly, even when away from the source of help. It is like learning to chop wood in the country as an adolescent, or to diagram sentences in grade school: practice helps. At first there may not be any pattern to the process.

Elderly individuals may take "wild shots." For example, sometimes they may think effectively and clearly, but as often, thoughts may seem scattered. Then all of a sudden the brain seems to function better (more clearly). Sometimes thoughts come so fast that answers appear to almost everything and the elderly individual feels confused again. Sometimes an elderly person may feel in an "alcoholic glow" and move from bitterness or loneliness to loving the whole human race in a wildly impractical fashion. With time the older person may learn to trust the nurse or physician and hit a balance with the moments of fearfulness lessening.

One elderly woman said that as a little child she had learned to walk but was still afraid to try it on her own. For months she insisted on holding on to someone's hand. Then her mother, short of time or patience to walk with her, rolled up the hem of the child's skirt into a ball, stuffed it into her hand and said "Hold onto that." The girl walked all over the house

204   clutching a chunk of her own skirt instead of a hand and balanced perfectly.

Health care workers who practice advocacy health care with the elderly hold out their hands until the patients do not need that kind of help anymore. Sometimes, briefly, the patients may think they do and "hang onto the skirt again" for a bit of security. But soon they can walk alone as they have been doing for 8 or 9 decades, are proud of their accomplishments again, and not scared by momentary failures of confidence.

There is a very fine line between "can't" and "won't", and it is not always easy to discern it.

● ● ●

Compassion, patience, a sense of proportion, humor, and adequate awareness of the dynamics of human behavior are a circle of safety in which to gather strength; the elderly person needs a health care worker who is an advocate and a friend.

Adult Health Conference: Community-Oriented Health Maintenance for the Elderly

Chiyoko Furukawa, R.N., M.S.
Assistant Professor
University of New Mexico
College of Nursing
Albuquerque, New Mexico

THE PRACTICE OF HEALTH CARE for the elderly is generally directed toward acute care with little recognition of the equally important area of health maintenance. This situation concerns the health needs of 10% of the total population of about 25 million people age 65 years or older in the United States. Furthermore, the elderly population can be expected to increase in the coming years, as it has since 1900 when it constituted only 4% of the total population.[1(p5)]

Although the increased life expectancy has brought forth a sense of accomplishment, health care services to meet the needs of the elderly have not progressed as rapidly as the population growth. In addition the family system that supported and cared for the aging in the past has

The author extends grateful appreciation to Beth Hutchison, R.N., Adult Health Conference Coordinator, Boulder County Health Department, for assistance and for providing the 1978 data of the Adult Health Conference.

206

changed. Today many elderly persons struggle alone to maintain their daily living pattern and need support to sustain their lifestyles. It is estimated that 95% of older noninstitutionalized people living in a normal community depend on others or community resources for their survival.[2]

To explore the plight of the aging, the White House Conference on Aging was held in 1961 and again in 1971.[3] Most significantly the conference stressed the principle of health care as a basic right and the development of a comprehensive system of health services in communities with elderly populations. In line with this philosophy, community health care agencies and other health care providers reported initiation of services to improve the health care and maintenance of the elderly.[4-6] These programs focus on optimal functioning, early detection of illness, health teaching and counseling, and community resources for other necessary assistance to improve the quality of life for the elderly.

This article reports on the Adult Health Conference (AHC) program of the Boulder County Health Department, which was specifically planned for ambulatory persons 65 years or older with some participation by persons 55 to 64 years old.

COMMUNITY PROFILE

Boulder County is a combination of urban, rural, and mountain communities located in north central Colorado. The 1970 census of the county was 131,899[7]; current estimate places the population at 196,200.[8] About 50% of the population resides in the city of Boulder, where the University of Colorado and various scientific research facilities are located. Boulder is also the county seat.

Health care facilities consist of three hospitals and six nursing homes. Two of the hospitals are in the city of Boulder and the third is in Longmont, the next largest town. The physician services are concentrated near the hospitals, although a few are located in the rural and mountain communities: The health department and the Visiting Nurse Service of Boulder County work together to provide community health care to the general population and to the elderly, primarily through a program called Home Health Care.

Although the community's median income in 1970 was $8,093, the agency's experience showed most elderly lived on less, with the main source coming from Social Security.[7] The current financial status of this group of elderly remains essentially unchanged. Thus they depend on Medicare and Medicaid to pay for health care services.

The community's awareness of the needs of the aging is evident within the city of Boulder. There are two recreational centers and three low-cost housing complexes for the elderly. The outlying towns in the county—Longmont, Lafayette, and Louisville—also have organized recreational activities for the elderly, but only Longmont has provided the elderly with low-cost housing.

Table 1 shows the distribution of the elderly population only for the communities where AHCs were conducted. Therefore the population as indicated in the table is somewhat less than the population for the entire county.

The data show that the number of

Table 1. Elderly population distribution of the adult health conference sites, Boulder County 1970 and 1979

Community	Total population		Population 65 years & older		Percent population 65 years & older	
	1970*	1979†	1970*	1979‡	1970	1979
Boulder	66,870	83,082	4,362	5,810	6.5	7
Broomfield	7,261	23,707	177	1,000	2.4	5
Lafayette	3,498	10,143	315	800	9.0	8
Longmont	23,209	45,966	2,492	5,520	10.7	12
Louisville	2,409	5,600	358	750	14.9	13
Lyons	1,315	1,300	387	130	29.4	10
Nederland	492	1,011	Data Unavailable		—	—
Total	105,054	170,809	8,091	14,070	7.7	8.2

*US Department of Commerce, Bureau of the Census. *1970 Census of Population, General Population Characteristics, Colorado.* (Washington DC, US Government Printing Office, 1971).

†Leach J: Boulder County's population hits 200,000. *Boulder Daily Camera,* July 15, 1979; and Boulder Chamber of Commerce.

‡Directors of Senior Citizens Services Boulder County, 1979 population 65 years and older (personal communication with Beth Hutchison).

elderly increased in all the communities except Lyons. However, the percentage of elderly in terms of the total population decreased in Lafayette, Louisville, and Lyons and showed only a relatively slight increase at Boulder, Broomfield, and Longmont. This results because the increase in the elderly population at the first three sites did not keep pace with the growth of the total population, whereas in the latter three communities, the elderly population increased at a faster rate during the period studied.

PROGRAM RATIONALE

In the late 1960s the Boulder County Health Department recognized the need for a locally supported preventive health program for the ambulatory elderly because Medicare excluded this category of health care. Budget requests to initiate

the program were submitted to local resources each fiscal year until funding was finally obtained in 1972. There were several rationales for initiation of the proposed program.

The first reason was the belief that the segment of the population over 65 years old is the most vulnerable to chronic and debilitating diseases. It was subsequently reported that 67% of the elderly living outside institutions have chronic conditions,[2] and 86% have at least one chronic illness requiring health care.[1(p10)] Assuming these percentages and the 1970 census report,[7] approximately 5,000 to 7,000 people in Boulder County were potentially in this high-risk group.

Second, the elderly have long-established lifestyles that ought to be maintained and supported as long as possible by an ambulatory preventive program. This health service could assist in delay-

208 ing the physical and mental conditions potentially threatening to independent function. In most communities it is estimated that 81% of the elderly have few or no problems with mobility and are able to live independently while only 5% are institutionalized.[1(p11)]

Third, preventive health care to provide early recognition of illness, treatment of problems, and improvement of inadequate daily living patterns (ie, eating, sleeping, and socialization habits) to delay chronic illness was believed to be achievable. The experience of the visiting nurse service revealed that elderly people are reluctant to seek medical advice until they are really sick, have poor understanding of prescribed treatment and diet, commonly rely on self-medication by using over-the-counter drugs, and lack interest and participation in coping with health problems because of minimal realization of their health needs.

Another reason was that despite chronic illness, the elderly could achieve optimal living, within individual limitations, with the aid of professional health care teaching, guidance, and surveillance care. The education of the elderly about the community health care system often reinforces their ability to take responsibilities as well as to participate in meeting their own health care needs.[9]

PROGRAM OBJECTIVES

The program was initially designed to provide health maintenance care to 1,200 persons who were 65 years of age or older by applying nursing interventions to achieve the following objectives:

- Early detection of previously unrec-

ognized problems through the use of interviews, examinations, observations, and selected screening procedures;
- Surveillance of individuals with chronic conditions to ensure that they continue necessary medical care or prescribed regimens and to help maintain the level of health commensurate with the individual's ability;
- Provision of health care education in the areas of nutrition, exercise, safety, medical care, physical examination, and self-care. Sessions on health care topics are to be selected based on group interest and need;
- Use of community resources for services beyond the scope of nursing practice, but mutually identified as a need for optimal social and physical well being;
- Provision of follow-up nursing care to assist individuals with health care problems and to facilitate actions of community agencies to alleviate difficulties affecting the individual's wellness;
- Consumer referral of individuals in need of community health care services.

PROGRAM IMPLEMENTATION

A low-key approach was used to offer relevant services that emphasized con-

---

It was highly important that the elderly were treated with dignity and given the opportunity to make decisions affecting their lives.

sumer participation. It was highly important that the elderly were treated with dignity and given the opportunity to make decisions affecting their lives. Archer stresses "achieving an understanding of the needs, fears, and desires of the people as one of the first steps in program planning for health maintenance care."[10]

The program for the elderly was designated as the "Adult Health Conference," instead of the often-used "Well-Oldster Clinic," to deemphasize the clinic atmosphere and to avoid the notion that a person must be ill to participate in the program.

Phase 1

The program was implemented in three phases. Phase 1 was initiated in late 1972 in the rural communities of Lafayette, Louisville, and Longmont. These sites were selected because the elderly were already meeting for monthly recreational activities, requests for health services from the recreational directors were received, and accessibility to medical care was a problem for some individuals.

The notion of health care as a "piggyback service" to recreational activities became the theme for the informal approach to care in a nonclinical setting. Attending the recreational function was not a prerequisite to using the nursing service. The elderly were informed that the health services were not a replacement for medical care but rather a complemental service within the realm of nursing.

The health department nursing staff stressed that each individual must make the decision to use the service, and any

nurse-physician consultations about health problems were to be done with the individual's permission. This approach is supported by Hitchcock, who encourages professionals working with a community group "to listen to the client's expressed need for service rather then telling him what he needs."[11]

During phase 1 the nurses attended the recreational functions as participant-observers to collect information relevant to development of the program. This time was used to get acquainted and to establish rapport with the elderly group. Whenever professional services were requested, an interpersonal approach was used. This approach proved to be a mutual learning experience for the nurses and the elderly.

For example, the elderly were initially cautious in requesting service, because nursing care outside the clinical setting was an unfamiliar experience for them. This required the nurses to demonstrate their role in the health care system; to explain how they work with the individual, family, community, and health care team; and to provide information about other health services offered by the agency. The elderly also witnessed the cooperative spirit with which the recreational directors and the nurses functioned in their behalf. Most importantly the elderly were able to talk on any topic and found that the nurses were patient and willing listeners.

Phase 2

In phase 2, the action stage beginning in February 1973, nursing services were continued at the monthly recreational

210   functions. Two new sites, Broomfield and Longmont Spanish, were added during this phase. The support of the medical community was not sought, because the focus was on nursing service and experience showed that physicians as a group tended not to support community health programs. However, physicians were contacted individually as referrals were made, and information about the AHC was given at that time. Generally the physicians have accepted the program, and misinterpretations of the health service objectives have not occurred.

Group health education was introduced in phase 2. This included the publication of a brochure to describe the AHC and outline the health services. The brochures, which were also written in Spanish for the largest minority group in the county, were distributed to senior citizens groups, to the community, and to those whose work was related to the aging. Three physicians separately conducted free health talks on heart disease and arthritis at the various recreational sites. Three nutritionists representing various community agencies demonstrated low-cost meal preparation and discussed proper diet for those with heart conditions and diabetes. These health talks topics were selected by the elderly group.

Phase 3

Phase 3 began with a study to determine if a need for AHC services existed in the city of Boulder. The elderly in Boulder lived relatively close to medical care facilities. Thus the question was whether these elderly would participate in AHC services in addition to seeking medical care. The study indicated that they were interested in participating in the AHC if the services were offered at a convenient location. The respondents also revealed that they had a number of health-related concerns but did not see their physician until they were sick. Based on these findings, which supported the potential use of a health maintenance service by the elderly, an AHC program was initiated in Boulder.

The first two sites were the Golden West Manor (November 1973) and North Boulder Recreation Center (January 1974). The selection of these sites considered the availability of public and senior citizens' transportation services. Although Golden West Manor was a rent-subsidized housing unit for the elderly, participation in the health care services was optional for residents. Other elderly living in the vicinity were also invited to attend the health care services.

The unexpected large attendance at the two Boulder sites necessitated the implementation of an appointment system to avoid long waiting periods for the health care services. The appointments were made by the housing office and the recreation center; ongoing and periodic appointments were made at the conference sites. All AHC sites currently use the appointment system.

In addition, repeat health maintenance visits for routine consultation or care were extended from 1 month to 3 months or longer to properly manage increased attendance at the sites. However, a priority appointment was provided whenever a special problem or need developed.

THE ROLE OF THE NURSE

The philosophy for nursing care in implementing the AHC program was:

- Health care is a basic individual right.
- The elderly are individuals with concerns about social changes and the aging process.
- Clients' rights need to be protected.
- Health care practices require mutual goal setting.
- A holistic approach is necessary for the care of the individual, family, and community.

Wellness profile

The program was staffed by the nurses of the agency's Home Health Care Program, who were knowledgeable about the care of the aging, accepted the client advocacy role, and practiced nursing as an extension of the client rather than the physician.[12] Nursing care began by obtaining a health history that included the identification of past illnesses and current health status information, such as drug profile, nutritional and fluid intake pattern, height, weight, mobility and exercise status, emotional health, immunization level, and routine health care–seeking patterns.

After documenting the information, the nurse not only reviewed the overall health status with the client but also interpreted findings on any problem areas. Any abnormal findings were fully explained, and recommendations were made for further evaluation by a physician. Participation in the mutual decision-making process began at this time.

The elderly were given the option of contacting the physician themselves or of having the nurse call the physician for them.

Optimal benefit

Other nursing activities centered on teaching and counseling clients about optimal functioning, sustaining the chosen lifestyle, and obtaining the best benefit from the health care system. Follow-up activities, an integral part of the nursing services, included communicating findings and treatment goals with health care professionals, contacting community resources to obtain services, and making home visits for additional assessment and evaluation of complex health problems that required closer monitoring.

Because the nursing staff believed the community input and support were essential for the program, lay and nonagency nurse volunteers were recruited to assist in the delivery of the health services. Other community agencies for the elderly were encouraged to provide information pertinent to improving AHC services.

PROGRAM EVALUATION

Overall growth

Perhaps the most significant aspect of the program is its growth from 1973 to 1978. The nature of this growth is shown in Table 2, which gives a breakdown of individuals enrolled at the conference sites for the initial year and 1978. From the agency's standpoint the growth in total enrollment by the end of 1978 was

212 **Table 2.** Number and percent of individuals enrolled at conference sites, initiation year and 1978

Conference sites	Program initiated	Total enrollment		Population reached (%)		Enrollment growth (%)
		Initial year	1978	Initial year	1978	
Boulder						
Golden West Manor (BGW)	Nov. 1973	98	227	2.0	4.0	131
N. Broadway Recreation Center (NBR)*	Feb. 1974	115	179	2.3	3.2	56
North Portland Place (BNP)	July 1976	32	108	0.6	1.9	237
Walnut Place (BWP)	Feb. 1975	87	143	1.7	2.5	64
Subtotal	—	332	657	—	11.6	97
Broomfield (BFD)	June 1973	50	82	11.1	9.0	64
Lafayette						
Senior Center (LFT)†	Feb. 1973	78	69	16.4	9.2	−11
El Central (LEL)	March 1975	33	53	5.6	7.1	67
Subtotal	—	111	122	—	16.3	10
Longmont						
Senior Center (LGT)‡	Feb. 1973	130	425	3.7	8.2	226
Spanish (LTS)	Sept. 1973	45	84	1.3	1.6	86
Subtotal	—	175	509	5.0	9.8	190
Louisville (LSL)	Feb. 1973	62	128	12.7	18.1	106
Lyons (LNS)	April 1974	25	69	9.1	44.2	176
Nederland (NLD)	Sept. 1974	14	31	Not Available		121
Totals	—	769	1,598	—	—	107

*Bimonthly service–1975.
†Bimonthly service–1976.
‡Trimonthly service–1978.

most encouraging because it showed that the program goal of reaching 1,200 elderly was achieved, and the more-than-expected enrollment suggested a wide acceptance of the program by the elderly.

The results shown in Table 2 indicate an increase in enrollment at all sites except for the Senior Center at Lafayette (LFT). The 11% decrease at this site is attributed primarily to the transfer of the enrollees to the El Central (LEL) site, although there was a decrease of the 65 years or older group as a percentage of the total population from 1970 to 1979 (Table 1). Also, the total percentage increase in enrollment at the two Lafayette sites (LFT, LEL) was not only the lowest but was substantially lower compared with the other sites. The reason for this is not clear because Lafayette has a relatively large group of elderly population, as indicated in Table 1.

Monthly attendance

Another perspective of the program's growth is illustrated in Fig 1, which shows the average monthly attendance at

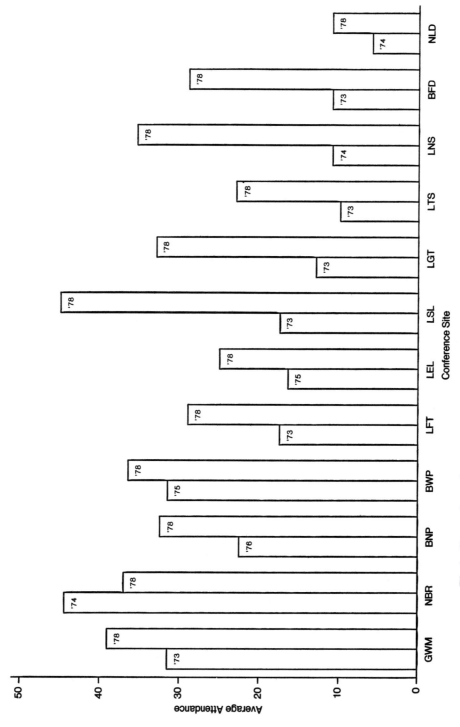

Fig 1. Comparison of average attendance per conference site (initiation year and 1978).

214 each conference site for the initial year and 1978. Whereas Table 2 denotes number of individuals enrolled at each site, Fig 1 indicates the average attendance, which can include repeated counts of any single individual. The increase in monthly attendance for all sites, except for North Boulder Recreation Center (NBR), is associated with the growth in enrollment and percent increase of the elderly population. The number in monthly attendance is roughly less than half of the total enrollees for the conference sites.

The reason for the decrease in monthly attendance at NBR despite an increase in the number of enrollees is unclear. Several factors may be contributing to the situation, such as the transfer of the enrollees to North Portland Place (BNP); the general health status of the enrollees at NBR requires less frequent monitoring; and the recreational aspect of the center attracts a more transient population that attends once rather than continuously.

Most conference sites, with the exception of Louisville (LSL), show an average attendance of about 25 to 30 per conference in 1978; this is considered to be optimum for efficient and effective service. To maintain this size of attendance, bimonthly conferences are conducted at Golden West Manor (GWM) and NBR, and trimonthly at Longmont Senior Center (LGT). However, the LSL site continues to have a monthly conference, which explains the relatively large attendance of 46 during 1978. The communities of Louisville and Lafayette are comparable in elderly population (Table 2) and the combined attendance

of the latter's two sites is about the same as the attendance at the monthly conference at the former site.

Although Lafayette had the lowest percentage increase in total enrollment (Table 2), its average monthly attendance (Fig 1) increased substantially from the initial year through 1978. This probably resulted because the enrollees at Lafayette (LFT, LEL) required more frequent surveillance of their health problems, particularly those individuals with diabetes, as indicated by abnormal urine-screening results.

Counseling sessions

A major thrust of the AHC was to counsel the elderly on promotion and maintenance of health. Fig 2 summarizes the relative frequency of health-related topics selected by the elderly for counseling sessions with the nurses. The information was collected during the first year of the AHC and shows diet, medication, and

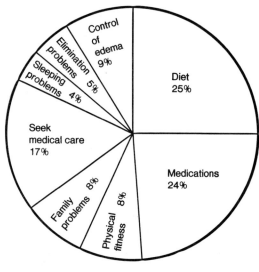

Fig 2. Frequency of health counseling topics.

advice on seeking medical care were the most frequently selected topics. Similar data for 1978 were not available, but discussions with the nursing staff indicate only slight changes from the results shown in Fig 2. One apparent change is a greater concern about medication than about diet and an increase in requests for advice about family problems. The last development may be because the elderly who have been enrolled in the AHC for some years feel more comfortable in expressing family concerns to the nursing staff.

Screening activities

Another goal of the program was to institute screening activities for the early detection of unrecognized health problems and to provide necessary health surveillance care. Table 3 shows the comparison of screening activities for 1973 and 1978 for only those communities where service was initiated in 1973. The results show that a large number of health screenings were conducted to identify health deviations. The screening activities are also used to monitor health status, to plan appropriate interventions, and to provide continuous care for individuals with chronic conditions. Thus the screening activities were also used as tools to assist the nursing staff to optimize health care.

Blood pressure analysis

The blood pressure findings summarized in Table 3 are based on two criteria. The first criterion, blood pressure ranging from 140/90 to 160/95, was used in 1978. It was not used in 1973 because the range was thought to be inappropriate in determining blood pressure abnormality for the elderly group. However, the criterion has been used since 1974 for identifying individuals with potential for developing hypertension and to periodically monitor blood pressure as a preventive measure. The second criterion, a blood pressure reading above 165/95, was used in 1973 and 1978 with a definitive protocol for management and follow-up care.

The 1978 findings, using the first criterion, revealed that approximately three fourths of the elderly screened had abnormal blood pressures. The results are consistent with the theory that the aging process tends to increase blood pressure and the incidence of hypertension.[13(p77)]

Although controversy exists regarding the normal range of blood pressure for the elderly,[14,15] the abnormal rate for the entire county using the second criterion was considerably less; it ranged from 15% in 1973 to 22% in 1978. The highest abnormal rate (30%) was found in Longmont. One reason for this is the management of hypertension at AHC on the request of the client's physician. Another factor may be attributed to enrollees with unrecognized hypertension. These situations also apply in Broomfield, where there was an increase in abnormal findings from 12% in 1973 to 19% in 1978.

The abnormal rate of 30% for Longmont is the only one that agrees well with the result of 29.8% reported for both sexes in the 65 to 74 age group by the National Center for Health Statistics.[16] In communities where minimal decreases in abnormal rates are found, there appears to be some relationship between

Table 3. Comparison of screening activities by community (1973 and 1978)

Variable	Boulder		Broomfield		Lafayette		Longmont		Louisville		Totals	
	1973	1978	1973	1978	1973	1978	1973	1978	1973	1978	1973	1978
Number of conferences	2	72	7	9	11	23	15	46	11	12	52	162
Blood pressures checked	61	2,318	74	248	145	560	207	1,399	149	450	1,659	4,975
Blood pressures above 140/90 and below 160/90	—	1,857	—	201	—	460	—	984	—	369	—	3,871
Percent abnormal	—	80	—	81	—	82	—	70	—	82	—	78
Blood pressures above 160/95	13	461	9	47	30	100	54	415	30	81	250	1,104
Percent abnormal	21	20	12	19	21	18	26	30	20	18	15	22
Urine checks (sugar and albumin)	28	497	9	23	32	63	59	495	16	88	305	1,166
Abnormal findings	3	51	0	2	5	9	14	30	1	8	43	100
Percent abnormal	11	10	0	9	16	14	24	6	6	9	14	9
Hemoglobin checks	32	482	14	31	44	66	74	482	37	81	321	1,142
Abnormal findings	0	45	2	2	5	4	20	37	6	10	46	98
Percent abnormal	0	9	14	6	11	6	27	8	16	12	14	9

the control of hypertension and the extent of medication and diet counseling.

Urinalysis

The results of the urine screening activity presented in Table 3 primarily pertain to glycosuria; findings of albumin abnormality were infrequent. This situation is contrary to reports that 50% of aging renal systems show gross abnormality and that some histologic abnormality is found in 97% of the elderly.[13(p142)] Therefore the urine nitrite test for bacteria screening was added in 1976 to monitor the vulnerable renal system. Urine screening for albumin is emphasized in hypertension management.

Lafayette had the highest abnormal urine findings (14%) in 1978, but a decrease from 16% in 1973. As mentioned, this community has several elderly persons with diabetes who require frequent monitoring for maintenance. This situation also applies to Louisville, where the abnormal rate increased from 6% to 9% during the 1973 to 1978 period.

The decrease in abnormal urine rate in Longmont from 24% in 1973 to 6% in 1978 is significant. The improvement was attributed to nursing efforts at the Longmont Spanish (LTS) site, where a number of diabetic elderly were found in 1973. Another reason may have been the increase in enrollment, which could have diluted the previously high abnormal findings from the LTS site. Because screening results are now tabulated by communities rather than sites, determining abnormal findings by sites is not possible (in contrast to 1973).

Hemoglobin

217

The hemoglobin screening results reported in Table 3 are based on criteria of 14 to 16 gm/100 ml for men and 12 to 14 gm/100 ml for women. The most significant decrease in abnormal rate was found in Longmont. Reasons for improvement were the same as those outlined for the decrease in the abnormal urine findings.

The highest abnormal hemoglobin result was at Louisville, where an elderly person diagnosed with anemia required monthly monitoring. Four of the ten abnormal findings were found in this individual.

The increase (0% to 9%) in abnormal hemoglobin results at Boulder is not considered significant because the 1973 results were based on a relatively small population. However, three persons diagnosed as having pernicious anemia were receiving bimonthly vitamin B-12 injections in 1978. These persons usually have abnormal hemoglobin, which accounts for the increase in the abnormal rate.

Medical care referrals

The medical care referral for diagnostic purposes and annual physical examination were important for the early detection of potential problems that could result in chronicity or prolonged recovery. The proponents of health maintenance programs agree that a comprehensive physical examination and a periodic reexamination are important means of maintaining the health status of older people.[17-19] Table 4 compares the number of individuals referred for medical care for the initial year and the fifth year of

218

Table 4. Number of individuals referred for medical care by community, 5-year comparison (1973 and 1978)

Individuals referred	Boulder		Broomfield		Lafayette		Longmont		Louisville		Totals	
	1973	1978	1973	1978	1973	1978	1973	1978	1973	1978	1973	1978
Individuals enrolled	130	657	35	82	67	122	106	509	48	128	386	1,498
Individual referred to physicians	44	200	7	18	32	48	49	69	29	31	161	366
Percent referral rate	34	30	20	22	48	39	46	14	60	24	42	24

the program. There was a substantial decrease in referrals, from 42% in 1973 to 24% in 1978. This suggests that many clients with health problems or in need of periodic examination were receiving physician care, particularly the core group of elderly people who were enrolled in the program since 1973. This especially applies to Longmont and Louisville, where the largest decreases in referral rate occurred. Another factor contributing to decrease in referral rate was the completion of the primary nursing course by the staff. This assisted in delineating health problems that could be safely managed without medical referral.

Lafayette had the highest referral for medical care at 39%. This high rate is partially the result of closer medical supervision required for treatment of one elderly person's anemia. Another reason may be related to the group's complex health status, which requires more frequent physician consultation.

Support services

The AHC program evaluation would not be complete without reviewing the other nursing activities that support the services at the conference sites. Because data collection methods have been modi-

fied over the years, exact comparative data cannot be presented. Therefore trends and changes of other nursing activities that have emerged from 1973 to 1978 will be discussed.

Home visits

Home visits occurred most often at the start of the AHC program, when a number of elderly people with chronic health problems were identified. These problems required more frequent supervision than the monthly AHC service but generally were not so critical as to require the services of the Home Health Care Program. Home visits are referred to Home Health Care because nursing staff efforts focus on the increasing need at the conference sites.

Community agencies

Referrals to community agencies remain a high priority. In 1973 a large part of the referrals were for financial assistance from social services because many elderly were unaware of this resource. The number of referrals for this assistance remains unchanged from 1973 despite the increase in enrollment. This suggests that the elderly are either already receiving assistance or are able to manage without social services.

As a result of the aging process, the elderly of the AHC are expected to experience mental and physical stresses. However, the referrals for mental health services, a resource that could help the elderly cope more effectively, did not increase appreciably during the 5-year period when health services were provided. This indicates that the elderly are still reluctant to accept services, and the nursing staff may be the primary support for mental health. Apparently more explanation is needed about the benefits of mental health counseling, particularly to decrease the stigma associated with

---

The elderly must learn to view mental stress as another type of health problem which is similar to physical ailments.

---

receiving care. The elderly must learn to view mental stress as another type of health problem that is similar to such physical ailments as diabetes and arthritis. The importance of preventing serious mental conditions by seeking early assistance must also be conveyed.

Dental and nutritional counseling has been added to the community services for the elderly. The presence of a dental hygienist and nutritionist at selected conference sites has contributed to a more comprehensive health service. The hygienist provides a thorough examination and makes referrals to dentists associated with Boulder Dental Aide, Inc, a voluntary organization. The elderly may choose a dentist from a list of participat-

ing dentists and receive a 50% discount on dental care.

The nutritionist assists the nursing staff with counseling on weight control and special diets, which were major concerns expressed by the elderly (Fig 2). Recent information gathered at the AHC shows that about 50% of the elderly are at least 20% overweight and are on special diets. These two points attest to the value of the nutritionist as a resource to the AHC services.

Other sources

Other referral sources available to the AHC participants are the services of the University of Colorado Speech and Hearing Department; physical, occupational, and speech therapists; Family Planning Clinic for Pap tests; alcohol counseling service; legal aid; the district attorney's consumer affairs department; and Retired Senior Volunteer Program. Some of these services require a fee for service either on a fixed or sliding scale basis.

COST OF SERVICE

The AHC services were offered free because the program was viewed as a counterpart of the agency's child health maintenance service. An initial budget of $500 was received in late 1972, and $10,000 was obtained in 1973 from local governmental sources. The budget allocation had grown to $40,000 in 1978, appropriated from the local government and the United Way.

Every effort was made in planning and implementing the program to operate the service efficiently and effectively while keeping quality care as a goal. The first-

220 year cost of the service was $3.66 per client visit, which increased to $5.40 in 1978. The cost per client visit was determined by considering administrative and staff time for planning, service, follow-up, and supplies. Because the existing community centers were used as conference sites, there were no support costs, such as rental and utilities fees. In-kind contributions by recreational centers and low-cost housing units were not included in the cost of the service.

The average total time for interviews, health counseling, assessment, and screening activities ranged from 15 to 30 minutes for each client per visit. Generally the initial client visit took longer because a health history to serve as baseline information was obtained. Successive follow-up visits usually become shorter if no new problems emerged.

CONCLUSIONS

Client and community involvement was sought and found to be an essential component of a successful and relevant health care service. The acceptance and use of the service depend on meeting the needs of the target population. Furthermore, the health care services needs must be identified by the clients who choose to use the service.

Nursing care to promote and maintain the health of the elderly in a nonclinical setting was found to be possible. For the program in Boulder County a majority of the established goals were met. First the program goal of reaching 1,200 individuals was exceeded in 1978. Second the screening activities, blood pressure, urine, and hemoglobin, assisted in identifying health problems and were effective tools to monitor chronic conditions. Another

aspect of the screening activity was that individuals with abnormal findings sought medical care early to prevent complications or chronic illness. Third, the group health care education on topics selected by the clients was effective in developing an awareness and responsibility for health care maintenance. Last, the cooperation and support from community agencies contributed to providing relatively low-cost health care services.

PROGRAM UPDATE 1979–1981

This section provides an update on the AHC program with information that has become available since the publication of the original article.

The AHC continues to offer health services to Boulder County's elderly population with 1654 clients receiving care during 1980. This is an increase from a total of 1498 enrollees in 1978. A client characteristic noted in the most recent years is that some individuals will not attend on a regular basis, but reestablish themselves more permanently in the program after a year or two. The exact reason for this is unknown, but this behavior suggests that the "healthy" elderly are able to manage self-care during the interim and return to seek further health services as they view the need.

Some changes in the AHC sites have evolved to meet the demands of increased enrollment and to assist with accessibility of care. For example, a low-income housing unit known as Regal Square was added as a new site in Louisville (LSL) in 1980. Another community of mobile homes recently anexed to Broomfield (BFD) city limits will have an AHC site in 1981 funded entirely by United Way.

A new senior citizens' recreational facility was especially built to meet the needs of the older population in Lafayette combining the Senior Center and the El Central site. This AHC site is now serving essentially the same population as in earlier years (Table 1), but will expand services by another half day per month using United Way support. The only community where services were discontinued during 1978 to 1980 was Nederland (NLD), apparently due to lack of consistent organization of the senior citizens' activities. However, the senior citizens spearheaded a reorganization in 1981 including the reestablishment of the AHC services. Currently, the conference is serving 20 to 30 clients per month.

The trend in the 80s, with regards to the elderly clients attendance of the Boulder AHC sites, is that they shifted from site to site for their own convenience. Thus, all the sites within the city of Boulder should be viewed as a whole and attempts to keep each site as a separate entity are no longer valid in terms of noting attendance.

The services of the AHC remain free to the communities' elderly people because financial support is available not only from the United Way, but also from the Boulder County Tax funds and the Visiting Nurse Association membership dues and donations. The latter is a new source of funding since 1978. The efficient and effective use of these funds remains a priority for the health services. Despite valiant efforts, the inflation in the last few years has caused the cost of an AHC visit in 1980 to be $9.50, an increase from $5.40 in 1978. With such increases in the cost, the ability to provide "free" health care to the older population on a continuing basis is a grave concern.

The nine years' experience with AHC revealed that quality of nursing care can be achieved when 20 appointments are scheduled per half-day site visit. If appointments exceed 30 per half-day, the clients are underserved because the nurses become overextended. Consequently, the large numbers of AHC attendance per site, as shown in Figure 1, are not possible when strict appointments are enforced to provide appropriate health care.

Another significant change reported by the AHC staff is in the health screening results. For 1980 and the first half of 1981, there was an increase in abnormal findings associated with blood sugar, hemoglobin, and urine tests. A partial explanation for this may be attributed to an increased emphasis in chronic disease management by the AHC. In many instances, clients use the AHC to monitor care regimen by requesting the health screening tests. The elderly clients remain under their physicians care, but because the nurses have learned to adequately manage the care of individuals with chronic illness, the tendency of over-referrals to physicians has decreased. In other words, the AHC nurses now recognize the parameters of care which they are able to provide safely.

REFERENCES

1. Butler R, Lewis M: *Aging and Mental Health: Positive Psychological Approaches.* St Louis, The CV Mosby Co, 1973.

2. Brotman H: The fastest growing minority: The aging. *Am J Public Health* 64:249–252, March 1974.

222

3. Callahan C: The White House conference on aging. *Nurs Outlook* 22:96–99, February 1972.

4. Storz R: The role of professional nurse in a health maintenance program. *Nurs Clin North Am* 7:207–223, June 1972.

5. Anderson E, Andrews A: Senior citizens health conference. *Nurs Outlook* 21:580–582, September 1971.

6. Weston A, Fairley I: Sixty and up health centers: Vancouver's first year of experience in geriatric screening and counseling. *Can J Public Health* 59:389–392, October 1968.

7. US Department of Commerce, Bureau of the Census: *1970 Census of Population, General Population Characteristics, Colorado.* Washington, DC, US Government Printing Office, 1971.

8. Leach J: Boulder County's population hits 200,000. *Boulder Daily Camera* July 15, 1979.

9. Brody S: Evolving health delivery systems and older people. *Am J Public Health* 64:245, March 1974.

10. Archer S: Health maintenance program for older adults. *Nurs Clin North Am* 3:730–732, December 1968.

11. Hitchcock J: Working in a non-health oriented setting. *Nurs Clin North Am* 5:251, June 1972.

12. Niland M: Understanding the elderly. *Nurs Forum* 11:273–289, November 1972.

13. Kart C, Metress E, Metress J: Aging and Health. *Biological and Social Perspectives.* Menlo Park, Calif, Addison-Wesley, 1978.

14. Masters A, Lasser R: Blood pressure elevation in the elderly patient, in Brest A, Mayer J (eds): *Hypertension.* Philadelphia, Lea & Febiger, 1961, pp 24–34.

15. Harris R: Cardiopathy of aging: Are the changes related to congestive heart failure? *Geriatrics* 3:42–46, February 1977.

16. US Department of Health, Education, and Welfare, National Center for Health Statistics: *Blood Pressure Levels of Persons 6–74 Years, United States, 1971–1974.* Series 11, no 203 DHEW. Washington, DC, US Government Printing Office, 1977.

17. Coe R: Assessment of preventive health practices for the aged. *Gerontologist* 13:345–348, June 1973.

18. Boyd R, Oakes C: *Foundation of Practical Gerontology.* Columbia, SC, University of South Carolina Press, 1973.

19. Rosen H: Modern medical care delivery for the aged: A program in total health maintenance. *J Am Geriatr Soc* 27:505–509, October 1972.

Index